Digital Futures and the City of Today

Digital Futures and the City of Today

New Technologies and Physical Spaces

Edited by Glenda Amayo Caldwell, Carl H. Smith
and Edward M. Clift

Series Editor: Graham Cairns, AMPS

intellect Bristol, UK / Chicago, USA

First published in the UK in 2016 by
Intellect, The Mill, Parnall Road, Fishponds, Bristol, BS16 3JG, UK

First published in the USA in 2016 by
Intellect, The University of Chicago Press, 1427 E. 60th Street,
Chicago, IL 60637, USA

A catalogue record for this book is available from the
British Library.

Copy-editor: MPS Technologies
Cover designer: Gabriel Solomons
Front cover image © Linda Matthews
Production managers: Gabriel Solomons and Jelena Stanovnik
Typesetting: John Teehan

ISBN 978-1-78320-560-8
ePDF ISBN 978-1-78320-561-5
ePub ISBN 978-1-78320-562-2

Produced in conjunction with AMPS (Architecture, Media, Politics,
Society)

Printed and bound by Hobbs, UK

Contents

Foreword

Graham Cairns

For architects, the city can still be a question of constructed buildings, a physical entity; whilst for human geographers, it is a place of human interaction and engagement. Similarly, for film-makers, it may be a site for action and futuristic nightmare; whilst for animators and computer programmers, it becomes a virtual world – a second life, a 'simulated' city. For sociologists, it is a defining aspect of cultural identity; whilst for political activists and theorists, it is a place to 'occupy' and the site of the polis. In the current urban context, however, the digital is now both evasive and pervasive. Almost every action we take in the contemporary metropolis is either recorded, encoded, interlaced with, or overlaid by, an electronic network that joins us to each other and to itself.

In this contemporary context, we are now familiar with the digitally laden experience of the contemporary public transport ride, and listen to urbanists as they envisage a future for the interconnected 'smart city'. We watch the design process of our buildings and environments become, in and of itself, a mediated engagement, as creative human actions merge with autonomous form to generate computer algorithms. Today, architects simulate user behaviour as a form of 'space syntax', while the contemporary *flâneur* navigates the city through Google Maps and a myriad of other Web 2.0 paraphernalia. Through counter-positioning discipline-centred perspectives, overlaying their research methods and fomenting opportunities for cross-disciplinary engagement, this book aims to offer insights into the contemporary and historical city, and its continually evolving relationship with emerging medias and technologies.

The context for this book – and the launch of this Intellect series – is a global network of activities investigating these issues. The Mediated City Research Programme involves conferences, workshops, research projects and related events which have fed into this engagement with Intellect and its publication of this book series. Led by the research group AMPS (Architecture, Media, Politics, Society) and its associated scholarly journal, *Architecture_MPS*, the Mediated City Research Programme is an ongoing international engagement of artists, designers, planners, architects, digital image-makers, computer programmers, film-makers and photographers. Already engaged in North America, Europe and Australasia, it positions the city as a dual physical and mediated phenomenon, and seeks to better understand and disseminate research on the contemporary city as a phenomenon increasingly experienced, rendered, designed and explored as both a physical and virtual entity. To this end, the engagement of AMPS on this Intellect Books publication series is a natural step for both parties.

The other books with which Intellect launches this series – *Filming the City: Urban Documents, Design Practices & Social Criticism Through the Lens* and *Imaging the City: Art, Creative Practices and Media Speculations* – similarly come from this engagement with AMPS. Inevitably, they offer their own particular insights into this multifaceted hybrid phenomenon. In this volume, however, the focus is split into three main areas, reflected in its three sections: 'Embedding – The digital in the physical world'; 'Applications – The use of the digital in the everyday'; and 'Studies and trials – Examples of community uses of digital technologies'. Split into these three related parts, this book offers overviews of the hybrid phenomenon that is the modern digital or smart city; examines live projects active across the world; documents experimental visions and ideas on the future of the hybrid metropolis; and finally, presents experimental projects engaging local communities in design through new technologies.

What this book, its associated series and the broader AMPS research programme all highlight, then, is an understanding that an invisible digital matrix has become interwoven into the physical infrastructure and sensorial experience of the contemporary city. This matrix alters our perception of the city, informs our behaviours and increasingly influences the physical designs we propose. It is also changing the nature of the design process itself by allowing more people to be involved, a greater range of voices to be heard and more complex interactions to be imagined. Obviously, it is also integrally linked to the very tools architects and planners use in the design process. This book slices through the wide array of issues now emerging in the digital era to critically examine key areas of activity for architects, designers, media specialists, communities and activists concerned with the futures of our cities. In short, it offers a multifaceted view of the complex integrated phenomenon that is the contemporary hybrid city.

Introduction

Glenda Amayo Caldwell and Carl Smith

The pervasive and ubiquitous nature of digital technologies have affected nearly all aspects of our daily lives, including the design and experience of the built environment. This book is a compilation of chapters that have been contributed by academics, practitioners and designers who reveal that this phenomenon is felt across the globe. The city of today is an interwoven series of physical spaces with digital layers of media and information. From the perspectives of architects, designers, media specialists, technologists, communities and societal activists, this book explores the hybrid city as it is today, and what the potential futures of our cities may look and feel like.

This book is one of the results of the AMPS Mediated City Research Programme, and draws materials from research held events in London and Los Angeles in 2014. Added to that mix are essays from a range of other disciplines and countries, who together offer critical discourses that explore the city as a physical, virtual, filmic, social and political construct. Split into three related sections, this book offers overviews of the hybrid phenomenon that is the modern digital or 'smart' city; examines live projects active across the world that present ideas on the future of the hybrid metropolis; and finally, offers experimental projects engaging local communities in design through new technologies. In short, the book offers a multifaceted view of the complex integrated phenomenon that is the contemporary hybrid city.

Section One – 'Embedding – The digital in the physical world' – begins with a contribution from Alessandro Aurigi, who writes about the struggles managing top-down urban approaches and bottom-up urban acupuncture. Proposing a smart urban acupuncture that mediates between the two through strategic and multidisciplinary work, he strikes a cautionary tone about the future of the 'smart' city.

Aroussiak Gabrielian from the University of Southern California examines how new means of navigating space can open up innovative possibilities in architectural practice. She investigates how navigational technologies (such as Google Street View), with rapidly growing databases of environmental imagery and other rich information sources, might be transformed from records for passive consumption to active agents of cultural production, enabling a means to reimagine the city as dynamic landscape.

Cláudia Sofia Gonçalves Ferreira Lima investigates the city of Porto's digital networks to see how they impact people's responses to, and perceptions of, the city. She discusses how architecture can be a catalysing element of virtual and physical relations, and what affordances of the physical and the virtual can be most effectively used to create positive impact.

Finally, Cristina Miranda de Almeida outlines her model of radical hybrid experience, which aims to address the issue of how individuals maintain their independence and individuality whilst becoming increasingly submerged within the mediated city through the continual use of their technologies. This tension is framed by the understanding that these technologies are now so essential for mediating life in the city that they create new forms of experience of matter, space, time, self/identity and action.

Section Two – 'Applications – The use of the digital in the everyday' – reflects on a combination of projects that explore the hybrid nature of technology-enriched urban spaces. Sandra Wilson and Lilia Gomez Flores investigate the issue of 'persistent identity,' where our identity is used to provide us with access to a growing range of services and benefits, thus increasing the need to 'manage' our identity. They analyse the interactions between individuals and their identities in the city, highlighting the requirement for new forms of literacy to demonstrate the many ways in which surveilled space alters human experience.

Gavin Perin and Linda Matthews examine the image of the city and the politics behind it. They consider the devices and technology employed to mediate the image of the city, such as the IP (Internet Protocol) webcam, to propose the possibility of three utopian subjects. Ultimately, these authors suggest that disciplines concerned with urban spaces and their image must reconsider the formal, spatial and material expectations brought to bear on their subjects.

Georgios Artopoulos and Nikolas Bakirtzis from the Cyprus Institute have contributed a chapter that highlights a transdisicplinary approach to the use of advanced digital tools for the negotiation of complex urban environments, particularly those that are rich with layered history, such as in Nicosia, Cyprus. Here, monuments are referred to as 'cultural lighthouses'. In an attempt to reconcile the invisible layers of information that are embedded in ancient structures, the researchers employ virtual reality to bring an awareness of the city to the inhabitants of Nicosia.

Melanie Chan looks at location-based applications to illustrate how their increasing ubiquity is creating a situation in which the technological mediation of everyday life is becoming ever more pervasive and persistent. She argues convincingly for a model that views a range of contemporary human activities, behaviour and social arrangements as being engendered by location-based applications. It is a template she uses to explore three key themes of our technologized existence: place, play and privacy.

In M. Hank Haeusler's chapter, the author introduces media architecture by exploring the infostructure of a digitally augmented bus stop in Sydney, Australia. The 'Bus Stop of the Future' project promotes media façades that reach beyond advertisement to provide more useful information (in this case, public transport information) to the passers-by. As with all the chapters in this section, it offers an example of how our everyday lives in the city are being transformed, invisibly and inexorably, by technology.

Section Three – 'Studies and trials – Examples of community uses of digital technologies' – enters the realm of community projects and the ways in which the public can be increasingly engaged in the design of the city. Kristen Scott examines a scenario in New York City in which local government is engaging the community in debates on health through an innovative mobile app. Focusing on issues such as sexual health and women's health, the technology she documents is having real beneficial impact and raising awareness among whole swathes of previously underinformed citizens of the city.

In a similar way to the essay that begins this book, the arguments of Marta Miguel, Richard Laing and Quazi Zaman suggest dangers in our embracing of technology. Looking at the ways in which citizens of the city can be encouraged to engage in its design and management through participatory processes, they suggest that it is fundamental to look at aspects other than the technological. Arguing that new medias and technologies can facilitate participation on a more practical level, they suggest that new technologies be based on an understanding of the human component of participation – something they explore through various workshops with local residents using traditional forms of exchange and communication.

Marco Zilvetti, Matteo Conti and Fausto Brevi offer a very different example of how technology engages life in the city and, in its own ways, contributes to its betterment. Centred on the role new technologies and medias are having on the development of new individual and city transport systems, they explore a range of innovations. Set to revolutionize modes of transport – from the personalized driverless car to mass long-distance transit – the technology they describe will not so much change the face of the city, but drastically alter our movements through it.

Finally, Glenda Caldwell and Mirko Guaralda extend the discussion on media architecture to question how urban informatics can be used to navigate useful social information, ultimately informing architectural and urban design through a project in Brisbane, Australia. They propose that there is further research to be done to investigate the opportunity for media architecture to change the way information is provided to the public as well as to provide avenues of feedback from the public back to designers and decision-makers.

A common theme from all the sections is a grappling with and acceptance of hybrid aspects in the modern city. It is evident that the digital, virtual, non-visible or intangible characteristics of technology are having a major impact on how we experience, navigate, see and feel the built environment which, until recently, was mainly a physical entity. Is it the invisible nature of the digital that makes it so perplexing? Although we cannot see the actual data that transfers the information, it is captured, visualized and transmitted through a range of devices, screens and materials that inherently influence how the city is perceived, conceived and experienced.

The hybrid city refers to the invisible versus the visible, the immaterial versus the tangible, the digital versus the physical. But how are all of these experienced simultaneously and individually? It is through the mediation of the hybrid cities that the authors of the chapters in this book offer novel insights and innovative approaches – alongside critical reflections and questions – in an attempt to better understand and grapple with the vastly changing nature of urban space. The future of the city is here; how we continue to learn from each other so as to make these urban environments more habitable, prosperous, enjoyable, comforting and overall better for everyone is an open and ongoing question. There are challenges, benefits and opportunities that need to be addressed, highlighted and celebrated. This book brings different voices together that contribute to the debate.

Section One

Embedding – The digital in the physical world

Chapter 1

No need to fix: Strategic inclusivity in developing and managing the smart city

Alessandro Aurigi

Introduction

The prevalent discourses around the concept of the smart city often describe it as a long-awaited revolution in urban planning and management that is needed to 'fix' increasingly large, wasteful, chaotic and unsustainable civic environments across the globe through the deployment of high technologies. The emergence of located informatics, the Internet of Things, the creation of 'urban operating systems' and the addition of sensing and intelligent functions to everyday objects and spaces will – it is argued – change rules and improve quality of life, urban attractiveness and the related economic development potential to fix an otherwise critical situation. These remedial aspects of the smart city are becoming entirely dominant in global debates, as well as in many proposed real-world initiatives involving large-scale interventions, including the shaping of brand new urban centres.

This chapter looks at how the current urge to evoke an urban crisis and the consequent need of major fixes – this time of the 'smart' type – is, essentially, nothing new. The history of urbanism, however, has shown how the push of top-down, idealized models and solutions has tended to make urban space and inhabitation 'stiffer' and less – rather than more – resilient. Reflecting on this can have important implications within the same battleground of the smart city's major selling point: successful urban management. The urban futures of large-scale smart city proposals so often discussed by large tech companies and their municipal clients tend to be based on hierarchy and centralization; a vision where 'big data' might be collected locally, but which serves centrally conceived and controlled systems. How really flexible and able to adapt is such a model of the smart city? A model where 'good' management is based on economy of scale efficiencies and expert algorithms can be called into question.

This contribution outlines an alternative outlook for future smart urban management and development. This stems from the ability of organizations to engage in low-risk, context-aware trial-and-error developments from which to continuously learn, enhancing adaptability. The city can then be looked at as a 'learning' organization that can thrive – and has historically thrived – on the dialogue between a series of smaller-scale interventions in the public's good interest and the holistic breadth of institutional involvement and planning. Urban designers have looked at ways to stimulate change and revitalization through localized design and construction, which has sometimes been effectively branded as 'urban acupuncture'. Similarly, a 'smart' approach can be more effective, grounded and sustainable only by articulating the institutional and 'acupunctural' dimensions successfully and strategically, through facilitation, incubation and coordination.

The call for the smart city

The 'digital city' movement of the second half of the 1990s thrived – with all the hype associated to it – at a time of economic growth and during a high-tech financial 'bubble'. This was characterized, amongst other things, by strong discourse over the 'death of distance' (Cairncross 1998) and the replacement of the physical with the digital (cf. Benedikt 1991; Negroponte 1995). Overall, there was an over-optimistic outlook at the base of those developments, one which identified the rise of an 'information society' and its knowledge economy as a greatly beneficial – and somehow unstoppable – revolution and opportunity on economic, social and environmental grounds.

The current case for pushing major smart city projects, however, is being taken forward against the backdrop of a strong financial crisis and a steep reduction in public spending for most post-industrial economies. For most cities of the global north, the burden of further investing in new technological infrastructure has become harder to justify. A set of more critical reasons is therefore employed.

As can be read on numerous websites, blogs and documents, the large-scale urban ICT platforms and 'solutions' being envisaged and marketed by large companies are described as urgently needed to avoid a crisis. The case for the smart city is therefore made by employing emergency, dystopian discourses that represent the urban condition as quasi-terminal, highlighting the need for technological fixes. Cities are described as 'ill-equipped to deal with the shift in population and lack the necessary scale of infrastructure required to support it' (Living PlanIT 2011). Anil Menon (2013) argues on the CISCO blog that 'With limited resources, obstacles that range from traffic congestion and pollution to infrastructure constraints and overcrowding are increasingly amplified – all of which requires a paradigm shift in how we approach and manage these types of situations'. Similarly, Schneider Electric (n.d.) argues on its website that 'Cities face huge challenges: congestion, pollution, blackouts, crime, debt and rising costs – while competing with each other for investment, jobs and talents. Cities need to become smarter: more efficient, sustainable and livable'. Meanwhile, GSMA (n.d.) remarks that, 'To ensure that the cities of the future are safe and healthy places to live and work, smart city initiatives are being established globally'.

Whilst statements might slightly differ depending on the actors and their agendas, some general traits of the smart city rhetoric can be identified. It can be argued that we have created cities that are too large (and ever expanding), polluted, unsafe and fundamentally out of control. Such a dystopia can be counterbalanced by the utopia of smart fixing. Digitally-assisted urbanity brings with it the benefits of the dematerialization of otherwise polluting processes (as Benedikt argued in 1991), universal services and, above all, expert systems which assist living and manage the otherwise spiralling chaos.

The constructed urge to fix the city

Feeling the need to fix the city in a major way, through the widespread introduction of innovative visions and interventions, is nothing new. But it often takes the declaration of some major crisis in order for this to be justified. As Dear argues in relation to the dawn of modernist urbanism:

> The origins of this emergent social rationality lay in the post-Civil War era, when reconstructionists worried how to discipline and regulate the urban masses, and how to control and arrange the spatial growth of cities (Boyer 1986: 9). It did not take long before a host of urban ills were associated with industrialisation and urbanisation, and an intense anti-urbanism was born.
>
> (Dear 1995: 31)

There have been many calls throughout history for applying fundamental changes to the way we conceive and organize the city. These have always been associated with societal transformations and technological advancements, and have created a synergy between the needs of functional adaptation and the ideological drive to affirm new ways of looking at, and dealing with, urban space.

Renaissance urbanists had to deal with a city which undeniably needed some updating (for instance with sanitation), but whose medieval morphology also contrasted ideologically with how the new 'man' and his place in the world were defined by humanist philosophy. A major fix had to be pushed through the geometrical device of central perspective, restoring a much-desired order to urban space. Various experiments of new, ideal towns were proposed and eventually built, such as Palmanova in Italy, designed in the sixteenth century by Vincenzo Scamozzi. However, instead of being a resounding success, the experiment surfaced all the limits of a rigid, over-planned approach that put ordered morphology before actual, messy civic life (Muir 2007).

Pre and post-Second World War modernist urbanism can offer another example of constructed 'crises'. As conceptions about society, technology and our present and future place in the world evolved, so did the accepted civic visions and needed 'remedies'. The neo-classical built environment was not compliant with the rapid acceleration in the progress of modern science and technology, and the rise of an increasingly rationalistic, 'mechanical' world. As a result, a major, unescapable crisis was declared:

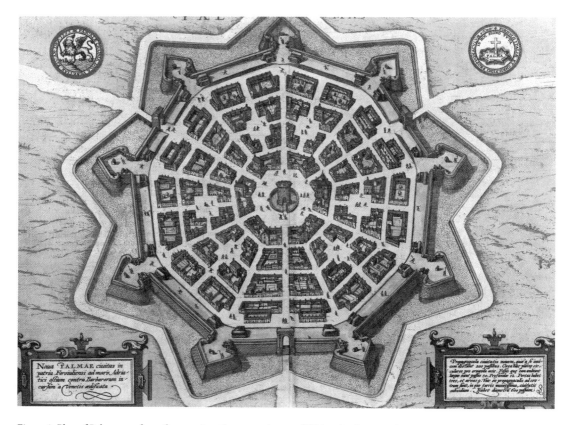

Figure 1. Plan of Palmanova from the seventeenth century (source: Wikimedia Commons).

[The man of today] finds himself still disconcerted, still inside the old hostile framework. This framework is his home; his city, his street, his house, his apartment rise up against him and, unusable, prevent his tranquil pursuit [...] of the organic development if his existence.

(Le Corbusier 2008: 307)

Certainly, cities as well as buildings needed upgrading and adapting, but this had again become more than a practical issue. A relatively unplanned, uncontrolled, organically developing city could only be dissonant with modernistic interpretations:

In the bibliography of the Chicago School compilation, The City (1925), Louis Wirth flatly asserted that: 'There is a city mentality which is clearly differentiated from the rural mind. The city man thinks in mechanistic terms, in rational terms, while the rustic thinks in naturalistic, magical terms'.

(Raban 1974: 181)

The chance to fix the 'usability' and legibility of the city came by reorganizing it into zones that could work together as the cogs of a rational machine, reducing irrational complexity. This was fixing by zoning: creating clear, fixed land uses and their relationships whilst pushing for the making of the 'international style' of an often context-neutral built space.

Smart fixes

The modernist legacy resonates strongly within the smart city movement. Rather than rejecting modernism tout court, postmodernist thinking and practice has embedded it in a wider perspective (Jencks 1996: 30). Moreover, with the machine paradigm first shifting from the physical to the digital, and then recombining the two through ubiquitous computing – or 'everyware' as Greenfield (2006) brilliantly defined it – the modernist vision can still hold. As Dear (1995: 31) notes, 'By the beginning of the twentieth century […] planning discourse had been realigned to emphasize "unity", "control" and "expert skills"'. The emergence of early discourses on the application of the Internet and virtual reality to urban spaces naturally ended up connecting and extending this logic of expert control to new, high-tech practices. Computer scientists joined in fuelling visions of top-down overview and control, envisaging what it now is called 'big data': 'When you switch-on your city Mirror World, the whole city shows up on your screen, in a single dense, live, pulsing, swarming, moving, changing picture' (Gelernter 1991: 30). This top-down control ability has inspired mainstream smart city discourse and proposals as their main selling points. In 1999, Bill Mitchell acutely observed:

> In the design of smart things and places, form may still follow function – but only up to a point. For the rest, function follows code. And if you need to alter these code-enabled functions, you don't rebuild, reshape, or replace material components; you just connect, fetch, and load.

(Mitchell 1999: 50)

'Coding' the city can thus become an augmentation – and a new lease of life, a 'remediation' (Bolter & Grusin 1999) – for functionalist planning approaches. Perspective and zoning are now remediated by algorithm, and the new 'ideal' city is a digitally-enhanced one.

In South Korea, for instance, cities like Songdo or Sejong City – the latter earmarked to become a national administrative centre of half a million people – have been conceived as smart cities, characterized by a strong impact of ubiquitous digital technologies over their successful management. It should not be too much of a surprise that in such plans a fundamentally modernist-looking master plan strongly relies on the twenty-first century smart fix. These cities are conceived very much as machines, with spatial, physical, digital and human gears, and an urban operating system. They are the ubiquitous city, or U-city. In the U-city, high technology is seen as directly – and deterministically – linked with the offer of a better lifestyle. The promotional video outlining various aspects of the 'smart' high quality of life promised in Sejong City refers to this approach as 'Happy City'. In smart Happy City, the *trait d'union* is the maintenance of a clean and efficient urban space through data gathering, central control and information broadcasting, and the ability to engage in a series of smart transactions. Citizens and visitors – and the difference between the two is interestingly non-existent – rely on a civic operating system to assist and give them directions, whilst international investors are happy to pour money into a

Figure 2. The master plan model of Sejong City (source: author)

safe and well-organized place. The words 'control' and 'expert' – as referable to the various urban expert systems – are entirely central to the city's vision for a functional 'happiness'.

Nevertheless, a sanitized smart city of big data and expert algorithms has its limits and drawbacks. As Manuel Fernandez (2012) puts it in his blog:

> Masdar, Incheon or Songdo are large projects that give us an idea of the nature and scale with which we are capable of intervening in this territory. But they are no more than contradictory ideas to the very concept of cities as places with memory, history and conflict.
>
> (Fernandez 2012)

Cities might just be too lively, messy and rich to reinterpret them as high-tech machines. However, they do need both management and the tools to adapt successfully to an ever-changing set of challenges. Indeed, cities are becoming more and more digitally-augmented as a result of widespread adoption of networked and mobile technologies. If not by some major paradigm shift and rational restructuring – however 'soft' and electronic – does it make sense to think of alternatives?

Beyond the ideal organization

When it comes to looking into models for managing institutions and companies, with a focus on making them responsive and adaptable to change, economist Tim Harford is critical about 'ideal' models of organization. These are described as based on a rational hierarchy of line management and communication:

> First [a leader] should take advantage of the fact that he's in a position to see the big picture. The more technology he devotes to this task, the better he can see how everything fits together, enabling him to coordinate what's happening on the ground [...]. The leader should also be surrounded by a supportive team with a shared vision of where the organisation is going. And to ensure that the strategy is carried out effectively, reporting lines should be clear. Information should flow to the top and be analysed, and instructions should flow back in response – otherwise nothing but muddle and chaos lie ahead.
>
> (Harford 2011: 41)

This amply resonates with 'mainstream' ways in which to see the smart city as the ultimate rational machine. A major feature of the smart city scenario are systems that are able to capture and analyse the data needed to construct the 'big picture' used by civic managers, who then 'coordinate what's happening on the ground'. However, Harford argues that 'ideal organisation' models can be counterproductive when adaptability is at stake:

Figure 3. Abandoned shops in Plymouth city centre (source: author).

> Every one of these [top-down control] assets can become a liability if the task of
> the organisation is to learn from mistakes. The big picture becomes a self-deluding
> propaganda poster, the unified team retreats into groupthink, and the chain of
> command becomes a hierarchy of wastebaskets, perfectly evolved to prevent feedback
> reaching the top. What works in reality is a far more unsightly, chaotic and rebellious
> organisation altogether.
>
> (Harford 2011: 42)

This has parallels in urbanism. The flexibility and ability of a city to learn and adapt is
clearly affected by the way it is conceived and managed, and by how its spatial organization
and regulations facilitate – or fail to do so – change and initiative. Rationally zoned cities
(i.e. places shaped through some top-down vision) seem to be particularly non-resilient,

unless they stray away from the purity of their initial model. In modernist Plymouth, UK, for instance, the rationally planned, all-commercial/shopping-dedicated city centre has crumbled under the pressures of economic changes. A growing number of downtown shops have closed down and now lay empty, as zoning constraints have imposed rigid land uses to entire quarters, thereby limiting alternative, bottom-up adjustments. Where shops close down and nothing else can happen, people will tend to use the streets less. This will disincentivize further business or retail uses; or, as Jan Gehl (2011: 75) puts it in a simple and powerful way, 'nothing happens because nothing happens'.

Beyond the top-down smart city

Urbanists have become sensitive to such a conundrum, and processes of civic design which are people and life-centred, rather than machine-inspired, are now being advocated: 'A much better strategy would be to consider initially the "Life", then the "Spaces", then the "Buildings"' (Gehl 2006: 75). For the smart city too, a vision where people and their lives are central and actively participating in the shaping of environment and systems is not to be taken for granted. Current visions of big, data-driven, smart urban systems rely on the power for large transactions of simple information; these may be derived from sensors, as well as produced by people's mobile devices acting as data 'feeds' to predetermined central systems. Prevalent big-scale proposals actually tend to be about smart tools having the agency's lion share. For instance, the Living PlanIT documentation is interestingly more concerned with the 'city' engaging with citizens than the other way around: 'One Urban Report™ and its associated PlaceApps will also dramatically improve the level of engagement a city has with its citizens' (Living PlanIT 2011). On the other hand, Greenfield argues that:

> [w]e want to use networks and sensing and computation and visualization to help people understand the power they already have over the circumstances of their lives, and to enhance that power. That's a pretty significant variance from the model of 'the smart city' inscribed in, say, Cisco's promotional material – which treats these technologies as tools for city managers, and ordinary people as, at best, individual data points.
>
> (Greenfield 2011)

Moreover, an emphasis on bottom-up qualitative influence could indeed extend to the designing of the systems themselves, rather than stopping at the information provision phase. It has been argued how:

> [t]he 'shared' digital city [model] does not just limit itself to acknowledging that citizens and local communities have information to provide or things to say within

a certain pre-defined framework. It implies that the framework should not be pre-defined at all [...] and that communities should be empowered to design their own digital city and prioritize its aims.

(Aurigi 2005: 21)

Similarly, Usman Haque promotes a citizen-centred discourse that highlights the importance of bottom-up, spontaneous interactions:

We, citizens, create and recreate our cities with every step we take, every conversation we have, every nod to a neighbour, every space we inhabit, every structure we erect, every transaction we make. A smart city should help us increase these serendipitous connections. It should actively and consciously enable us to contribute to data-making (rather than being mere consumers of it), and encourage us to make far better use of data that's already around us.

(Haque 2012)

Saskia Sassen (2011) – somehow linking with Gehl's argument on 'life and people first', but referring more specifically to the shaping of smart cities – has also envisaged configurations in which '[r]ather than allowing the technology to control the urban environment, the environment shapes the technology'.

So, what type of smart city approaches could this translate into so as to allow the successful management of a complex, humane, strongly contextualized and ever-changing organism?

Smart urban acupuncture for the adaptable city

The history of urbanism provides several examples of the push to apply major fixes to the city, as well as ideas for inspiring alternative ways to envisage the smart city. These are also relevant because it is important to keep in mind that, however augmentable by high technology, we are still dealing with real places and their qualities – and that is central to it all. What is interesting here is the need to affirm again how envisaging a 'circular' relationship between the shaping of physical, social and digital spaces and facilities is an immensely better way to frame any discourse and practice on the smart city, as opposed to the frequent deterministic and smart solution-based logic informing current debates. The overly nonchalant jettisoning of what we know about urban design in the name of an unexplored 'digital' world and its alleged new rules is not a good starting point towards shaping the digitally-augmented city (Aurigi 2013).

Processes and practices of spatial design can therefore help here. The concept and design practice of what has been referred to as 'urban acupuncture' indicates a series of minor but well-targeted interventions within limited, precise and valued existing contexts, each acting as catalysts for stimulating urban renewal. This has been formulated – in different ways – by the Finnish architect Marco Casagrande and the Brazilian architect and urbanist Jaime Lerner. Casagrande exemplifies 'acupuncture' by describing his own hands-on efforts to re-inject hope and energy into Treasure Hill, an urban farming community earmarked for demolition in the heart of modern Taipei. His approach – which proved popular and successful when implemented – aimed:

> [...] to reinforce the existing urban farming qualities of the Treasure Hill with state of the art high environmental technology solutions and so view the Treasure Hill settlement as a living laboratory of sustainable urbanism. The new technologies and solutions must respect the way of life of the Treasure Hill veterans – the active solar panels and mechanical biological treatment units of organic waste must make room for the grandmothers.
>
> (Casagrande n.d.)

Talking about the approach by Jaime Lerner, Landry notes how:

> [...] urban acupuncture involves identifying pinpointed interventions that by being accomplished quickly can be catalytic by releasing energy and creating a positive ripple effect. [...]. The fast acupuncture approaches had a purpose: 'preventing the inertia of complexity sellers, of pettiness and of politics from stifling critical opportunities and public projects'.
>
> (Landry 2006: 378)

Such concepts resonate strongly with the reflections in this chapter, to the point that they can be translated and extended into a digitally augmented version: a 'smart urban acupuncture' as a desirable approach towards the shaping of a more context-sensitive, experimental and adaptive smart city.

On the one hand, this relates with much of what is happening at the moment in urban informatics and located digital art. From the 'relational architecture' work of artist Rafael Lozano-Hemmer (Dekker 2009: 223–24) to media façade and urban screen installations such as 'Aarhus by Light' or the 'Confession Booth' by Dalsgaard and Halskov (2010: 2278–279), it would be easy to fall into the temptation of dismissing most of this work as transient and of low practical impact. Interventions like these can present many pluses in terms of potential for public and community involvement and participation (and be useful as critique and provocation). But they are also valuable as part of an adaptable approach to city management and design, offering potential for low-risk widespread experimentation and trial-and-error. They are characterized by context grounding, and the ability to obtain high-quality local feedback, organic development and the increased resilience that can come with it. Smart acupuncture provides an alternative to big data, big platforms and big control. These localized experiments can gain adoption and be further customized in an open-source way. Furthermore, they bring clear advantages from a point of view of being smart at managing the city in a facilitative way. They can succeed or fail, but carry lower overall risks when they go wrong; hence even failures are safe enough and good for overall learning. They allow many different ideas to be tried out, are highly agile and initially independent of each other, so they can add resilience to the city. They are born or embraced locally, and work for – and within – a specific place, people, culture and set of assets. These experiments do not try and apply any major fixes, and tend to be more additive than curative, more suggestive than definite. Thanks in part to their scale and relative transitional nature, they can also be 'interstitial', boosting a much-needed urban feature:

> Interstices represent what is left of resistance in big cities – resistance to normativity and regulation, to homogenisation and appropriation. They embody, in a sense, what is still 'available' in the city. Their provisional and uncertain status allows for hint, a glimpse of other ways of creating a city that are open and collaborative, responsive and cooperative.
>
> (Nicolas-le Strat 2007: 314)

Within current debates, Anthony Townsend (2014) has recently argued in favour of a vision for the smart city as characterized by extreme flexibility; in this way, it 'can be rapidly re-purposed [whilst promoting] activities that cultivate a maker-culture [through] a community [which] will embrace its role as a civic laboratory for testing the smart solutions it seeks to create'. Interestingly, even from within large corporations, awareness exists towards the benefits of more flexible and engaged approaches, potentially aligning with an acupuncture discourse where larger institutions can play an important role. IBM's former smart city 'architect' Rick Robinson, for instance, advocates 'refactoring' the software and applications that can populate augmented urban space:

> Agile approaches embrace the fact that when we start to create a new system, we don't know exactly what the final result should be. Traditional approaches to software development attempted to address that challenge through the lengthy analysis of stakeholder requirements. In contrast, agile approaches address it by quickly presenting a first working solution to stakeholders for feedback, and asking them what should be changed. The final solution is co-created by developers and stakeholders through many iterations of that process.
>
> (Robinson 2013)

The smart city of strategic inclusivity

What we have just discussed suggests that it would be easy but dangerously reductive to associate urban acupuncture – and its smart variance – with a bottom-up approach (as opposed to the top-down variant of the corporate smart city). Casagrande's discourse, on the one hand, suggests that local laboratories of contextualized augmented urbanity can revitalize grassroots energies. Lerner's approach to urban acupuncture complements this strategy by introducing and valuing institutional roles. His vision involves a proactive and vigorous participation of institutions and local government in facilitating and supporting local change, as well as disseminating and extending good practice. It is important to note how Lerner's own personal successes in promoting acupunctural interventions were crucially dependent on the proactive and facilitative involvement at the institutional level. He describes how the quick and impactful local projects in Curitiba – such as the Opera de Arame, built in an abandoned quarry – happened due to his own influence at the institutional level, in addition to the municipality's involvement (Lerner 2014: 111).

Approaching the design and production of a more adaptive smart city therefore needs to take into account two seemingly contrasting dimensions: it needs the strategic, empowered and public good-oriented ethos that an institutional involvement should provide; whilst at the same time it needs the agility, inclusivity and trial-and-error benefits of local, acupunctural interventions.

Strategies need to abandon their focus on corporate, city-scale fixes to the 'whole' in order to value and facilitate experimentation at the local, neighbourhood level. Such context-sensitive strategies require the multidisciplinary, holistic and recombined intelligence of artists, built environment and design professionals, social scientists, computer scientists and indeed community organizations, rather than being limited to the solutions offered by a large IT company. Nevertheless, projects and ideas will still benefit from coordination, dissemination and the empowerment available through the presence of institutions and large companies too. These can have a vital role in making things real and more impactful by facilitating the networking of local initiatives, extending the sharing of good practice, supporting the incubation of innovation and creativity, understanding spatial implications better, and being able to learn more deeply from many socially embedded trial-and-error experiences.

A successful example that resonates well with this vision was the approach of the Office of the New Urban Mechanics in Boston, USA. As Townsend (2013: 214–15) describes it, this had been set up as a municipal-funded agency that 'instead of micro-managing […] stayed strategic' by steering design and policy through a civic overview, whilst encouraging localized prototyping and mobilizing bottom-up ideas through 'an almost guerrilla approach to smart-city building'.

Figure 4. The Opera de Arame in Curitiba, Brazil (source: author).

Conclusions

Although there are many initiatives within the urban informatics arena that try to develop aspects of the smart city from the bottom up, prevalent discourses and drives by large municipal and industrial players indicate a need for all-encompassing, corporate projects. We have seen in this chapter how such need is invoked through the construction of a discourse of crisis and emergency, and how, after all, this is nothing particularly new in the history of civic transformations. However, this chapter has argued that major sudden fixes to urban environments – despite being fascinating prospects – have not worked well, and in fact created serious adaptability deficits for cities. Our most successful and liveable places remain those that have developed organically and progressively, rather than from a quick, major and rigid plan of change. The city is never a terminally ill patient in need of major surgery, and questions must therefore be raised about similar potential pitfalls in smart city development.

This means that rather than 'adding' major new systems to the city and deterministically expecting positive change, it would be far better to create the conditions for high adaptability, fostering the unfolding of new context-sensitive and gradual ecologies of space, people and high technologies. In this sense, fragmentation is good: it can allow many new and diverse interactions between the three above-mentioned components to be trialled, with reduced risks for the city as a whole, increased resilience and a more ecological unfolding, thus benefitting from the wisdom of place and community.

This is where the concept of a 'smart urban acupuncture' can come in. Beyond labelling, this implies a rethinking of the processes involved in shaping and designing the smart city. Fragmenting this into local labs and projects ensures experimentation, a rich range of ideas and contextual, organic, adaptive development. But, to close the loop, this also needs to be enriched by multidisciplinary, holistic strategic thinking (rather than single-expertise monologues), and facilitated by municipalities, large institutions and businesses. So, far from envisaging an absence of institutional or industrial presence, what this chapter is trying to highlight above all is the need for smart city visions to transcend any top-down versus bottom-up dualism. Smart urban acupuncture in the city is likely to be much more effective if supported and maximized through multidimensional, multi-agency strategies so as to become organically and inclusively smart, and foster an ecology of innovation.

References

Aurigi, A. (2005), 'Competing urban visions and the shaping of the digital city', *Knowledge, Technology and Policy*, 18: 1, pp. 12–26.
—— —— (2013), 'Reflections towards an agenda for urban-designing the digital city', *Urban Design International*, 18: 2, pp. 131–44.

Benedikt, M. (1991), 'Introduction', in M. Benedikt (ed.), *Cyberspace First Steps*, Cambridge, MA: The MIT Press, pp. 1–25.

Bolter, J. D. and Grusin, R. (1999), *Remediation: Understanding New Media*, Cambridge, MA: MIT Press.

Cairncross, F. (1998), *The Death of Distance: How the Communication Revolution Will Change Our Lives*, London: Texere Publishing.

Casagrande, M. (n.d.), 'Urban acupuncture', http://thirdgenerationcity.pbworks.com/f/urban%20acupuncture.pdf. Accessed 20 May 2014.

Dalsgaard, P. and Halskov, K. (2010), 'Designing urban media façades – Cases and challenges', in *Proceedings of the SIGCHI Conference on Human Factors in Computing Systems*, Atlanta, USA, 10–15 April, New York: ACM, pp. 2277–286.

Dear, M. (1995), 'Prolegomena to a postmodern urbanism', in P. Healey, S. Cameron, S. Davoudi, S. Graham and A. Madani-Pour (eds), *Managing Cities: The New Urban Context*, Chichester: Wiley-Blackwell, pp. 27-44.

Dekker, A. (2009), 'City views from the artist's perspective: The impact of technology on the experience of the city', in S. McQuire, M. Martin and S. Niederer (eds), *Urban Screens Reader*, Amsterdam: Institute of Network Cultures, pp. 223-232.

Fernandez, M. (2012), 'The intelligence of a city is on the streets', http://www.ciudadesaescalahumana.org/2012/03/the-intelligence-of-city-is-on-streets.html. Accessed 5 March 2013.

Gehl, J. (2006), 'Life, spaces, buildings: And in said order, please', in M. Moor and J. Rowland (eds), *Urban Design Futures*, Oxon: Routledge, pp. 70-75.

————— (2011), *Life Between Buildings: Using Public Space*, London: Island Press. First published 1971.

Gelernter, D. (1991), *Mirror Worlds*, Oxford: Oxford University Press.

Greenfield, A. (2006), *Everyware: The Dawning Age of Ubiquitous Computing*, Berkeley: New Riders.

————— (2011), 'You are the smart city', http://blog.cosm.com/2011/06/you-are-smart-city.html. Accessed 5 March 2013.

GSMA (n.d.), 'Connected City', http://www.gsma.com/connectedliving/gsma-connected-city/. Accessed 14 November 2013.

Haque, U. (2012), 'Surely there's a smarter approach to smart cities?', *Wired*, 17 April, http://www.wired.co.uk/news/archive/2012-04/17/potential-of-smarter-cities-beyond-ibm-and-cisco. Accessed 5 March 2013.

Harford, T. (2011), *Adapt: Why Success Always Starts with Failure*, London: Abacus.

Jencks, C. (1996), *What is Post-Modernism?*, Chichester: Academy Editions.

Landry, C. (2006), *The Art of City Making*, London: Routledge.

Le Corbusier (2008), *Toward an Architecture*, London: Frances Lincoln Edition. First published 1928.

Lerner, J. (2014), *Urban Acupuncture*, Washington: Island Press.

Living PlanIT (2011), 'Cities in the cloud – A Living PlanIT introduction to future city technology', http://www.cisco.com/web/about/ac78/docs/Living_PlanIT_SA_Cities_iWhitepaper.pdf. Accessed 18 November 2013.

Menon, A. (2013), 'The Smart City Council – Accelerating an exciting growth', https://blogs.cisco.com/news/the-smart-city-council-accelerating-an-exciting-future/. Accessed 24 February 2014.

Mitchell, W. J. (1999), *E-topia: Urban Life, Jim – But Not As We Know It*, Cambridge, MA: MIT Press.

Muir, E. (2007), *The Culture Wars of the Late Renaissance: Skeptics, Libertines, and Opera*, Cambridge, MA: Harvard University Press. Nicolas-le Strat, P. (2007), 'Interstitial multiplicity', in C. Petcou, D. Petrescu and N. Marchand (eds), *Urban/Act*, Montrouge: aaa – PEPRAV, pp. 214-318.

Negroponte, N. (1995), *Being Digital*, London: Coronet.

Raban, J. (1974), *Soft City*, London: Picador.

Robinson, R. (2013), 'Refactoring, nucleation and incubation: Three tools for digital urban adaptability', http://theurbantechnologist.com/2013/03/27/refactoring-nucleation-and-incubation-three-tools-for-digital-urban-adaptability. Accessed 18 September 2013.

Sassen, S. (2011), 'Talking back to your intelligent city', http://voices.mckinseyonsociety.com/talking-back-to-your-intelligent-city. Accessed 1 June 2013.

Schneider Electric (n.d.), 'Smart cities', http://www2.schneider-electric.com/sites/corporate/en/solutions/sustainable_solutions/smart-cities.page. Accessed 24 February 2014.

Townsend, A. M. (2013), *Smart Cities: Big Data, Civic Hackers, and the Quest for a New Utopia*, New York: W. W. Norton & Company.

——— ——— (2014), 'Utopolis: A manifesto for smart city development', *The European*, 20 March, http://www.theeuropean-magazine.com/anthony-townsend--2/8244-a-manifesto-for-smart-city-development. Accessed 8 April 2014.

Chapter 2

Reimag(in)ing the city: Street View as storyspace

Aroussiak Gabrielian

Introduction

Contemporary architecture and allied design fields are largely data-driven practices – either in the form of parametric scripts or environmental metrics. This has tended to overshadow conversations on cultural meaning and the shaping of daily life. The following chapter focuses on how new media, including the database as 'cultural form', can contribute to the meaningful design of the built environment (Manovich 1999: 80–99). It examines how navigational technologies – most specifically Google Street View, an indefinitely growing database of environmental imagery – might be transformed from records for passive consumption to active agents of cultural production; or, a means to reimagine the city as dynamic landscape.

The etymology of the word 'landscape' can be traced to the Old English *landskip*, which referred not to land itself, but a picture of it; and the Dutch *landschap*, which was used to refer to sixteenth to seventeenth-century paintings of primarily pastoral scenes. It is thus a term that inherently implies mediation (cf. Cosgrove 1985; Daniels & Cosgrove 1988: 1–10). Today, the idea of landscape persists as a mediated reality, yet one that is largely 'experienced' through the intervening agents of our computer screens. This chapter sets up a dialogue between the built environment and its representation by exploring landscape not as a grounded 'reality', but as a technologically-mediated experience.

Specifically, the following examines how people see, consume and have the potential to construct landscape through the populist mapping technology Google Street View. The focus is design, and how this means of navigating space can open up possibilities for new ways of practicing architecture and landscape architecture that do not rely on the professional commission, but rather allow an explorative wander through the monumental and mundane to uncover opportunities for imaginative intervention. This does not mean to suggest such interventions are inspired by observed 'problems' or 'constraints' (to use the language of conventional practice), but by the captured moments of daily life that trigger new stories of people and place.

Street View is dissected particularly for its potentials as a cinematic medium, or a spatio-temporal representation of the built environment, that may be integrated into landscape practices to generate such new design futures. The chapter addresses how new media theory and practice – specifically database narrative, interactive cinema and world-building – might inform the design of 'storyspaces' emergent from Street View exploration. Ultimately, the research attempts to transform Street View's applicability from a utilitarian navigational tool to an active agent of reterritorialization.[1]

The mediated landscape

Before moving forward, it is important to further situate landscape in the context of media and representation. Geographers, in particular (such as Carl Sauer, J. B. Jackson, Kenneth Olwig, Denis Cosgrove, etc.), have long been debating the term's ambiguities as both abstract representation and physical manifestation of human settlement. Denis Cosgrove, for instance, traces landscape not as formal morphology or territory itself, but as a 'way of seeing', focusing most on *landschap* painting traditions, and the framed or bounded perspectival scenes that distance the 'viewer' from the material world. In *Social Formation and Symbolic Landscape*, Cosgrove argues:

> Landscape is [...] a way of seeing, a composition and structuring of the world so that it may be appropriated by a detached, individual spectator to whom an illusion of order and control is offered through the composition of space according to the certainties of geometry.
>
> (Cosgrove 1985: 55)

Cosgrove's is actually a Marxist argument, in which the development of perspective and particular map and survey techniques (for parcelizing land) is reflective of the shift from the 'natural economy' of feudalism to that of capitalism (or from land's use value to exchange value). He explains:

> *Landschap* painting was a genre imported from the Netherlands that became popular among landowners seeking to represent newly acquired or consolidated estates, many of them witnessing a struggle between the customary rights enjoyed by a feudal peasantry and the property rights claimed for landowners in an emerging capitalist land market. Technically, the creation of landscape images was closely aligned with estate survey and mapping, and many artists were also surveyors and map makers. Mathematics, measure, and perspective provided the spatial language of landscape.
>
> (Cosgrove 2004)

The seventeenth century was also a time when maps were cleansed of their symbolic and associative content, and space was objectified into a neutral field of Cartesian or fixed spatial coordinates. As part of the Enlightenment project, landscape – as the unit of geographic measure – gave us 'the ability to see the globe as a knowable totality' (Harvey 1991: 246). Geometry (etymologically connoting 'earth measure') drove the science of map projection and techniques of cadastral surveying that made these mathematical abstractions possible. This imperial and totalizing vision of the globe presented landscape as an object to be parcelized, owned and controlled (Harvey 1991: 240–59). Thus, the framed painted scene, the measured and parcelized map, and the static constructed perspective were all forms of 'landscape as mediation' that inherently privileged vision and the all-encompassing eye, despite the immersive nature of the world it represented.

While Street View clearly presents an alternative to traditional mapping techniques, it mediates the world through power structures (as a 'product' of one of the world's largest technology corporations), while simultaneously providing a kind of democratizing access to its expansive database. Challenging the totalizing top-down view of the traditional map, it is a world not seen in the perspective of its everyday citizens, but from a slightly elevated vantage point that provides more depth of visibility. However, what is captured and made accessible is highly choreographed by the street networks (some expanding exceptions include the off-road trekking feature and the ocean floor mapping) and by its calculated method of data collection. Most significant, is it is a navigable world to be 'experienced' in 'movement', thus breaking down the 'sovereign eye' of the constructed perspective (Cosgrove 1985: 48). While still a visual medium, Street View's 360-degree image capture dissolves the frame that distances the viewer or subject from the 'object' of contemplation.

Imaging the city

Jean Baudrillard (1981) famously rejected the contemporary relevance of Borges' fable, 'On the exactitude in science' (1946), in which cartographers drew a life-size map so detailed that it covered the territory exactly, but which frayed and fell into ruins over time, leaving only shreds of the map still discernible in the deserts. Baudrillard (1994: 1–2) inverted this tale to insist on the precession of simulacra, stating 'it is the map that precedes the territory', and continuing, 'today it is the territory whose shreds slowly rot across the extent of the map'. Baudrillard's ideas resonate more forcefully today than ever, with mapping technologies that trace the surface of the earth and make this data widely accessible. Artists and designers whose primary medium is landscape must recognize that representational mediations quite often precede and often substitute any experience of the physicalities of the so-called 'real' territory. While the hard data Street View collects may be more precisely mapped by geospatial 3D scanning technologies, the accessibility, DIY potential and navigational interface of Street View – along with the material, social and phenomenal qualities that it captures – provides a whole new platform of possibilities for landscape perception and production.

Since change is inherent to landscape, and because landscapes are typically perceived or experienced in movement and through time, developing new and excavating old time-based representational tools must continue to adequately describe a subject that exists in constant flux. Cinematic techniques (cinema is primary to the expanded field of media arts) are critical to this effort due to the range of associations with landscape (time, mood and atmosphere, or affect, narrative, scene, etc.). This investigation contextualizes Street View as a cinematic medium, most particularly because it captures the world in movement ('cinema' derives from the Greek *kinema*, meaning 'movement'). Its output additionally provides an imaged re-presentation of the atmospheric and material variety of the phenomenal world. It is thus also inherently connected to landscape, whose etymology bears strong 'scenic' associations (see above). Street View's navigational methods are closely aligned with cinematic practices, including sequencing, panning, tracking, etc. Most fundamentally, its documentary-like quality catalogues the effects of humans' environmental values, as well as reveals the use, misuse and appropriation of space by inhabitants performing acts of everyday life.

The landscape of Street View

Though Google Earth originated as a synoptic medium, the Street View function, which continues to expand exponentially, has permitted anyone to access 'below the thresholds at which visibility begins' (deCerteau 1984: 92–93). The populist tool has dramatically altered humans' relationship to the globe, 'bringing the exotic to our doorstep while rendering the distant familiar' (Cosgrove cited in Corner 1999: 117). Street View's limitless extension depends on Google's continued recruitment of willing users to contribute to its global database in a kind of guerrilla mapping of places these individuals choose to capture. Thus, rather than the supposed neutrality of this robotic gaze, Street View has become a rich repository of human values.

Street View presents the world from the perspective of the car in motion or, more recently but less ubiquitously, from the person on foot, on bicycle, etc. Despite appearing unmediated, the method of capturing this data and processing it for our consumption is highly abstracted. Photographs taken from 360-degrees are stitched together into 'flat' panoramas, which are then projected onto a sphere to simulate 'reality' (cf. Google 'Turning Photos into Street View' n.d.). As a contemporary mode of seeing and 'experiencing' landscape, Street View – with its biases, distortions of time and space, and occasional fortuitous imprecisions – simulates the world while remaining distinct from it as its own truth or 'autonomous reality' (Gadamer 1975: 135; cf. Baudrillard 1994).

At the same time, however, Street View could not be more 'real' – it presents the world laid bare. Without judgment, its detached gaze captures the rawness of humanity, and the use, misuse and appropriation of space by inhabitants obliviously performing acts of everyday life. While the tourist typically travels to parts of a city that have been constructed for their view and consumption, travelling through Street View provides access to back-of-house or typically hidden realities that provoke new questions about society and the relationships between power and landscape construction. Moreover, it raises continued questions about voyeurism and forms of surveillance (as a contextual reference, see Mitchell 1994; Jameson 1991).

This social dimension is a compelling and under-explored aspect of this powerful tool for the field of landscape architecture. Street View's infinitely shifting panoramas enable an anthropologic study of place. Anthropologists have begun excavating Street View for the ethnographic data it unexpectedly and 'neutrally' captures. Artists such as Jon Rafman also mine Street View for the uncanny moments of social encounter in the landscape (see Figure 1).[2] These situational moments become the starting point for the design methodology proposed here.

This research does not simply advocate the design of opportunistic places made accessible by Street View. Instead, design here is presented as storytelling (or 'cinematic storyboarding'), building on the social, atmospheric, material and spatial information fortuitously captured by Street View – information that would not be accessible by point-cloud technology. Because the footage registers only moments in the temporal continuum, it provokes the imagination to consider possible narratives that both support and transform these fleeting glimpses. Recognizing the cinematic potentials of the medium and what it makes visible, the research thus proposes designs, not for the fixed and physical notion of site, but rather the spatio-temporal and provisional quality of situations.

Figure 1.1. 'Autonomous reality'. Street View images revealing its glitches, distortions of time and space, and occasional fortuitous imprecisions (source: Jon Rafman).

Figure 1.2. 'The practice of everyday life'. Everyday situations captured by Street View. (source: Jon Rafman).

Landscape as database

As a vast storage of data, or 'collection of items on which the user can perform various operations', Street View is also a straightforward example of the database that has become symbolic of our 'computer age' (Manovich 1999: 80). Much has been debated on the subject of 'database aesthetics', and where narrative and data collections intersect in the framework of new media, specifically new cinematic media. Arguing for the database as a symbolic or cultural form, media scholar Lev Manovich (1999: 219) goes so far as to suggest that the database is 'a new way to structure our experience of ourselves and of the world'. He additionally evokes Borges' tale, arguing 'now the map has become larger than the territory. Sometimes, much larger' (1999: 225). As Street View captures not just the physicality of the territory, but also glimpses of the life that exists within it, the map has indeed become larger than the territory – especially given that its newer archival functions allows users to navigate places at different moments in time.

As stated in the beginning of the chapter, contemporary architectural professions are myopically reliant on data sets to determine form and performance. The 'data' presented via the Street View interface, however, might be equally 'objective' and ever-expansive, yet the Street View database (like every database) is 'crafted' so that data is organized, viewed, navigated and searched in a particular way. Despite its deviation from the traditional map, Street View is still very much a map of the world, with specific abstractions, omissions and codifications providing new ways of seeing (and thus understanding) the world. By enabling movement through the projected panoramas, the 'user' is able to wander through the world's constructed spaces like a psychogeographer's drift, crafting one's own meanders into sequential or montagic experiences that generate endless stories of people and place. It might be closer to Deleuze and Guattari's (1987: 10–13) concept of a 'tracing' rather than a 'map': in their *A Thousand Plateaus*, tracing refers to an objective and exacting practice, yet here it is up to the 'user' to create the map as a reimagining of place.

What is interesting about Manovich's essay and subsequent writings (as well as critical responses to it) is the relationships drawn between database and narrative, the latter associated with 'the tyranny of linear thinking that we have been subjected to since the 19th-century in both literature and cinema' (Vesna 2007: xv). While both Manovich and his critic Grahame Weinbren agree on the limitations of sequential narrative in a world of expansive thought and experience (Manovich relating its 'tyranny' to the 'assembly line of industrial society'), they both seek to find some synthesis between the rise of the database and the richness of the story. The reference to the Fordist assembly line is useful here as the economic structure of today has shifted away from the singularity of Fordism to the endless plurality of consumerist society. This therefore parallels the transition from linear narrative – which exhibits a beginning, middle and end – to 'multilinear structures' (Weinbren 2007) or 'interactive narrative' (Manovich, who continues to define 'database narrative' as even more specific).

Weinbren uses the example of Salman Rushdie's *Haroun and the Sea of Stories* (1990) as a reference for multilinear narrative structures that should characterize our age. In Rushdie's story, each ocean current contains a different story 'and because the stories were held here in fluid form, they had the ability to change, to become new versions of themselves and to join up with other stories and so become yet other stories' (Rushdie cited in Weinbren 2007: 61). Weinbren (2007: 61) goes on to suggest that Rushdie's Ocean – which Rushdie calls 'the biggest library in the universe' – is most certainly a database. Street View provides the same possibility for a radical opening up of the singularity of the traditional narrative structure (as well as the singularity of the static map). Manovich cites cultural theorist Mieke Bal's (cited in Manovich 1999: 228) criteria for narrative: namely an actor and a narrator; the three levels of text, story and fabula; and its contents, which should be 'a series of connected events caused or experienced by actors'. While the idea of narrative is used more loosely here, perhaps using 'story' and 'storyspace' (rather than 'narrative') allows for the lack of adherence to these standards. Weinbren (2007: 66) also challenges these conventions, arguing that it is 'events' that make stories, not the description of them. As such, it is the situations – the sociospatial circumstances uncovered by Street View – that stimulate stories for which a world is imaginatively transformed. Street View is therefore the ultimate 'interactive narrative', offering endless opportunities for choice, with the infinite possible itineraries opening up equally infinite design scenarios.

As Street View 'consumers' – to return to de Certeau's *The Practice of Everyday Life* (2011) and his chapter, 'Walking in the city' – we tactically overturn the metanarrative by tracing our own sequences through space (and time). Rather than 'walkers' in the physical sense, we may translate the everyday practice of de Certeau's text into a 'walk' through Street View. As de Certeau (1984: 93) notes, the city's 'ordinary practitioners [...] follow the thicks and thins of an urban "text" they write without being able to read it [...]. The networks of these moving, intersecting writings compose a manifold story that has neither author nor spectator'. The infinite trajectories created by the 'walker's' (i.e. user's) endless choice through Street View likewise create the infinite 'story currents' of Rushdie's Ocean.

In its basic sense, landscape itself – like Rushdie's Ocean – could be framed as a database or a 'collection of items in which the user can perform various operations: view, navigate, search' (Manovich 1999: 219). Landscape, like the Ocean of the Streams of Story, contains endless 'story currents' that have yet to be uncovered. One might ask, then, why we might frame this 'walk' through the mediation of Street View rather than be prompted by a fully embodied presence in the physical world. In this case, Street View collapses space so we can start the story in Manhattan and migrate to Mumbai, crafting new ways of connecting such places through physical proposals that are prompted by the momentary Street View capture. This expansive sense of accessibility extends to the question of design and authorship, challenging the status of the professional designer, and allowing 'users' (or 'everyday practitioners') to participate in story creation and reimagining the physical shape of the world. In addition, the neutrality of the Street View capture and the vastness of coverage offer opportunities for each 'user' to endow place with value and meaning.

This type of design practice – where there is no predetermined site and programme – is well-aligned with sensibilities of landscape, a medium that itself is in a perpetual state of transformation. Landscape architects must accept open-endedness and persistent change, recognizing no landscape is ever itself 'complete'. Without claiming a strictly dichotomous relationship, architecture is certainly more closed and scripted, thus perhaps not as appropriate a lens through which to use Street View as a design tool.

Landscape as navigable space

The Street View process of capturing imaging data (using eighteen lenses to take 360 degrees of imagery in the horizontal dimension and 180 degrees in the vertical; cf. Google 'Turning Photos into Street View' n.d.), as well as the experience of navigating it via our computer screens, is structured by particular movement, duration, and speed, thereby aligning it with specific cinematic techniques. Just as the camera's frame in film and photography controls and constructs narrative, the specific navigational methods (or ways of moving through Street View) reveal distinct situations that become ideational seeds for design.

Returning to Manovich and his section on 'navigable space' in *The Language of New Media* (2001), it is his description of the movement through gamespace – specifically *Doom* (1993–) and *Myst* (1993) – that provides a foundation for thinking about narrative as emergent from spatial exploration. The two games – among the first of their kind though with a plenitude of subsequent spinoffs – 'present the user with a space to be traversed, to be mapped out by moving through it' (Manovich 2001: 245). Street View similarly presents the user with such space wherein the narrative emerges from the particularities of a specific traverse (as one 'map' of infinite possibilities). In other words, it is movement through 'space' that yields the narrative, not predetermined characters and events. Manovich relevantly elaborates on his discussion of games:

In contrast to modern literature, theater and cinema, which are built around psychological tensions between characters and movement in psychological space, these computer games return us to ancient forms of narrative in which the plot is driven by the spatial movement [...]. Stripping away the representation of inner life, psychology, and other modernist nineteenth-century inventions, these are the narratives in the original ancient Greek sense, for, as Michel de Certeau reminds us, 'in Greek, narration is called "diagesis": it establishes an itinerary (it "guides") and it passes through (it "transgresses").'

(Manovich 2001: 246)

Later in the chapter, Manovich references the example of the *Aspen Movie Map* (1978), designed by the MIT Architecture Machine Group, 'as the first interactive virtual navigable space'. It is actually an early precursor to Street View in that the programme allowed the user to 'drive' through the city of Aspen, CO using a joystick. The MIT team constructed the space by taking pictures of the environment every three metres (Manovich 2001: 259). It is through such mediations that we are able to explore the world in a new way and potentially imagine it otherwise. Clearly, a world captured at three meter intervals re-presents it in a way both familiar and alien, allowing us to recognize and realize aspects of our surroundings that remain otherwise overlooked, as well as provoking our imaginations as we see things anew.

Design: Mapping and the landscape imagination

With this contextualization of Street View within media theory, it is now necessary to situate it in the discourse of landscape. Because the reader might be unfamiliar with the intellectual foundations and practices of landscape architecture, it first seems essential to frame design through this lens. Specifically, mapping is essential to the landscape architectural project. As in geography, 'landscape' in 'landscape architecture' refers both to representation and actual territory (which is itself culturally mediated through physical transformation). While most confuse landscape architecture with landscaping, horticulture or gardening, landscape architecture as a profession emerged from, and has developed into, a field that synthesizes vast social and ecological systems to generate designs that enhance the quality and performance of the built environment. 'Performance' in this context means the infrastructural capacity to function ecologically, and to catalyse public life and new forms of socialization. Because of the breadth and complexity of these systems, mapping becomes instrumental to the practice of landscape architecture. In fact, it was landscape architect Ian McHarg, in his seminal book *Design with Nature* (McHarg 1969), who pioneered the overlay mapping methods that evolved into geographic information systems (GIS). While McHarg's rational and synoptic process emerged directly from the legacy of the Enlightenment, it was in the 1990s that McHarg's pupil, landscape architect James Corner, began redirecting the instrumentality of mapping from a positivist or deterministic science to an agent of creativity (cf. Corner 1999). It is this evolved perspective that will be addressed briefly here in the context of Street View and its imaginative capacity.

According to Corner, landscape architecture requires an understanding of territory and site in order to make transformative impressions on it:

[M]apping is returned to its origins as a process of exploration, discovery and enchantment. This is less a case of mapping to assert authority, stability and control, and more one of searching, disclosing and engendering new sets of possibility. Like a nomadic grazer, the exploratory mapper detours around the obvious so as to engage what remains hidden.

(Corner 1999: 225)

By opening up our interpretation of the world, we are inspired to see it anew; to see relationships emerge that trigger our reconception of it. Mapping landscape – through practices of drawing territorial systems and their relationships – becomes part of the design process as both a reading of place (reflective) and an opening up of new ways of understanding it (projective). In landscape architecture, the map negotiates between a given reality and an idea, and between an idea and its physical embodiment. In other words, it both follows (through interpretation of a given circumstance) and precedes the world it represents. Corner's essay 'The agency of mapping' (1999) appears in the book *Mappings* (Cosgrove 1999); this collection attempts to diversify the history of cartography, which had long focused exclusively on scientific measure and objective representation as 'markers of universal rationality and progress' (Cosgrove 1999: 8). While Street View is itself constructed on these ideals of 'objectivity' and calculation, it is the individual navigator as 'exploratory mapper' that 'discloses new sets of possibility' (1999: 225).

In his introduction to *Mappings*, Cosgrove makes the distinction between the closed certainty of the map (noun) and the active and exploratory process of mapping (verb):

Another form of mapping is the creative probing, the tactical reworking, the imaginative projection of a surface [...]. Thus the map excites imagination and graphs desire, its projection is the foundation for and stimulus to projects. Mapping Paradise or Hell can have no function other than to guide the viewers' faith and direct their conduct towards life after death. All utopias require mapping, their social order depends upon and generates a spatial order.

(Cosgrove 1999: 16)

An exploration through Street View likewise provides the 'stimulus to projects', prompting transformative design ideas based on new discoveries and connections drawn through the particular navigational story. Corner concludes:

Mapping is a fantastic cultural project, creating and building the world as much as measuring and describing it [...]. In describing the 'agency' of mapping, I do not mean to invoke agendas of imperialist technocracy and control but rather to suggest ways in which mapping acts may emancipate potentials, enrich experiences and diversify worlds. We have been adequately cautioned about mapping as a means of projecting power-knowledge, but what about mapping as a productive and liberating instrument, a world-enriching agent, especially in the design and planning arts?

(Corner 1999: 213)

Landscape as storyspace

Such a framing of mapping becomes a precursor to recent cinematic fascination with 'worldbuilding'. Initially born out of the genres of science fiction and fantasy, worldbuilding is the cinematic practice of designing environments from which narratives or stories emerge, rather than the conventional process of designing an environment that supports the prewritten script. The fabricated world is primary and the 'characters' simply support

Figure 2. Sequential navigational method and detail of yielded storyspace. Uncovered historic markers in this everyday vegetal strip inspired the integration of proliferated physical markers that embody, register and trigger memory and the passage of time, and stimulate dialogue and debate.

the world, but the narrative again derives from the exploration of that world. In *Building Imaginary Worlds: The Theory and History of Subcreation,* Mark J.P. Wolf describes how:

> Worlds, unlike stories, need not rely on narrative structures, though stories are always dependent on the worlds in which they take place. Worlds extend beyond the stories that occur in them, inviting speculation and exploration through imaginative means. They are realms of possibility, a mix of familiar and unfamiliar, permutations of wish, dread, and dream, and other kinds of existence that can make us more aware of the circumstances and conditions of the actual world we inhabit.
>
> (Wolf 2014: 17)

Figure 3. Elevational navigational method (lateral tracking) and detail of yielded storyspace. Navigation through Street View captured various graffiti artists tagging this urban block. The generated storyspace fabricated a circumstance which required new forms of exhibiting or experiencing this accretional street art. The urban ('rock')-climbing programme gives passers-by the opportunity to view both the art and its wider surroundings in new and provocative ways.

Figure 4. Volumetric navigational method (panning horizontally and vertically from a stationary position) and detail of yielded storyspace. The physical proposal focused on creating moments of pause and reflection within the volume of this space. In this storyspace or design scenario, a hammock infrastructure provides a place of surprise amidst the atmospheric phenomena captured by Street View's off-road 'trekkers'.

While clearly entirely fabricated worlds such as Oz – the 'first transmedial world' – and *Minority Report* (Spielberg 2002) – the first commercial feature-length film to use worldbuilding techniques[3] – provoke curiosity, desire and dreams, Street View brings the distant close and provides a frame through which we see the familiar in a new light. Its momentary captures of sociospatial information provide other forms of provocation and imaginative stimulus. In other words, what Street View teaches us is that we do not necessarily need to begin with alien worlds to generate stories, but can use the wonders and curiosities of what exists to inspire exploration and the creation of new realities, new 'situations', new narratives, new storyspaces. Figures 2 through 5 show how fortuitous discoveries in Street View, and particular cinematic methods of navigating the interface, inspired design narratives related to new ways of perceiving and experiencing the everyday spaces around us.

Figure 5. Archival navigational method and yielded storyspace. Archival navigation is defined by access to and collection of past footage of the same location, offering a kind of archive of both built content, as well as the evolution of use and ecological change over time. The storyspace strategy is therefore the construction of a new narrative based on a projected and imagined future that builds on this transformative past. While this particular update was discovered fortuitously, the archival function has been formalized as a new Google Street View feature as of April 2014. This archival data allows one to not only view singular places in time, but permits the user to move expansively through the city of the past (permitting a kind of time travel). Discovering the traces of withered vine prompted the planting of the wall of this forecourt. This new ecology was further enhanced by the introduction of bird dwelling units that have colonized the wall, creating a new habitat for migratory birds, and provoking new forms of human engagement with the city.

Conclusion

As navigational technologies such as Street View become a more ubiquitous part of our contemporary existence, we must continue to probe their potential for reimagining the city as dynamic landscape. Such technologies inspire new methods for designing the physical environment, yet the hopes here are that those methods privilege social values and cultural meaning, rather than utilitarian responses to data sets and structures.

The chapter is likewise intended to provoke the professional designer into re-evaluating the role of the architect (or landscape architect) in the authorship of space. Anyone can create their own 'map' through Street View and begin to imagine how such places might be otherwise; or how these glimpses into everyday life might have evolved or might perpetuate through an understanding of the physical environment. Whether travelling the streets of far-off places or the streets of one's childhood, Street View (as a participatory framework) allows users to craft their own meanders or story currents. Again, the idea is to consider design not simply as a response to site, programme and performance demands, but as a form of storytelling – exploring how imaginative spatial ideas can both prompt new design narratives, and how sociospatial circumstances uncovered by Street View might trigger new stories of people and place.

New media and cinematic methods can contribute to the meaningful transformation of daily life – from the repetitious and mundane to the imaginative and wondrous. While the storyspaces generated from the practices promoted here are not necessarily within the 'feasibility' of actual execution, challenging the tried and true can serve to challenge these conventions through time. The intention of this chapter is thus not to emphasize the final products of design, but the process or method of working, thereby questioning how these new technologies might ultimately benefit physical dwelling.

References

Bal, M. (2009), *Narratology: Introduction to the Theory of Narrative*, Toronto: University of Toronto Press.

Baudrillard, J. (1994), *Simulacra and Simulation*, Ann Arbor: University of Michigan Press.

Borges, J. L. (1975), 'On exactitude in science', in *A Universal History of Infamy* (trans. N. T. de Giovanni), London: Penguin.

Certeau, M. de (2011), *The Practice of Everyday Life*, Berkeley: University of California Press.

Corner, J. (1999), *Recovering Landscape: Essays in Contemporary Landscape Theory*, New York: Princeton Architectural Press.

Cosgrove, D. (1984), *Social Formation and Symbolic Landscape*, Madison: University of Wisconsin Press.

———— (1985), 'Prospect, perspective and the evolution of the landscape idea', *Transactions of the Institute of British Geographers*, 10: 1, pp. 45–62.

———— (1999), 'Liminal geometry and elemental landscape', in J. Corner (ed.), *Recovering Landscape: Essays in Contemporary Landscape Architecture*, New York: Princeton Architectural Press.

———— (2004), 'Landscape and landschaft', Lecture delivered at the *Spatial Turn in History Symposium*, German Historical Institute, London, 19 February.

Daniels, S. and Cosgrove, D. (eds) (1988), *The Iconography of Landscape*, Cambridge: Cambridge University Press.

Deleuze, G. and Guattari, F. (1977), *Anti-Oedipus*, New York: Viking Press.

———— (1987), *A Thousand Plateaus*, Minneapolis: University of Minnesota.

Gadamer, H.-G. (1975), *Truth and Method*, New York: Seabury Press.

Google (n.d.), 'Share your photo spheres on Google Maps', http://maps.google.com/help/maps/streetview/contribute/#all. Accessed 1 June 2013.

———— (n.d.), 'Turning photos into Street View', www.google.com/help/maps/streetview/learn/turning-photos-into-street-view.html. Accessed 1 June 2013.

———— (n.d.), 'Where is Street View available', http://maps.google.com/help/maps/streetview/learn/where-is-street-view.html. Accessed 1 June 2013.

Harvey, D. (1991), *The Condition of Postmodernity: An Enquiry into the Origins of Cultural Change*, New York: Blackwell.

Jameson, F. (1991), *Postmodernism, or, The Cultural Logic of Late Capitalism*, Durham, NC: Verso.

Jenkins, H. (n.d.), 'All over the map: Building (and rebuilding) Oz', unpublished manuscript.

Manovich, L. (1999), 'The database as symbolic form', *Convergence: The International Journal of Research into New Media Technologies*, 5: 2, pp. 80–99.

———— (2001), *The Language of New Media*, Cambridge: MIT Press.

Mitchell, W. J. T. (1994), *Landscape and Power*, Chicago: University of Chicago Press.

Rafman, J. (n.d.), '9-Eyes', http://9-eyes.com. Accessed 19 July 2013.

Rushdie, S. (1990), *Haroun and the Sea of Stories*, Granta Books in association with Viking Penguin.

Vesna, V. (2007), *Database Aesthetics: Art in the Age of Information Overflow*, Minneapolis: University of Minnesota Press.

Weinbren, G. (2007), 'Ocean, database, recut', in V. V. Bulajić (ed.), *Database Aesthetics: Art in the Age of Information Overflow*, Minneapolis: University of Minnesota Press.

Wolf, M. J. P. (2014), *Building Imaginary Worlds: The Theory and History of Subcreation*, London: Routledge.

Notes

1. The term 'reterritorialization' (preceded by deterritorialization) comes from *Anti-Oedipus* (Deleuze & Guattari 1977), and is related to the transformative processes of capitalism, power and identity as the world globalizes. It was subsequently adopted and adapted by anthropologists and geographers (among others). While none of these fields frame reterritorialization as a creative endeavour, but rather a socio-spatial process, here it is used as both. This suggests that Street View is an instrument for transformation related to the globalization of media, as well as a tool for taking what has been deterritorialized (e.g. globalization flows replacing the space of places) and consciously transforming space into new ways of dwelling in the world.
2. In addition to Jon Rafman, various other artists, such as Paul Cirilio, use Street View as a creative impetus, particularly to address issues of privacy and surveillance.
3. *Minority Report* is interesting as a 'design fiction' in the sense that its envisioning of Washington D.C. in year 2050 actually inspired the design and patenting of a range of new technologies. The fabricated world catalysed new ways of imagining the world in which we exist. The hope here is that 'design fictions' or 'storyspaces' emergent from Street View might ultimately inspire new ways of structuring the physical world around us.

Chapter 3

Information, communication and the digital city

Cláudia Sofia Gonçalves Ferreira Lima

Introduction

Cities are places of contrasts at all levels, mixing and divergent; they bear both opportunities and failures, comprising different inner worlds. Understanding the city is to understand the visible and invisible layers that compose and represent its environment. The city can be analysed as a form of communication produced to represent and inform the city agent's visions and beliefs. Even before the written word, distant messages were conveyed by fire and smoke at the speed of light (Brown & Duguid 2002). Communicating has evolved from spoken and written words to contemporary means of communication through visual and performative narratives and the Internet – now a dominant source of information – changing the ways in which people understand the city.

Using the city of Porto as a case study, this chapter looks at ways of communicating and informing the city, as well as the creation of symbols, the conveyance of messages, and the consequences that these have for city life. It introduces a debate about the era of information and communication technology (ICT), and its most pronounced impacts on the technological and globalized city and urban society. Given that information is critical for everyday life in the global city, this chapter offers an investigation of ICT in the context of Porto. To do this, the reader is offered an architectural perspective of media (as an important information and communication form) in order to study virtual spaces and alternative realities to the city, which provide mediated experiences of the city. Here there is some degree of tangency between virtual and physical worlds, where architecture can act as a catalyst of virtual and physical relations, as well as be mediated by the urban realm.

Technology, information and networked societies – along with the process of globalization – have defused and invaded people's lives over the last two decades. The city has become a flow of networks with many meanings, conveying countless messages through mediums such as newspapers, billboards and graffiti (Mitchell 2005). City spaces provide the bandwidth for the flow of information between people, spaces of exchange, competition, learning and communication. As digitized and informational commodities increasingly invade the city, people's experience of the city becomes mediated by the visual cues increasingly populating the urban environment in the form of light, colour and movement (for example, advertising, street and traffic information, people's movements, and many other stimuli).

Information networks have a great impact on cities and offer many possibilities for interconnections between people. Ultimately, this investigation tries to offer a more general analysis of the effects of information and communication technology on city life by reviewing some current work on cities' mediated experiences through networks of electronic information, with a focus on the Web as the most up-to-date medium of information widely used to represent cities and their virtual services. Because the city's institutions and leaders are more aware than ever of the importance of the Internet as a means to represent and promote the city, this chapter looks at Porto's digital networks, and how these impact people´s response to, and perceptions of, the city.

City multiform 'plexuses' and messages

Massey, Allen and Pile (1999) have argued that a city has many fluid and cross-cutting realities. Imagining the city in this way is to look at it as a range of superimpositions – both visible and invisible – and when these superimpositions change, different groups of people and worlds may come into proximity. The authors examined the ways in which the city is represented through these superimposed worlds, as well as the rhythms and patterns of the cities' networks that divide city life on an everyday basis (Massey et al. 1999). They also explored the symbolism of the built environment, contrasting juxtaposed aesthetics against issues of exclusion or inclusion (1999: 55). Most of all, the authors (1999: 71) proposed that cities are the intersections of a series of narratives, with each having a distinct story to tell, as well as their own significance and coexistence. Reducing a city to a point on a historical timeline is to deny its very continuum of growth (1999: 171). Experiencing the city first-hand clearly encourages a more comprehensive perceptual understanding of its particular settings. However, other drivers do exist that communicate the city through invisible layers.

Venturi, Izenour and Brown (1977) share the understanding that the city (in this case, Las Vegas) relies on an informational medium composed of artificially created façades. Las Vegas is a city of spectacle, evident in the billboards of the famous 'strip', and the historicizing of fantasy architecture in the form of motels and casinos. Here, the primacy of symbols and signs is taken as a commercial strategy; by decomposing the city into its main symbolic elements, city space itself becomes the main character of the narrative. Thus perception, as symbolization, becomes a dimension of the narrative of the city. Here, architecture is examined as a form of communication, where methods of 'commercial persuasion and the skyline of signs' (Venturi et al. 1977: 6) serve the purpose of enhancing the civic and cultural orders of the city.

The city is thus understood as a place with a wide range of meanings, with objects that can convey given messages. This is an age of digitized realities whose sub-worlds can be created and experienced either individually or as a collective. The city is therefore dependent on a complex information network of TV screens, cinematic billboards,

Figure 1. City plexuses and messages.

music, mobile phones and other miniaturized commodities, with architecture and public space providing the set for such network interactions. However, evocation of cities often provides stereotypical images about places people have never visited. This allows them to build partial perceptions of other cities using images from secondary sources of information (Burgess 1990: 143), such as media or software (Vale & Warner Jr. 2001).

The age of the 'invisible' city

The city is greatly dependent on infrastructures such as water, electricity, gas and transport systems. In the globalized world, city life has been over-immersed with applications of this particular trope: 'on-ramps' to the information highway, speed bumps, construction sites, toll booths, highwaymen and hotels. The metaphor seems to make immediate sense and has quickly become taken for granted as an image of this new network (Druick 1995).

Along with transport, communication technologies have allowed for a deeper transformation in the growth of cities and the globalization of their economies. The existence of the informational society is important for understanding the ways through which technologies are socially constructed, the ways in which they are put into use, and the effects and impacts of the power relations within their development (Dixon et al. 2005). The greater the 'bandwidth' (i.e. the channel through which information passes), the more impact ICT has in people's relationships with jobs and other everyday activities that have an electronic congener. ICT has significantly impacted city dwellers, either through urban networks, the economy, urban life or other various dimensions. Porto Digital is one example of a bandwidth infrastructure in the city of Porto. It aims to bring people together and closer to information about their city, in an attempt to develop a wider network of virtual relations. It is a network that unifies several existing networks in the city, expanding to cover a larger area with optical fibre and wireless communication spots.

Telecommunications have been considered as demonstrating the plasticity of space, stretching, deforming and compressing according to the city agents' needs (Sassen 2000). In other words, space can be reconfigured by telecommunications. Reducing the costs of transmitting and accessing technology has changed the ways in which people relate with the built environment. For example, easy access to communication, information and music via cell phones has provoked a more distant relation between people and the city, especially in public spaces: people move faster and are less aware of their surroundings. The city's spatial structure, as well as its planning, thus becomes more entwined with knowledge, information and technology (Castells 1997). City spaces provide the bandwidth for telephone and mobile phone networks, wireless and cable systems, Internet and video networks, and music and miniaturized commodities (Graham & Marvin 2000). The cultural realm of the city also becomes more flexible and fleeting, with the emergence of transient and symbolic communication mediums increasingly mediated by networks of electronic media (Castells 1997).

Is it pertinent to ask if physical spaces are being replaced by virtual public spaces? In essence, public spaces gather a multitude of features that allow people to connect with other people. They are a social production that facilitates a relationship with the built environment, although we also increasingly have mediated experiences there through the city's existing visible and invisible networks. The virtual domain is not a replacement for the physical world. Nevertheless, it can add to the city's diverse representational forms, acting as another source of information and augmenting its experience (for example, by allowing the virtual recreation of places that have an actual physical reference).

The city is increasingly a system of virtual spaces that are connected by the information superhighway (Mitchell 1996). It is a place that provides the settings for communication and is itself a conductor of flows of information (Mitchell 2005). The city becomes a commodity in which there is an increasing dominance of software over materialized form. In *City of Bits*, Mitchell (1996) explores architecture and urbanism in the context of the telecommunication revolution. He argues that we make technology and, in turn, it makes us. Mitchell (1996: 3) provides an interesting exploration of the 'city of Infobahn' through an analysis of computer-aided design (CAD), geographic information systems (GIS), software development and e-commerce, and the miniaturization of the 'instruments of human interaction'.

As such, the digital city is similar to an information ecosystem that keeps changing, eliminating those that can no longer can adapt. This is the invisible city of the twenty-first century; a city of the electronic information age. Mitchell (1996: 5) argues that our task is now to imagine and create 'digitally mediated environments' for the type of life and communities we want. This becomes important for understanding the possible impacts that informational commodities have in the experiences 'that give shape and texture to our daily routines' (1996: 5), along with access to economic opportunities and public services. Hence the city is more than the physical achievements of our own desires and actions, and more than the physical order brought about by our collective acts: it is also a place for potentially developing memorable architectural environments that enable a better knowledge and understanding of places, where invisible information flows, mobile environments and messages populate our lives.

The mediated city: A virtual experience

It was after the Second World War that communication technologies paved the way for the formation of the global village. Global communication systems – specifically electronic media – have created unified business communities. This was the greatest restructuring of the city´s economy since the Industrial Revolution, with information becoming the biggest form of wealth. Today, the global village is understood as a metaphor of the Internet and the Web. This enables the idea of a unified global community wherein there are little or no barriers to information access and exchange of goods.

According to Castells (cited in Dixon et al. 2005), the rise of the network society in the late twentieth century led to a new social structure emerging – a new layer between and within societies: the 'space of flows'. This space of flows was based on temporal and spatial organizations of social practices: 'the material organization of time-sharing social practices that work through flows; flows of capital, information, technology, interactions, sounds and images' (2005: 24). The Internet is a global network of computers, encompassing electronic transactions, exchange (communication) and representation. As in real neighbourhoods, virtual communities allow interaction and communication, albeit at a distance: services and goods can be electronically traded, while images, sounds and texts form part of the Web's complex network.

Emphasizing this perspective, Piazzalunga (2004) contends that digitally configured space (resulting from technology) can provide other meanings for our experience. Furthermore, this sort of space promotes a unique way of reading the processes of architecture. The city becomes constantly virtualized and its perceptions derive increasingly from its representations. The city can be visited through a website where public spaces are experienced as if people were actually there.

The digital city is like an information ecosystem that is constantly changing, yet which is also trying to adapt to as many users as possible. This is the 'invisible city' of the twenty-first century – that of the electronic information age. Boj and Diaz (2008) claim that the use of augmented reality systems will enable new ways of understanding the city. They question how city space will respond to the fast assimilation of 'technological devices in urban spaces, the advances in ubiquitous computing and embedded technologies' (2008: 145). They make the case for new developments in mixed reality technologies that bridge the digital and physical worlds. Here, two-way interaction, enabled by three-dimensional computer graphics, creates a new configuration of hybrid space between the physical and the digital. This could also be termed 'augmented reality'.

Ishida (2000) also explores city metaphors developed in information spaces. The author argues that digital cities, as spaces for public communication and social information networks, will change alongside the advance of computer and network technologies, where the Internet provides a valuable platform for the global spread of information about every aspect of life: 'Digital cities integrate urban information (both achievable and real-time) and create public spaces for people living in the cities' (2000: 7). These can be created for commercial, tourism, welfare, educational and political purposes, attracting people because they can experience a space that belongs to them for as long as they stay connected. The digital city does not offer a substitution of the physical city, but a complementary space of social, political and cultural manifestations.

Digital Porto: The city as a digitized commodity

Aside from being able to provide mediated experiences of places, digital cities have also become important for urban planning and community participation, with two-dimensional and three-dimensional mappings of real cities and interactive e-platforms. The Web has obviously had a significant impact on people's perceptions and understanding of cities. Moreover, digital information is increasingly used by a large number of people in globalized cities, rapidly overtaking traditional forms of dissemination and becoming more readily available.

There has been an increasing amount of digital information about the city of Porto over the past twelve years. With the understanding that places are better promoted through the use of communication media, the city's institutions and leaders have initiated a series of digital-based projects aimed at informing and communicating the city, offering training and support in various areas of interest. Under the national initiative of Cidades Digitais ('Digital Cities'), financed by POS-Conhecimento (Operational Program of Informational Society), the project aims to develop an informational and knowledgeable society at the regional level. It also attempts to stimulate applied regional skills that generate economical value for each region, raise the quality of life, as well as promote competitiveness and sustainable development.

Porto Digital is one of the many digital cities aimed at contributing to the evolution of an informational and knowledgeable society with global reach. The project aims to reach

Figure 2. Trindade metro station. Real-time information about Porto and the rest of Portugal.

communities with real and virtual interests at both the local and global level: dealing with work and competitiveness; simplifying and facilitating interaction with local power; and providing access to information, culture and leisure.

Porto Digital has six key milestones (Porto Digital 2015):

1. A broadband infrastructure aimed at spreading the use of this network to other entities (i.e. a unified network that does not just reach those who participate in Porto Digital). This extends the network to other areas of the city, with about 53 kilometres of optical fibre and a number of antennas for wireless communication (incorporated in buildings in such a way as to reduce maximum visual impact).
2. Three computer centres – CM Porto (Porto City Council), Porto University and AEIOU (news portal) – that host various Internet sites of the project.
3. A set of transactional websites about e-governance, employment, culture and tourism, real estate, businesses, etc.

4. A set of informative sites also available on mobile devices, such as counselling and social support, mobility, 3D virtual tours, etc.
5. Computer equipment placed in a select group of schools and non-profitable institutions.
6. The employment and vocational-oriented City of Professions within the historic centre of Porto.

According to Porto Digital (2015), the relevant benefits for the city include increasing intercommunication between university hubs (with relatively small charges for Internet access, as well as smaller charges for the council once it becomes networked) and technology companies situated in the wider region, and creating more precise traffic information and information about the city in mixed media. Porto Digital offers links to many official websites about the city of Porto, such as Porto City Council's (CMP)

Figure 3. Porto´s City Hall (used as part of a 3D competition) and Avenida dos Aliados (whose metro station represents an altered public space).

'Tourism and Culture' site. From here, people can also 'travel' to 'Portorama', a registered-users-only cyberspace where people can upload and share photographs of Porto, giving their idiosyncratic views of the city.

Design professionals recognize that the experience of space only has meaning from the standpoint of motion. As a result, they have looked for other perceptual tools that approach the design of movement, such as film or three-dimensional animation. The use of these mediums has helped the public to better understand the idea that the relationship between space and their movement in it is an important generator of experience. Porto Digital created an initiative that shows how three-dimensional virtual models can be used to represent the city in a more virtually accessible manner.

The Porto Digital website aims to create a virtual experience of the city using key buildings of Porto, and is intended to make the city more accessible to people from around the world that use the Web as a vehicle for experiencing cities. For this, a competition – 'Porto em 3D'/'Porto in 3D' – was launched that envisioned the creation of three-dimensional electronic models of paradigmatic buildings, enabling a better understanding of the physical city as a mediated experience. Only eleven buildings were proposed to be transformed into digital models when the competition began in 2006. By 2015, thirteen virtual models of significant places were available online (albeit viewable separately). By providing their specific location, this project could be maximized if incorporated into the sub-project of virtual tours of Porto.

In order to reach Porto Digital's proposed milestones, the city underwent some physical transformations. For this, the urban realm and architecture played a key role in incorporating the suitable infrastructures for the virtual networks. For instance, optical fibre cables were placed in existing underground conduits, while others were placed accordingly to existing regeneration plans for specific areas of the city. The acquisition of network interfaces or wireless access points enabled the creation of a residential wireless data network, meaning access to numerous networks was now available in public spaces and buildings such as the airport, shopping centres, conference centres and public gardens (Porto Digital 2015).

Another example of virtual information on Porto is Cidade das Profissões ('City of Professions'). Also created in 2006, this was a project to freely support the inhabitants of the city in areas of information and counselling about professions, jobs, training and entrepreneurship. This project was borne from the international network of cities of professions created in France during the 1990s (Réseau Cités des Métiers). It aims to promote citizens' employability and entrepreneurship by developing their skills and promoting knowledge about the world of work, enhancing their ability to adapt to market changes. This project is supplementary to the existing services in the city of Porto, developing alliances and partnerships that contribute to the quality and relevance of its activities. It provides individual counselling about jobs, internships, training and entrepreneurship; free Internet access, meeting venues, training and recruitment; monthly workshops, seminars and informational sessions; and projects for schools and

Figure 4. Largo de São Domingos, a public square with wireless access.

other institutions. The City of Professions conceives products for those with specific informational needs, as well as thematic games, newsletters and other informational kits made available to users and spread throughout the partners' network. People can also access a blog via the website that acts as a virtual centre for counselling and information, allowing them to share ideas and view specific events in the city.

The Porto Digital project falls within a major aim of the Porto Master Plan, launched by the city council in partnership with PortoVivo SRU – a public funded company leading the urban regeneration of downtown. As well as developing a communication plan and motivating all agents to contribute to the revitalization process, the project allows citizens to contribute knowledge and ideas, thereby reducing conflicts caused by lack of information. The communication plan focuses on six thematic promotional representations of the city. The first is about portraying Porto as a city of 'science and innovation', with a focus on business opportunities and scientific creation, and supported by universities and research centres. The second focuses on Porto as a city of 'retail', promoting shopping/commercial events. The third represents a city of 'tourism and leisure', promoting the city as a tourist destination by connecting travel agencies, private individuals and the Portuguese tourism exchange. The fourth is about representing Porto as a 'culture and entertainment' centre, communicating different cultural and businesses' activities/initiatives in the city. The fifth presents Porto as a city of 'mobility', promoting public transportation, information about roads and car parks, and making the city more environmentally friendly. The sixth representation is about 'housing' promotion amongst students, young people, entrepreneurs, and creative and knowledgeable professionals (Porto Master Plan n.d.: 26). The communication plan, together with Cidade das

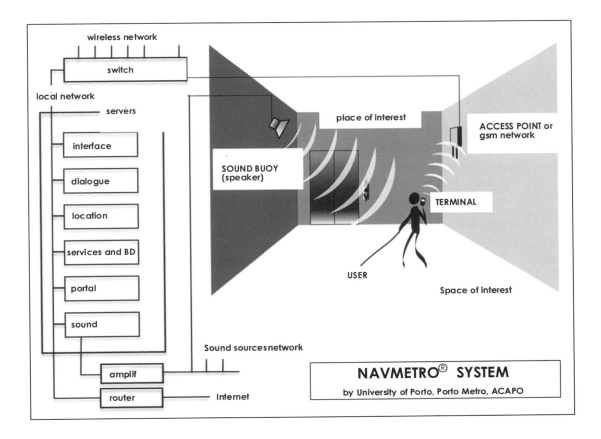

Figure 5. NAVMETRO system diagram.

Profissões and Porto Digital, show that city agents in Porto are increasingly aware of the importance of virtual platforms for reaching wider audiences, as well as for conveying the images they think best represent a positive, future-led and innovative city.

A very important achievement in the field of ICT – and one that also answers the particular aims of the city of 'mobility' (the fifth theme in the communication plan) – was made by the Metro do Porto SA in partnership with ACAPO (Blind and Amblyopic Portuguese Association) and the FEUP (Engineering Faculty of Porto University), who provided an information and navigation service for blind and amblyopic travellers in all metro stations. NAVMETRO is a technological innovation developed by different scholars, academics and professionals aimed at making the metro's network more accessible and guaranteeing fair use for all citizens, especially those who are visually impaired. This innovative tool allows users with visual impairment to be oriented through the network, including providing assistance when buying and validating tickets; helping with orientation inside the station; and providing generic information about the metro lines, schedules and tickets. NAVMETRO works as a voice and sound orientation system by using mobile phones to guide users through several routes inside the metro station. At various decision points, a bird song is emitted to maintain the thread of spatial orientation (ACAPO 2009).

From these examples, one can recognize the substantial impact of ICT on creating representations and mediated experiences of Porto. Digital platforms have become important disseminating tools, instigating people to closer participation in city life and its physical transformation process.

Final considerations

The ways in which ICT impacts cities and people varies according to different spatial and social contexts. It is clear that ICT is a by-product of the globalized world; as such, the phenomenon can only be equated within this spatio-temporal framework.

Information about places is now readily available via digital platforms on the Web, where the invisible layers of the city can be accessed in the virtual realm. Accordingly, the physical city is increasingly supplemented by the digital city, where information is made available at all kinds of levels.

Some of the ideas about digital information exposed in this chapter have been based upon existing work and research on the city and its informational networks, thus questioning the current hypothesis of the possibility of physical space being surpassed by cyberspace. It is true that with globalization and the technological advances of the last part of the past century, information networks have invaded people's lives, both in private and public spaces: cable television has entered the home; widescreen TVs have flooded the city landscape; modern optical fibre and digital television allow faster access to information; and GPS has provided better geographical navigation and orientation.

However, these instruments – or informational tools – have come to exist in a parallel condition to the physical city, rather than having been created to dissolve it. These information networks exist according to the demands of an increasingly fast-paced society, where real-time events, information and data are divulged through any of the existing networks of information to reach the individual realm.

Physical spaces will always be the platforms that provide the city with flows of people, information, and communication – some of which are visible layers, while others are invisible. People's experience of the city is increasingly mediated by these networks, but never entirely replaced by the virtual experience. There are new spaces in the informational city where new experience conditions are established (such as the virtualization process, virtual presence and augmented reality). Buying, selling, booking appointments, visiting museums, chatting and many other human activities can be mediated through information systems and made effective in virtual environments.

Experience can occur beyond the purely presential concept. As Christine Boyer (1994) argues, the prevalence of sight over other senses has had a strong effect on the emergence of virtual reality technologies. She advocates that this phenomenon will fragment the relationship between people and the city. Others propose that the information age will bring about the end of 'press, television, and mass media; the end of brokers and other intermediaries; end of firms, bureaucracies, and similar organizations; end of universities; cities and regions; and the end of nation-state' (Brown & Duguid 2002: 16). However, there is evidence to support the fact that communication technologies increase contact and information exchange between people. Thus, the idea that virtual spaces will replace physical space and the interpersonal relationships will disappear is far from being proven. To claim that cyberspace will replace the physical space of the city is simplistic. Even as the co-modification of information increases, not all people have access to such technologies and not all that use them are shut away from city life. What is true is that there are increased searches for information digitally, especially if people want to know about places before directly experiencing them.

Digital cities should be 'physical space-oriented, encouraging people to go out' (Aurigi 2005: 62). They are strictly virtual sites that inform about their real counterpart. Consequently, they may also prompt people to directly experience cities. Electronic information about cities and technological advances in dissemination allow indirect experiences, and help shape people's perceptions of cities before they have been experienced first-hand. Ultimately, it is now hard to think of life without technology, as it has become embedded in everyday city activities: 'integrated within a complex network of human actors and technical artefacts [...] leading to the recombination of new spaces and times' (Dixon et al. 2005: 26).

In the case of Porto, electronic information about the city has been increasing due to the appreciation that the Internet is the most used and updated media for representing, informing and communicating the city. By 2015, many websites existed for the promotion of many aspects of the city: including community blogs and forums for promotion of debate about local issues; and dedicated tourism websites containing information ranging from the history of the city to the most detailed list of activities going on in Porto. Digital cities have also become instruments where the city is produced and communicated by the city´s agents according to their priorities.

The question arises as to how our everyday digital tools will impact on the physical realm. The growing awareness of the potential for varying kinds of ICT to be applied to planning, transportation, education and others has allowed Porto's city council to adopt an information and telecommunication infrastructure that is better able to generate an accessible community of knowledge and creation. ICT have a profound impact on people's perceptions of the city, enabling mediated experiences. They are therefore important (and increasingly used) tools for promoting cities at a global scale, suggesting representations that aim to match the city agent's beliefs and expectations about them (as discussed throughout this chapter and more specifically in terms of image change).

The case of Porto illustrates how digital and electronic information about the city has invaded everyday life – from physical space to dedicated city e-spaces. City spaces have provided the physical infrastructure for the virtual world, stretching and bending accordingly. However, it is unlikely that people will become increasingly distant from urban life as the city adapts to the technological era. On the contrary, observational evidence proves that the physical city surpasses the virtual one: Porto is an increasingly lively city, especially in the historic centre and downtown. On the other hand, the peripheral areas of the city still have mobility and accessibility issues, due to weak connections between distinct urban areas and lower public investment.

References

ACAPO (2009), 'Navmetro – 'Navegação assistida para pessoas cegas e com baixa visão na rede do metro do Porto'/'Assisted navigation for blind and weak vision people in the metro network of Porto', http://www.acapo.pt/index.php?option=com_content&view=article&id=235:navmetro&Catid=1:noticias&Itemid=189. Accessed 22 April 2014.

Aurigi, A. (2005), *Making the Digital City, The Early Shaping of Urban Internet Space*, Hampshire: Ashgate.

Boj, C. and Diaz, D. (2008), 'The hybrid city: Augmented reality for interactive artworks in the public space', in C. Sommerer, L. C. Jain and L. Mignonneau (eds), *The Art and Science of Interface and Interaction Design*, vol. 1, Berling: Springer-Verlag, pp. 141–61.

Boyer, M. C. (1994), *The City of Collective Memory: Its Historical Imagery and Architectural Entertainments*, London: MIT Press.

Brown, J. S. and Duguid, P. (2002), *The Social Life of Information*, Cambridge, MA: Harvard Business School Press.

Burgess, J. (1990), 'The production and consumption of environmental meanings in the mass media: A research agenda for the 1990s', *Transactions of the Institute of British Geographers New Series*, 15: 2, pp. 136–61, http://www.jstor.org/stable/622861. Accessed 12 January 2010.

Castells, M. (1997), 'An introduction to the information age', *City*, 2: 7, pp. 6–16.

Cidade das Profissões (2014a), 'Home page', http://cdp.portodigital.pt/. Accessed 16 April 2014.

——— ——— (2014b), 'Objectivos'/'Objectives', http://cdp.portodigital.pt/sobre-o-portal/ objectivos. Accessed 15 April 2014.

Dixon, T., Thompson, B., McAllister, P., Marston, A. and Snow, J. (2005), *Real Estate and the New Economy: The Impact of Information and Communications Technology*, Oxford: Blackwell.

Druick, Z. (1995), 'The information superhighway, or the politics of a metaphor', http:// bad.eserver.org/issues/1995/18/druck.html. Accessed 20 February 2010.

Graham, S. and Marvin, S. (2000), 'Urban planning and the technological future of cities', in Wheeler et al. (eds), *Cities in the Telecommunications Age: The Fracturing of Geographies*, London and New York: Routledge, pp. 71–98.

Isenstadt, S. (2001), 'Recurring surfaces: Architecture in the experience economy', *Perspecta*, 32, pp. 108–19, http://www.jstor.org/pss/1567288. Accessed 5 February 2010.

Ishida, T. (2000), 'Understanding digital cities', in T. Ishida and K. Isbister (eds), *Digital Cities: Technologies, Experiences, and Future Perspectives*, London: Springer, pp. 7–17.

Massey, D., Allen, J. and Pile, S. (eds) (1999), *City Worlds*, London and New York: Routledge.

Mitchell, W. J. (1996), *City of Bits: Space, Place and the Infobahn*, Cambridge, MA: MIT Press.

——— ——— (2005), *Placing Words: Symbols, Space, and the City*, London: MIT Press.

Piazzalunga, R. (2004), *Virtualização da Arquitetura/Virtualization of Architecture*, Campinas: Papirus Editora.

Porto Digital (2015), 'Home page', http://www.portodigital.pt/. Accessed 15 April 2014.

Porto Master Plan (2005), 'Executive summary', Porto Vivo Sociedade de Reabilitação Urbana (SRU), www.portovivosru.pt/pdfs/Masterplan_EN.pdf. Accessed 3 March 2014.

Sassen, S. (ed.) (2000), *Global Networks, Linked Cities*, London and New York: Routledge.

Vale, L. J. and Warner Jr., S. B. (eds) (2001), *Imaging the City: Continuing Struggles and New Directions*, New Jersey: The Centre for Urban Policy Research.

Venturi, R., Izenour, S. and Brown, D. S. (1977), *Learning From Las Vegas: The Forgotten Symbolism of Architectural Form*, Cambridge, MA: MIT Press.

Chapter 4

From the iron cage to the mediated city

Cristina Miranda de Almeida

[S]pecialists without spirit, sensualists without heart;
this nullity imagines that it has attained a level of civilization never before achieved.

(Weber 1905)

Introduction

In 1903, Georg Simmel wrote 'The metropolis and mental life'. In this short text, Simmel posed deep questions about how modern life was impacting our sense of individuality and individual autonomy. He also stressed how necessary it was for the individual 'to maintain the independence and individuality of his [her] existence against the sovereign power of society, against the weight of the historical heritage and the external culture and technique of life' (Simmel 1903). The chapter will focus on the questions posed by Simmel at the beginning of the twentieth century so as to reflect on the impact of city mediation 112 years after Simmel's text. The aim is to refocus Simmel's question to how individuals in a mediated city maintain the independence and individuality of their existence against the technique of life. In this sense, the concept of 'technique of life' is updated here to refer to the very digital information and communication technologies that mediate life in the contemporary city.

Simmel defends the idea that there is a fundamental aspect that persists across history: 'the resistance of the individual to being levelled, swallowed up in the social technological mechanism' (Simmel 1903). He was writing during an historical moment of transformation, in which city life was being rationalized due to a marked increase in its size:

Punctuality, calculability and exactness, which are required by the complications and extensiveness of metropolitan life, are not only most intimately connected with its capitalistic and intellectualistic character but also colour the content of life and are conductive to the exclusion of those irrational, instinctive, sovereign human traits and impulses which originally seek to determine the form of life from within instead of receiving it from the outside in a general, schematically precise form.

(Simmel 1903: 13)

So, how are people today resisting being swallowed up by the pervasiveness of the mediated environment in cities where computers are 'like pigments in a wall paint' (Castells 1996)?

After Simmel, Max Weber wrote *The Protestant Ethic and the Spirit of Capitalism* (1905), in which he coined the term 'iron cage' (in German *stahlhartes Gehäuse* can also be translated to 'shell as hard as steel'). The iron cage (Weber 1905) is a metaphor of the rationalization process in progress, particularly in western capitalist societies. The idea is that the iron cage is shaped by teleological efficiency, rational calculation and control bars that trap people; thus the 'rationalization' of life is the key point in the transformation from premodern to modern society. The rationalization process felt by Weber presents a Janus-like face: it resulted in the introduction of a more equal and efficient society, but it also opened the door to pervasive strategies of control in which we are immersed, particularly in mediated city environments.

Weber became concerned with social actions, and the subjective meaning that humans attach to their actions and interaction within specific social contexts. He also believed in idealism, which is the belief that we only know things because of the meanings that we apply to them. In 1999, Neil Gershenfeld published 'When things start to think', and Kevin Ashton used the term 'Internet of Things' in a presentation at Procter & Gamble. When we talk now about Internet of Things, we are basically referring to devices, things and living beings that can communicate, sense information and generate data flows and streams – a phenomenon that has been exponentially increasing lately, transforming itself into what is called 'big data phenomenon'.

Each historical time has a different sensorial regimen that influences the subject's experience according to scientific, technological, cultural, economic and other vital, historically determined paradigms. According to Simmel, the psychological foundation of metropolitan individuality is a result of the intensification of emotional life due to the features of external and internal stimuli.

> When one enquires about the products of contemporary life with reference to their inner meaning – when, so to speak, one examines the body of culture with reference to the soul, as I am to do concerning the metropolis today – the answer requires the investigation of the relationship which such a social structure promotes between the individual aspects of life and those which transcend the existence of single individuals. It will require the investigation of the adaptations made by the personality in its adjustment to the forces that lie outside of it. The psychological foundation, upon which the metropolitan individuality is erected, is the intensification of emotional life due to the swift and continuous shift of external and internal stimuli.
>
> (Simmel 1903: 11)

We can revisit this affirmation to analyse our circumstance today, in which Internet of Things also includes 'actants' or biocybrids[1] (Domingues, Hamdan & Augusto 2010) that are able to contribute to the data pool with the aid of geolocalized devices. In doing so, we may ask ourselves: (1) What sort of relationship is promoted between the individual aspects of life and those which transcend the existence of single individuals in this social structure? and (2) What adaptations do people make to the forces that lie outside of them?

The role of technology, the action of subject, and the relationship between technology and subject are all historically dependent. The Internet of Things is being embedded in all dimensions of urban life, bringing to people new forms of experience – including human and non-human actors, or actants (Latour 1987, 2005; Law & Hassard 1999) – that are given agency in everyday life and opening new opportunities to knowledge building.

Michael Callon (1991, 1995, 1997) and Bruno Latour (1987, 2005) developed the actant–network theory. The concept of actant, as defined in this theory, is any thing or being that has capacity to act, such as objects, inscriptions, artefacts, concepts, institutions, environments and other non-human living beings. In concrete, Latour (1987) states that actants can network and associate to form actant networks that connect, influence and empower each other. The actants' form of interaction is called 'heterogeneous engineering' (Law 1987; Law & Hassard 1999; Latour 1987, 2005).

In the hyper-connected age, the limits between offline and online, between the physical body and the digital self, are blurred in numerous ways, and society is immersed in hybrid environments that are being shaped as a result of the manipulation of genes, atoms and bits. In these hybrid environments, notions of space, time, matter, identity, relationship, work, leisure, self-expression, privacy, reputation, motivation and attention are being deeply affected.[2] The impact of these changes is particularly felt in relation to gender, age and cultural differences, as well as deficits of respect, fairness, attention and obstacles regarding self-expression.

When the physical (i.e. bio and atoms) and the digital dimensions of reality blend, a hybrid reality is formed. This hybrid reality does not fall inside the scope of society's perceptive window in a generalized way. There is little social awareness about what a hybrid reality is, or about the challenges, opportunities and benefits that emerge from it.

According to Simmel, one of these challenges is a need to balance intellectual and emotional aspects in any kind of relationship. So, how is this balance taking place now?

All emotional relationships between persons rest on their individuality, whereas intellectual relationships deal with persons as with numbers, that is, as with elements which, in themselves, are indifferent, but which are of interest only insofar as they offer something objectively perceivable.

(Simmel 1903: 12)

Forms of knowledge creation, storage, distribution and retrieval are changing quickly. What affects knowledge affects everything else, particularly in terms of the phenomena of big data and the Internet of Things. Simmel's affirmation reminds us how crucial it is to give importance to the emotional side along with the intellectual one in relation to knowledge. This can provide a clue as to how to make sense of big data and open doors to art. Art is a field that can turn a city into an interface for geolocalized narratives supported by mobile and environmentally embedded technologies.

Creative narratives can have a profound effect on how we experience knowledge (e.g. real time, interactivity, always-on, geolocalized, oversaturated, blasé), on who creates and manages meaning (e.g. humans and actants), and on what type of content is added or developed (expert and non-expert content; simultaneous emergence of bottom-up and top-down forms of knowledge).

The problem

Simmel identified the notion of the blasé attitude, a recurring feature in the psychological traits associated with urban environments, defined as indifference towards the distinctions between things; that is to say, the 'meaning and the value of the distinctions between things, and therewith of the things themselves, are experienced as meaningless' (Simmel 1903: 14):

> There is perhaps no psychic phenomenon which is so unconditionally reserved to the city as the blasé outlook. It is at first the consequence of those rapidly shifting stimulations of the nerves which are thrown together in all their contrasts and from which it seems to us the intensification of metropolitan intellectuality seems to be derived.
>
> (Simmel 1903: 14)

Simmel was referring to the dominance of rules and standards relating to reason, science, instrumentalization, measurement and rationalization. This process is framed by the centrality of intellectual functions (in detriment of emotion and intuition) that resulted in a 'homeless mind' (Berger 1974). Nowadays, we can analyse the accelerated impact of the Internet on matter, time, identity, self and environment. This process is another step in this same rationalization process taking the form of globalization.

Nevertheless, the dimensions of this process are not yet clearly understood. In particular, considering matter only from the point of view of its physicality is not enough to analyse the rational layers that are being embedded into everything. From living beings to urban ecosystems, the rationalization process is embedded on the very flesh of our cities and bodies. We measure and visualize everything: our steps in the city, heart rates and our emotional reactions during social mobilizations (for example, tweets during the 15M movement).

The embedding of the Internet in the core of our physical and social realities is an intensification of rationalization processes. It affects not only the subject's experience, but also the very definition of matter. As a result, new analytical tools are required to take into consideration the very dissolution of screens into the physical world, the blending of digital into matter, and the emergence of digital matter as a new layer that intimately merges with nature. According to Thomas S. Popkewitz and Fazal Rizvi (2010), to 'explore the irony embodied in globalization as a quality of the homeless mind is to explore the entanglements of distant events and spaces with the immediacies of everyday life'. For these authors:

> Globalization becomes both a perceived source of anonymous 'forces' that have no historical 'home' or author and something that enables planning for interventions in daily life. Numbers as the construction of categories of equivalence 'act' to establish globalness. Sameness becomes inscribed as difference that stands outside history. The irony of the practices of globalization lies in its simultaneous relocation into practices that link the collective belonging qualities given to society with home – the homeless quality of reason makes homes!
>
> (Popkewitz & Rizvi 2010: 264)

This must be the same feeling of sameness, lack of discrimination and blasé attitude highlighted by Simmel in 1903.

Although these methods of dealing with numbers and data are pervasive, contemporary urban administrations and other local and regional institutions are not fully aware of all actors interacting with data, nor how it is produced, mined and represented by them. For example, data is considered basically a human product, but non-human actors and actants (Latour) are also taking part in the weaving of the Web and big data pool. Even animals are sending tweets to update platforms about their movements. At the same time, although data is globally mined, data treatment is localized, and there is little collaborative transversality to compare how different cities take cross-border group of stakeholders into consideration when it comes to projects. Data visualizations are rendered in a partial, fragmented and (not always) scientific way by designers, artists and developers. These parties are mostly linked to private sectors, who lack a full perspective on the social complexity that is involved in the representation of urban data and how it affects citizenship. In the same way, there is a lack of transversality in relation to fields of activities, thereby reflecting the fragmentary approach above-mentioned.

Research question and objectives

So, what are the main factors shaping the change that results from the inscription of these processes (rationalization, instrumental rationality, globalization) on matter and the urban environment? The research questions posed by this situation relate to the transformations formed when atoms, genes and bits merge in relation to the previous model of experience. What are the features of these new forms of materiality, sensitivity and action? The hypothesis is that a hybrid kind of interval is opening up between different layers of reality: namely analogue versus digital dimensions; nature versus culture; here versus there; past versus future; 'I' versus others; and human versus non-human. In this recombination process, a new kind of reality emerges – a 'radically hybrid reality'. In this reality, new experiences of matter, space, time and self/identity are being created in a twilight zone that merges private and public spheres, individual and first-person with collective perspectives, local with non-local relationships, human with non-human actions, physical and digital matter, and nano- and macro-scales of matter with different scales of time and space. Radical hybrid reality is thus shaping a materialism that displays a new physicality in relation to matter, time, space and self.

In order to better understand this emerging form of materiality, this chapter will assess the impact of the manipulation of these three elements (atoms, bits and genes) in relation to five dimensions: form, matter, space, time and self.

The first objective of what follows is to offer a more inclusive analytical model – called the 'Model of Radical Hybrid Experience' – to make visible some essential dimensions of this kind of reality. This model encompasses a hybrid materiality so that society can better situate itself in relation to a reality in which the digital dimension seamlessly blends with physical matter and the world gains agency.

The second objective is to introduce a few examples of how interactions between people, social processes, things and environments are undergoing a transformation triggered by technology.

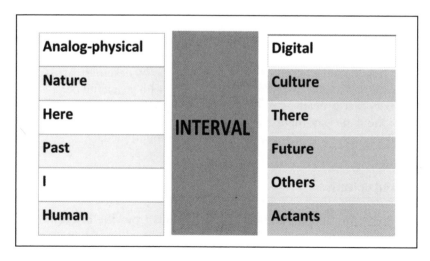

Figure 1. The hybrid interval of new materialities, temporalities, spacialities and sensibilities.

In order to construct this model, this research is grounded in the intersection of art, ICT and the urban experience from a constructivist viewpoint and uses the actor-network theory (Latour 1987, 2005; Law & Hassard 1999).

The Model of Radical Hybrid Experience as applied to the mediated city

Radical Atoms

Using an iceberg metaphor as its base, the Tangible Media Group distinguishes three kinds of interfaces for the interaction between analogue and digital dimensions. The first form corresponds to the idea of graphic user interface (GUI) or 'painted bits'; this only allows users to see digital information through a screen (as if information were below water) and interact with forms 'below water' through remote controls (e.g. mouse, keyboards and touchscreens). The second form is tangible user interfaces (TUI) or 'tangible bits'. This is the form that is most similar to an iceberg, with one part submerged and a second part that emerges into the visible realm. In relation to digital information, it means that part of the information is manifested in the physical sphere (e.g. as physical computation), which allows direct interaction with the exposed part of the iceberg. The third kind of interface is 'Radical Atoms'; this form enables direct interaction with physical manifestations of digital information, as though the whole iceberg has been extruded out of water.

The concept of 'Radical Atoms' is key to understanding this subject. According to Lakatos and Ishii (2012), 'Radical Atoms should fulfill the following three requirements: 1) transform their shape, 2) conform to constraints, and 3) inform their ability, in order to utilize dynamic affordance as a medium for representation, while allowing bidirectional input to control the shape and thus the underlying computational model'. This conceptualization opens the possibility of exploring the different levels of how digital information is embedded in the physical dimension of reality, and how hybrid materials are being formed when bits and atoms meet.

Although the concept of Radical Atoms is crucial to understand some of the processes that are being experienced, it not enough to understand all the features involved in the new forms of materiality and sensitivity. In this chapter, we respond to this problem by expanding this concept to construct a broader framework; this should be better able to support our understanding of how the radical hybrid media ecology and landscape are taking shape and affecting our experience.

In order to construct the framework of radical reality, it is necessary to focus on a few case studies from art and design in which the recombination of atoms, genes and bits configures the radical reality. Some of these cases relate to more than one category in the model, but are inscribed only in one category to serve as examples that highlight the feature being addressed. These case studies will be structured around five analytical categories: namely matter, space, time, self/identity and action.

In order to analyse radical experience in hybrid environments, it is suggested we look at five dimensions that, when crossed with the manipulation practices of genes, atoms and bits, constitute the basic dimensions of a radical extension model (Figure 2).

Radical experience

The radical features that can be observed in the Model of Radical Hybrid Experience (Figure 2) relate to form, matter, space, time and self. Some of the dimensions have sub-dimensions. Examples are given and briefly analysed in each; some of these could have been used for more than one dimension, but have been situated in just one for clarity.

Radical experience of form: Between natural and digital
In relation to form, a hybrid reality appears in the interval between analogue and digital dimensions. One example is data-based forms of 3D printing that can be even more radical when form includes genetic manipulation. One example is the possibility to grow our own limbs (William 2014).

Radical experience of matter
In relation to matter, a hybrid reality emerges in the interval between nature and culture. They also emerge in processes of simulation of nature and the appearance of new kinds of nature (including hybrid materials or substances), and are the result of manipulation of different scales of matter (Kac n.d.). One example of new kinds of matter brought about by scale manipulation is the so-called 'lotus effect' (cf. Barthlott & Ehler 1977), which refers to properties of water repellence and self-cleaning present in some materials as a result of their nano- and microstructures.

Radical experience of space: Between 'here' and 'there'
Simmel (1903) pointed out that the most significant features of a metropolis and our bodies is the functional extension beyond its physical borders:

> The most significant aspect of the metropolis lies in this functional magnitude beyond its actual physical boundaries and this effectiveness reacts upon the latter and gives to it life, weight, importance and responsibility. A person does not end with the limits of his physical body or with the area to which his physical activity is immediately confined but embraces, rather, the totality of meaningful effects which emanates him temporally and spatially. In the same way the city exists only in the totality of the effects which transcend their immediate sphere.
>
> (Simmel 1903)

Analogue dimensions		Interval in the radical model	Examples of radical hybrid experience
1. Form		Radical form: interval between analogue and digital data-based form	Bio-printing, grow your limbs [3]
2. Matter Radical matter: interval between nature and culture simulation, new nature, hybrid materials, scales	Matter-Substance	New nature	Natural History of Enigma, Petunya, Eduardo Kac [4]
	Matter- Scale	Nano and micro scales	Lotus effect [5]
3. Space		Radical space: interval between here and there. Geo-localization, tele-presence	The Tunnel under the Atlantic, (Maurice Benayoum and musical creation by Martin Matalon) linked the space of Pompidou Centre (Paris) and the space of the Museum of Contemporary Art (Montréal) in September, 1995
4. Time		Radical time: interval between past and future. Real Time, always on, now, long now Real time smart cities	According to Laura Beloff Appendix shows that connections became part of our identities, making visible our dependency to everything natural and artificial
5. Self Radical Self: interval between I and 'other', identity, point of view, control and first-person perspective. Self-knowledge.	Point of view	Radical point of view: Displacement of point of view, multiplicity and transformation of point of view	The Machine to Be Another is an experience of swapping perceptions and points of view, a technology-based performance in which participants swap their points of view with the aim to build empathy
	Control	Radical control: interval between self control and social control	Nike iPhone iPad-health control. Health apps and self knowledge are part of the trend known as quantified self, based on first person perspectives
	Self-agency-identity	Radical actors: interval between I and 'others'/actants	Some sharks have been tagged to their locations and send an alert about their position, as well as size and species, to Surf Life Saving Western Australia's (SLSWA) Twitter feed
	Self-action	Radical action: interval between local and tele-action	ECloud: Real time weather from different places in the world controlling polycarbonate tiles that move according to data in a certain pattern

Figure 2. Model of Radical Hybrid Experience.

This statement could have inspired the artist Maurice Benayoun – a pioneer of telepresence in art – in his televirtual event 'The Tunnel Under the Atlantic' (Benayoun 1995). During this event, Benayoun remotely connected people in the Pompidou Centre in Paris with the Museum of Contemporary Art in Montreal, thereby creating a virtual tunnel underneath the Atlantic Ocean. People on both sides of the virtual tunnel were simultaneously in a local and a global dimension, feeling at the same time a belonging to a 'here' and a 'there'. Telepresence technologies have opened up new forms of space and time hybrid experience. The interval between here and there is a hybrid dimension in which both virtual/physical and local/distant dimensions merge.

Radical experience of time: Interval between past and future
The artwork 'Appendix' by Laura Beloff (2011) is a complex example of different kinds of hybrid experience. In this section, the analysis will be focused on the aspect of radical time, and specifically particular how experience emerges in the interval between past and future:

> The Appendix is a networked robotic tail designed for a human. It investigates the relation between body, technology and human to his surrounding world, which is increasingly based on technological features and connections. [...] The work Appendix makes visible our dependency and connectedness to other people, things, nature and to various systems. [...] The current version of the tail has two real-world data connections: (1) Connection to nature phenomenon; the tail is receiving real-time data of the wave height of the sea, which is seen on the tail as an upward movement; (2) Connection to a system; the tail is following real-time data of a city public transport system and signals with a specific gesture the current/real-time direction of a tram.
>
> (Beloff 2011)

Radical experience of self: Between 'I' and 'other'
Simmel emphasized the need to compensate for the suppression of the personal layer (initiated by the rationalization process) with a rise in expression of individualities, peculiarities and extremities of the personal. Nowadays, this process is increasingly more accelerated:

> [L]ife is composed more and more of these impersonal cultural elements and existing goods and values which seek to suppress peculiar personal interests and incomparabilities. As a result, in order that this most personal element be saved, extremities and peculiarities and individualizations must be produced and they must be over-exaggerated merely to be brought into the awareness even of the individual himself. The atrophy of individual culture through the hypertrophy of objective culture lies at the root of the bitter hatred that preachers of the most extreme individualism,

in the footsteps of Nietzsche, directed against the metropolis. [...] When both of these forms of individualism which are nourished by the quantitative relationships of the metropolis, i.e. individual independence and the elaboration of personal peculiarities, are examined with reference to their historical position, the metropolis attains an entirely new value and meaning in the world history of the spirit.

(Simmel 1903)

The hypertrophy of objective culture that Simmel refers to is taking place as displacements from a fixed point of view to radical points of view (cf. 'The Machine to be Another' [Ehrsson et al. 2014]); from self-control and social-based self-control (see the application Nike+Running); and from 'me'/'I' to 'others' (see how sharks are being used by Australian marine biologists to save lives).

Tendencies in radical experiences

In order to understand the manifestation of the contemporary processes of rationalization that structure this model, these examples can be analysed in relation to five tendencies: physical-digital blending; global-local merging; universal practices of knowledge construction; the dissolution of interfaces; and first-person perspectives. We are now going to explore the features of each tendency.

Physical-digital blending
The first tendency is the merging of physical and digital layers of data into the physical environment, thereby enabling reality to be augmented. Computing is becoming ubiquitous, pervasive and invisible; alongside this, environments, things and beings are becoming increasingly wirelessly networked, geolocalized and tagged. In parallel, the frontiers between biological, mechanical and electronic parts of organisms are being blurred.

Global-local merging
The second tendency is society's access to continuous (always-on and real-time) global-local forms of interaction. The possibility to electronically code physical objects, beings and environments and tagging systems (e.g. RFID, QR codes, etc.) opens up the possibility for cities to integrate an emotionally subjective layer into the urban tissue, thus enabling direct access to social networks from urban contexts, equipment and institutions. This offers an extraordinary opportunity for including interactive bottom-up creativity and knowledge construction processes in the core of everyday life, as supported by mobile social media. As a consequence of these aspects, matter is gaining agency in this 'strange reality'.

Universal practices of knowledge construction
The third tendency is for both humans and non-humans to produce data and share content. In doing so, the challenges presented to digital inclusion trigger new forms of media illiteracy. This process is supported by the development of cloud computing, which enables the pervasiveness of knowledge. In this process of knowledge construction, opportunities and challenges for interdisciplinarity, multidisciplinarity and transdisciplinarity appear.

Dissolution of interfaces
As a fourth tendency, it is essential to consider what happens to interfaces. Interfaces are 'disappearing', dissolving into the environment as a result of a process of miniaturization and pervasiveness of micro-electromechanical devices (MEMs) such as smartdust, smart motes, nanobots, artificial intelligence, bio-inspired organisms, smart micro-organisms and drones. These turn environments into smart tissues and bio-interfaces (i.e. the use of smart micro-organisms and devices) embedded in tangible natural or artificial environments that substitute for computer screens. As a consequence, technology makes itself more invisible.

First-person perspectives
The fifth and last dimension in the process is the emergence of first-person perspectives in the use of technology. An example of this is the uploading of date-personal biophysical (biometric) data onto online self-tracking platforms .

According to Simmel (1903), alongside the liberalistic ideal and the division of labour brought about by the Industrial Revolution, individuals have been liberated from historical bonds, opening the door to the emergence of individual expression as a criteria of value:

> [I]ndividuals who had been liberated from their historical bonds sought now to distinguish themselves from one another. No longer was it the 'general human quality' in every individual but rather his qualitative uniqueness and irreplaceability that now became the criteria of his value. In the conflict and shifting interpretations of these two ways of defining the position of the individual within the totality is to be found the external as well as the internal history of our time. It is the function of the metropolis to make a place for the conflict and for the attempts at unification of both of these in the sense that its own peculiar conditions have been revealed to us as the occasion and the stimulus for the development of both. Thereby they attain a quite unique place, fruitful with an inexhaustible richness of meaning in the development of the mental life. They reveal themselves as one of those great historical structures in which conflicting life embracing currents find themselves with equal legitimacy.
>
> (Simmel 1903: 19)

Although originating more than a century ago, the outcome of the confluence of these tendencies is taking form today as the phenomena of 'selfies', in the multisensorial translations of data into physical phenomena and matter (cf. Bellof 2011), and in the shaping of new kinds of identity, materiality, sensibility, temporality and spaciality. In our data-driven lives, a kind of data obsession is emerging. An increasing substitution of words by multisensorial experiences is evident in this process, along with a hypertrophy of first-person perspectives combined with collective processes of sharing and knowledge formation.

Contributions and conclusions

Simmel's (1903) text helps to pinpoint the root of the change that is forging experience in the mediated city, and reflected in the analytical model based on the interrelationship between five dimensions (form, matter, space, time and self) and three spheres of action (genes, bits and atoms).

Current trends are giving birth to a more intense phase of the rationalization process, which started with the Industrial Revolution but is still somehow invisible. The factors that shape this new phase need to be addressed by institutions at all levels in order to prevent new kinds of digital illiteracy. Transformations affect how people and institutions behave, reflect, interact, socialize, create and distribute knowledge. If we want to understand the needs that are being forged, it is necessary to comprehend the nature of the relationship between technology and society when a new materialism is formed. Only by taking into consideration the change in the nature of reality itself (and matter in particular) can we lay the foundations for regulatory and policy-making dimensions that really touch the essential core of the problem posed at the beginning of this text.

Such issues impact all social sectors – from individuals and corporations to institutions – triggering the need to develop tools for transdisciplinary actions, collaboration, policy-making and creative explorations.

The Model of Radical Hybrid Experience offers a structure to fully grasp how the merging of the physical-digital-biological is turning urban environments into lively interfaces that support strange interactions and heterogeneous forms of knowledge construction. Rendering the features of this 'strange' reality visible will make the most of the benefits of the inscription of the Internet in the everyday lives of individuals, groups, businesses and institutions.

Alongside the impact of digital technologies, definitions of matter, time, space, self and action are realizing a new complex phase that suggests transdisciplinary collaboration. As much as the impact of previous technologies suggested a radical change to society (for example, electricity and the printing press), the impact of the digital is unquestionably bringing about a radical new shape to our constitution. Radical changes demand other forms of literacy, so that all the benefits, challenges and opportunities that are opening up do not turn into problems in our mediated cities.

References

Barthlott, W. and Ehler, U. (1977), 'Lotus Effect® Self-cleaning façade paint and render finish', https://www.youtube.com/watch?v=sCjmpyQlHYM. Accessed 2 March 2014.

Beloff, L. (2011), 'Appendix', http://www.realitydisfunction.org/appendix/. Accessed 29 May 2014.

Benayoun, M. L. (1995), 'Tunnel Under the Atlantic', http://www.benayoun.com/. Accessed 20 December 2015.

Berger, P. (1974), *Homeless Mind: Modernization and Consciousness*, New York: Vintage.

Bolter, J. D. (1996), 'Virtual reality and the redefinition of self', in L. Strate, R. L. Jacobson and S. Gibson (eds), *Communication and Cyberspace: Social Interaction in an Electronic Environment*, New York: Hampton Press.

Callon, M. (1991), 'Techno-economic networks and irreversibility', in J. Law (ed.), *A Sociology of Monsters: Essays on Power, Technology and Domination*, London and New York: Routledge, pp. 132–61.

—— —— (1995), 'Four models for the dynamics of science', in S. Jasanoff (eds.) *Handbook of Science and Technology Studies*, Thousand Oaks: Sage, pp. 29–63.

—— —— (1997), 'Society in the making: The study of technology as a tool for sociological analysis', in W. E. Bijker, T. Pinch and T. P. Hughes (eds), *The Social Construction of Technological Systems: New Directions in the Sociology and History of Technology*, Cambridge, MA: MIT Press, pp. 83–103.

Castells, M. (1996), *The Rise of the Network Society*, Oxford: Blackwell.

Domingues, D., Hamdan, C. and Augusto, L. (2010), 'Biocybrid body and rituals in urban mixed life', *Congreso Internacional Mujer, Arte y Tecnologia en la Nueva Esfera Pública-CIMUAT*, Valencia, Spain, 3–4 November, http://www.slideshare.net/camilahamdan/domingues-diana-hamdan-camila-augusto-lecibiocybrid-body-and-rituals-in-urban-mixed-lifecimuat-espaa-ddominghamdanaugust-apresentacao-2010. Accessed 2 June 2014.

Ehrsson, H., Mercurio, M., Duinen, H. and Preston, C. (n.d.), 'The Machine to be Another', http://www.themachinetobeanother.org/?page_id=818. Accessed 9 February 2014.

Ellard, C. (2014), 'Cities and their psychology: How neuroscience affects urban planning', *The Guardian*, 4 February, http://www.theguardian.com/cities/2014/feb/04/cities-psychology-neuroscience-urban-planning-study. Accessed 9 February 2014.

Gershenfeld, N. (1999), *When Things Start to Think*. New York: Henry Holt & Co.

Hansmann, U., Lothar, M., Nicklous, M. S. and Stober, T. (2003), *Pervasive Computing: The Mobile World*, Böblinger: Springer.

Hiroshi, I. and Brygg, U. (1997), 'Tangible bits: Towards seamless interfaces between people, bits and atoms,' in *Proceedings of the ACM SIGCHI Conference on Human factors in Computing Systems*, Los Angeles, USA, 18–23 April, New York: ACM, pp. 234–41.

Jenkins, H. (2006), *Convergence Culture*, New York: New York University Press.

Kac, Eduardo (n.d.), 'Natural History of the Enigma', http://www.ekac.org/nat.hist.enig. html. Accessed 10 May 2014.

Kerckhove, D. de (1995), *The Skin of Culture: Investigating the New Electronic Reality*, Toronto: Summerville House Publishing.

Lakatos, D. and Ishii, H. (2012), 'Towards Radical Atoms: Form-giving to transformable materials', in *CogInfoCom IEEE 3rd International Conference on Cognitive Info Communications*, Kosice, Slovakia, 2–5 December, http://tmg-trackr.media. mit.edu:8020/SuperContainer/RawData/Papers/521-Towards%20Radical%20 Atoms%20%20Form/Published/PDF. Accessed 12 May 2014.

Latour, B. (1987), *Science in Action: How to Follow Scientists and Engineers Through Society*, Milton Keynes: Open University Press.

—— —— (2004), *Politics of Nature: How to Bring the Sciences into Democracy*, Paris and Milton Keynes: Editions La Découverte and Open University Press.

—— —— (2005), *Reassembling the Social: An Introduction to Actor-Network-Theory* (Clarendon Lectures in Management Studies), Oxford: Oxford University Press.

Law, J. (1987), 'Technology and heterogeneous engineering: The case of the Portuguese expansion', in W. E. Bijker, T. Pinch and T. P. Hughes (eds), *The Social Construction of Technological Systems: New Directions in the Sociology and History of Technology*, Cambridge, MA: MIT Press, pp. 111–34.

Law, J. and Hassard, J. (1999), *Actor–Network Theory and After*, Oxford: Blackwell.

Negroponte, N. (1999), *Being Digital*, New York: Knopf.

Pepperell, R. and Punt, M. (2000), *The Postdigital Membrane: Imagination, Technology and Desire*, Bristol: Intellect Books.

Popkewitz, T. S. and Rizvi, F (eds) (2010), *Globalization and the Study of Education*, Oxford: Blackwell.

Poslad, S. (2009), *Ubiquitous Computing Smart Devices, Smart Environments and Smart Interaction*, London: John Wiley & Sons.

Simmel, G. (1903), 'The metropolis and mental life', in Gary Bridge and Sophie Watson (eds) (2002), *The Blackwell City Reader*. Oxford and Malden, MA: Wiley-Blackwell.

Weber, M. (1905), *The Protestant Ethic and the Spirit of Capitalism*, Cambridge: Cambridge University Press (2000)

Weiser, M., Gold, R. and Brown, J. S. (1999), 'The origins of ubiquitous computing research at PARC in the late 1980s', *IBM Systems Journal*, 38: 4, p. 693.

Williams, Riannon (2014), 'The next step: 3D printing the human body', *Daily Telegraph*, 11 February, http://www.telegraph.co.uk/technology/news/10629531/The-next-step-3D-printing-the-human-body.html. Accessed 5 October 2014.

Notes

1. Domingues, Hamdan and Augusto (2010) proposed the concept of biocybrids to relate to the merging of bio and digital signals (flesh, cyberdata and physical space).
2. The ICT-31 call in Horizon 2020 is focused on these aspects, particularly the topic 'Human-Centric Digital Age: R&D'.

Section Two

Applications – The use of the digital in the everyday

Chapter 5

Identity management, premediation and the city

Sandra Wilson and Lilia Gomez Flores

Introduction

We are now experiencing an era of 'persistent identity' (Poole 2010), in which our identity is constantly 'on'. Almost all our movements are routinely and smoothly monitored while we interact with CCTV cameras, withdraw money from ATM machines, swipe identity cards for entering buildings, and buy goods and services using credit/debit cards. Within a highly digitalized society, our identity is key to giving us access to a growing range of services and benefits, thereby increasing the need to 'manage' our identity.

Identity management (IM) is a term only recently coined (since approximately 2004), and yet it is slowly permeating our daily lived experience. Post-9/11, governments and corporations are placing a greater emphasis on security in an attempt to prevent more terrorist attacks of every kind. Along with the fact that we conduct an increasingly large part of our everyday interactions remotely – online via either computers or mobile devices – this has forced the development of various forms of IM solutions.

The nature of cities is constantly changing and being contested in a continuous, never-ending process of mediation from different disciplinary points of view. In this chapter, we analyse the interactions between individuals and their identities in the city from an angle of premediation. It is here that possible future experiences are first encountered through popular media, affecting our relationships with the urban environment.

Identity management

As part of our research (IMPRINTS 2014), we searched and analysed different scenarios of IM, which indicated that there were three forms of human interaction that need identification or authentication (Figure 1):

1. Between individuals.
2. Between individuals and organizations.
3. To give individuals access to their possessions (objects) and or/spaces.

In addition, these scenarios present three different instruments to introduce ourselves (identify) and prove who we are (authenticate):

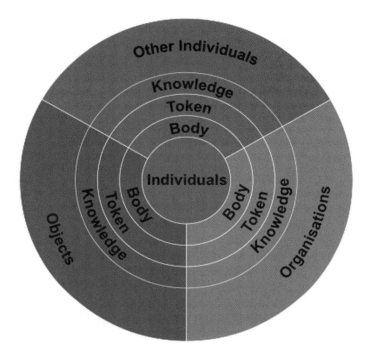

Figure 1. Forms of IM

1. Based on knowledge or memory (e.g. PIN codes, passwords).
2. Based on tokens (e.g. passports, customer cards, smartphones).
3. Based on body features (e.g. biometrics, implants).

The combination of interactions and instruments constitutes a 'field' of representation and mediation. All the scenarios have positive/optimistic and negative/pessimistic varieties.

Our research found that, as a method of authentication, passwords and PIN codes are usually considered neither very convenient, nor very safe. As such, some people expect that they will merge with other authenticators and eventually disappear. We will therefore focus this chapter on the use of tokens and body-based biometrics.

Smart token scenarios

The use of RFID and microelectronics such as Arduino enable the creation of a variety of smart tokens. An example is the London Underground Oyster Card, which allows its users to travel around the London transport system relatively easily. Nowadays, RFID is used in several other token systems, such as smart bracelets for use at festivals (BBC Newsbeat 2012). Already used in Europe, designers say the wristbands wipe out ticket fraud and touting, and can be loaded with cash to pay for goods on-site. This has parallels with the use of 'smart watches' like 'Rumba Time' (Price 2011), which lets you carry medical and payment information on your wrist. Clothing is also expected to be utilized increasingly for health and leisure information, as well as by other types of organizations. SmartLife (2014), for example, has developed an advanced wearable computing technology that interfaces seamlessly with the body to provide remote, real-time, always-on access to body data (via smart pants). The company's patented SoftSensor smart fabric incorporates ultra-thin dry sensors that deliver highly accurate information on a broad range of vital signs and body movements. These data may then be transmitted via connected devices to enable innumerable cloud-based hyper-personalized services in markets such as healthcare, sports, hazardous environments and the military. Supermarket chain Walmart (Murph 2010) have placed RFID in individual garments to help apparel managers know when certain sizes and colours are depleted and need to be restocked. In S. Korea, commuters can now shop at virtual supermarkets by mobile-scanning QR codes on murals of groceries plastered across metro platforms (YouTube 2011). The groceries are then delivered to the commuters' homes shortly after they return. Thousands of students in Brazil are now required to wear a shirt that text messages their parents when they do not show up for class (Nguyen 2012). The T-shirts work in a similar way to the tracking devices sometimes used to locate lost pets: a chip that is built into the clothing provides data to a central computer programmed to send updates to parents about their child's whereabouts via text message. Whenever the child enters the school, it instantly sends confirmation of the arrival; if they do not show up within 20 minutes of classes starting, parents will receive an alert that says: 'Your child has still not arrived at school'.

Interestingly, some individuals are starting to hack these RFID chips for their own purposes. In London, for example, the Urban Wizard (Whitby 2012) has removed the chip from his Oyster Card and placed it at the end of his 'magic' wand, wowing spectators with his supposed magic and 'wizardry'. These chips have also been placed into rings (although Transport for London has fined those caught doing so, as the cards are technically Transport for London's personal property!).

When implanted within the body, RFID chips can also carry financial information or provide access to spaces (for example, within nightclubs and bars), as well as providing access to cars, homes or workspaces (RFID Journal 2005). However, we do not have to be chipped or carry a mobile device in order for our bodies to be recognized within the city.

Body-based biometrics

The research exposed an increasingly common situation in which people gain access to urban spaces, and government or corporate services through authenticating body-based biometric features (e.g. fingerprints, palms, iris, face, voice, gait, etc.). Driven by a strong and growing industry, the use of biometrics in urban settings is rapidly expanding; ever more bodily features are being used for authentication, including body odour and buttock prints, but more significantly, DNA.

Fingerprints are now commonly used in many schools and colleges to pay for lunch or sign in for classes (YouTube 2008). Japanese company OMRON (OMRON Global 2012) has now developed hand gesture recognition in conjunction with face recognition technologies. Alongside other biometrics, such as fingerprinting, iris recognition is now commonplace in airports and at borders around the world. Tools such as face recognition are now in the US workplace; for example, Garden Fresh Restaurant Corp (Ganeva 2011), which runs franchises of the buffet restaurants Souplantation and Sweet Tomatoes, announced it had installed this technology at 122 locations across 15 states in 2011. Cognitive biometrics studies how different individuals might be identified by their brain's reactions to various images, such as one's mother (Freeman 2012).

Gunshot recognition (Safety Dynamics 2014) is another recent development. In this case, microphones can pick up the sound of a shot being fired in a metropolitan area within one second of the shooter pulling the trigger; a camera then zooms in on the location and authorities instantly have some idea of who and what they are dealing with:

'So in most cases, the shooter hasn't even begun to drop their arm yet and we're already looking at the scene,' said Wayne Lundeberg, Chief Operating Officer of Safety Dynamics: a Tucson-based company with gunshot detection technology in the US and Mexico.

(Safety Dynamics 2014)

This is also the area where the strongest public and political concerns for the future have been expressed, especially with respect to a potential loss of privacy, issues surrounding data protection and the export of these technologies to oppressive regimes. It is within the area of art practices that we find most discussion about these issues and their increasing leakage into other areas of public life. CV Dazzle (Harvey 2014) by New York-based artist Adam Harvey, for example, is a camouflage created from computer vision algorithms, allowing users to avoid the legal issues associated with the wearing of masks through a clever use of make-up and hair styling (Figure 2). The name originates from a type of camouflage used during the First World War. This approach has not yet featured in an act of public resistance; however, culture and fashion magazines (e.g. DIS, a fashion art and commerce publication) have used it in their styling. In an interview for theartblog.com, Adam Harvey (cited in Armpriester 2011) describes CV Dazzle as

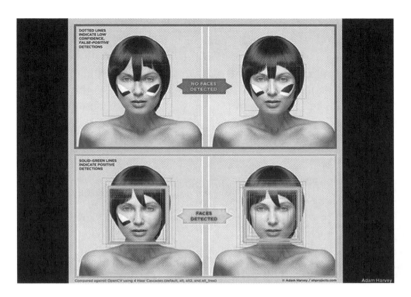

Figure 2: 'CVDazzle' by Adam Harvey.

'the ticket into the invisible class – men, women and children deleting themselves from the digital eye'.

Similarly, the FAGFACE mask by American artist Zach Blas (2014) – part of his Facial Weaponization Suite – develops forms of collective and artistic protest against biometric facial recognition (and the inequalities these technologies propagate) by making masks in community-based workshops that are used for public intervention. The mask is a response to scientific studies that link determining sexual orientation through rapid facial recognition. This mask is generated from the biometric facial data of many queer men's faces, resulting in a mutated, alien facial mask that cannot be read or parsed by biometric facial recognition technologies.

In a video interview with the authors last year, Blas highlights how some of these forms of IM are being used without an individual's knowledge or authorization. For example, in 2001, the Tampa Bay police used facial recognition technologies to search for criminals and terrorists during the Super Bowl, resulting in several arrests (but no charges). Blas also highlights the dangers of these technologies and databases being used for other purposes, such as to identify homosexual men purely from their faces.

This opposition has also been expressed in the sousveillance movement. Steve Mann (2004) established a differentiation between surveillance and sousveillance: 'surveillance' is French for 'to watch from above'; it typically describes situations where person(s) of higher authority (e.g. governments, institutions, police, etc.) watch over citizens, suspects or shoppers. Foucault (1977) described it as the higher authority to be 'godlike', rather than down at the same level as the individual party or parties under surveillance. Mann, meanwhile, describes it as the capture of multimedia content (audio, video or the like) by a higher entity that is not an equal of or a party to the activity being recorded. The author has suggested 'sousveillance' as French for 'to watch from below': the term refers both to hierarchical sousveillance (e.g. citizens photographing police, shoppers photographing shopkeepers, and taxi passengers photographing cab drivers), as well as personal

Figure 3. Pranav Mistry wearing the SixthSense device.

Figure 4. Pranav Mistry and the SixthSense device interacting with the city.

Figure 5. Pranav Mistry and the SixthSense device interacting with other people through the Internet of Things.

sousveillance (e.g. bringing cameras from lamp posts and ceilings down to eye-level for human-centred recording of personal experience). Sousveillance has two main aspects: hierarchy reversal and human-centeredness, and these often interchange (for example, someone who drives a cab one day may be a passenger in someone else's cab the next). The artist Wafaa Bilal (Hicks 2012), for example, has implanted a camera in the back of his head to 'watch-the-watchers', exploring sousveillance as a way to balance the sense of power and control.

Other developments include wearable cameras like the one used for the SixthSense (see Figure 3), developed by Pranav Mistry (2012). SixthSense is a gestural interface device comprising a neck-worn pendant that contains both a data projector and camera. It combines the cameras with illumination systems for interactive photographic art, and also includes gesture recognition (e.g. finger-tracking using coloured tape on the user's fingers). All this combined technology gives the wearer a sense of control and interaction that goes beyond sousveillance – although sousveillance is an always-present option. It gives the user the opportunity to navigate the city creating his/her own experiences with the urban environment and its inhabitants (see Figure 4). It has the possibility to wirelessly connect to the Internet of Things, smoothly weaving connections between the wearer and other people and/or objects by retrieving available online information, such as personal data and product characteristics (see Figure 5).

Premediation

In the aftermath of 9/11, Grusin (2010) observed a new media pattern emerging in the United States and then expanding worldwide. He called it 'premediation' and explained that it 'works to prevent citizens of the global media sphere from experiencing again the kind of systematic or traumatic shock produced by the events of 9/11 by perpetuating an almost constant, low level of fear or anxiety about another terrorist attack' (Grusin 2010: 2). Premediation is also described as the way in which multiple futures are brought to life in the present. Many of the scenarios discussed above are also being premediated within film and television, the most obvious example being the film Minority Report (Spielberg 2002) starring Tom Cruise, which provides examples of iris recognition being used to target personalized advertising whilst shopping. Research partners Turner, van Zoonen and Harvey (2013) highlight how film and television are key contributors to this process of premediation, whereby the scenarios they present do not prescribe certain meanings around IM, but create and delineate a so-called 'imaginative horizon'. News, popular culture and social media are no longer concerned with a representation of recent or live events, but are obsessing instead about what might happen next, including future identity management scenarios in the city.

We can see examples of ID tokens being premediated in the first *Bourne Identity* (Liman, 2002) film, where Jason Bourne has a stash of fake ID (its location revealed in the first place by an implant in his hip); while in RED (Schwentke 2010), another former CIA operative takes a sledgehammer to the foundations of his house, unearthing a box filled with cash and IDs. In terms of biometrics, *Gattaca* (Niccol 1997) demonstrates how blood tests are not only used to determine a person's identity (in cases where it is the only – or only certain – way) so as to permit access to buildings on a daily basis, but citizens are also effectively graded from conception according to their genetic make-up. This premediation of IM practices and technologies associated within the city has an impact on both our experience of the city and the ways in which it is mediated, regardless of whether these practices and technologies exist in any given reality or not.

Mass media, user-generated content and (pre-)mediation

It is important to make a distinction between what is considered mass media and what is deemed user-generated content (UGC). Although they both usually go together, they are not interchangeable. According to Wimmer and Dominick (2013), mass media is defined as 'any communication channel used to simultaneously reach a large number of people, including radio, TV, newspapers, magazines, billboards, films, recordings, books, the internet, and smart media such as smartphones, smart TVs and tablets'. On the other hand, Kaplan and Haenlein (2010) describe UGC as the sum of all ways in which people make use of social media. Some of the most famous social media platforms are Facebook, Flickr, YouTube, Myspace, Twitter, etc. The term, which achieved broad popularity in 2005, is usually applied to describe the various forms of media content that are publicly available and created by end users. According to the Organisation for Economic Co-operation and Development (OECD 2007), UGC needs to fulfil three basic requirements in order to be considered as such: (1) it needs to be published either on a publicly accessible website or a social networking site accessible to a selected group of people; (2) it needs to show a certain amount of creative effort; and (3) it needs to have been created outside of professional routines and practices. The first condition excludes content exchanged in e-mails or instant messages; the second excludes mere replications of already existing content (e.g. posting a copy of an existing newspaper article on a personal blog without any modifications or commenting); and the third omits all content that has been created with a commercial market context in mind.

The twenty-first century has seen a shift in power regarding information and what people believe, how they believe it and from whom they decide to believe it. Social media and UGC have empowered citizens by allowing them to receive, post and comment on almost everything using digital technologies. In 2012, using Hurricane Sandy as an example of a current event, Grusin (2012) blogged about the premediation occurring through news, social media and UGC outside the realm of mass media (such as movies, books, TV shows, etc.) and the impact that this had: 'socially networked media like Twitter, Facebook, YouTube, blogs, Tumblr, Instagram, and others all participate in the remediation and premediation of news across the globally networked world'. His blog included notes on how this premediation of Sandy leapt beyond the virtual reports of news into the real world, affecting people and their interaction with the cities touched by the hurricane: 'a full 24 hours before Sandy's expected landfall, subways and roads were closed; flights were cancelled; schools were cancelled; government offices were closed; people were evacuated; power may be shut off in anticipation of Sandy's disrupting it' (Grusin 2012). He concludes that news, social media and UGC work together to premediate a specific event: 'premediation works to prepare people affectively for what might be coming [...]. Premediation helps to bring Sandy into being not to prevent it'.

Beyond natural catastrophes and current news, people seem to be empowered by social media and UGC when engaged in their own daily premediation while navigating the cities where they live. Social media platforms like Waze, for example, use passive and active UGC to premediate navigation routes, presenting different alternatives to other drivers wanting to avoid traffic or to 'shave' minutes using alternative roads. Waze connects drivers to one another, creating local driving communities that work together to improve the quality of everyone's daily driving. The Waze website explains how the platform works:

> Waze is all about contributing to the 'common good' out there on the road... After typing in their destination address, users just drive with the app open on their phone to passively contribute traffic and other road data, but they can also take a more active role by sharing road reports on accidents, police traps, or any other hazards along the way, helping to give other users in the area a 'heads-up' about what's to come.
>
> https://www.waze.com/about

Foursquare is another social media platform that uses UGC to tell other citizens where to find the best places in the city to eat, drink and go clubbing, etc. Users can grade the different services they use and post comments on them; they can also receive suggestions of more places to explore within the city based on their previous posts and the zones within the city they frequent (this last aspect is enabled through the use of GPS on users' mobile phones).

Apple is already planning to launch their Proactive application on iPhones and other mobile devices, linking together several social network platforms such as Foursquare, Yelp and Nokia's HERE. In addition, their augmented reality application will aim to help users navigate the city in a more personal, customized way. Proactive will compete with interactive Google Maps by providing people with live news on public transportation services and a points of interest (POI) system. Apple has developed a pair of new features around the POI system: an augmented reality view for local listings, as well as a feature dubbed 'Browse Around Me'. The augmented reality feature allows users to hold up their iPhone in their Maps app, and point the camera toward a particular business or area. Pointed towards a café, for example, the screen could show a virtual view of menu items or daily specials. If the user points their phone toward a street, a virtual outline of local businesses, restaurants, shopping stores or coffee shops could appear. As a separate feature, the Browse Around Me button could simply show points of interest on an overhead map that are more tailored to previous searches and user preferences.

Through the use of social media and UGC people are premediating the city for themselves and their fellow citizens, presenting them with different alternatives and scenarios while using mobile technologies.

Conclusions

Bauman (2006) coins the concept of 'liquidity' in different social and political contexts, whereas Lyon (2010) applies it to 'the reduction of the body to data'. According to this latter theory, human bodies are continually being reduced to digital information. This allows data to constantly flow from a governmental context (such as CCTV cameras operated by the police) to commercial environments (such as airport checkpoints) to private surveillance (like nanny cams).

Within the scenarios described here, we can see a growing emphasis on body-based biometrics such as face recognition, fingerprinting and DNA, where the understanding of identity is fixed to one data subject. As such, they are considered static because they can create a one-to-one correspondence 'restricting people to one record or records to one person' (Wayman 2008). This also signifies a significant shift in our understanding of the nature of identity from 'what we are' to 'who we are', where previously our identities were expressed through what we wear, our tastes in music, etc. This is also a normalization of administrative techniques that were once reserved for criminals, and is largely being introduced without public discourse or consultation either by large corporations (e.g. Google Glass) or governmental initiatives (e.g. the use of facial recognition at public events). The authors were recently associated with hacking the 'Human Computer Interaction' conference in Toronto, creating the 'quantified toilet' – a fake sensor installed in the Toronto Convention Center and other civic venues that would automatically analyse 'deposits' in the toilets to detect a person's gender, drug and alcohol levels, pregnancy status, sexually transmitted infection status and... smell (Golbeck 2014). The intervention was designed to engender thought and discussion regarding the issues of surveillance, data and privacy. The Twitter response highlighted how there was a lack of mechanisms to raise any opposition to these types of initiatives. IM practices and technologies have then placed the city in a panoptic effect scenario run not just by the government and the authorities, but also by commercial brands.

Through sousveillance, we can also observe what Mann, Fung and Lo (2006) called a 'reverse panopticon', in which the observed become the observers and then the observed once again (depending on the roles they are playing at the time) in an infinite, never-ending cycle. Within this panopticon, premediation works both socially and politically. One of the effects associated with premediation appears to be a limiting of the power of urban citizens to move to action (Grusin 2010: 42–43, 71–72). It is only through some art practices and sousveillance that we can observe an attempt to raise awareness of the negative consequences of these developments (e.g. loss of privacy/anonymity), and what might constitute objections to these technologies and practices within the city. Despite this, there are no signs of resistance from citizens to the increased level of identity management or its shifting nature within our cities. As such, even the increase in UGC appears to conform to Grusin's (2010: 46) notion of premediation, which he likens to the phenomena to a video game where, although there are an infinite number of future possibilities available, only some are supported and encouraged: 'although within these premediated moves there are an infinite number of different possibilities available, only some of those possibilities are encouraged by the protocols and reward systems built into the game'.

However, the nature of identity – through social networking or in the use of wearable technologies and tokens such as garments and watches – can be perceived as more fluid and dynamic through personal expression, where unique and individual tokens can be embedded or customized through technologies such as RFID. Identity within the urban landscape of the city is therefore moving towards a more fixed interpretation.

Our identities and their subsequent management are therefore incessantly changing according to the context and the technologies mediating them: from a social context like Facebook to a commercial one via RFID, to official interactions like face recognition and CCTV endlessly identifying who we are.

These different IM practices and technologies create different 'atmospheres' within the urban landscape that have an 'emotional impact' on humans. The term 'atmosphere' is embedded in our daily experiences; it induces 'moods, emotions, feelings, thoughts, judgments, perceptions, sensations, and all manner of social relations and associated practices' (Ellis, Tucker & Harper 2013). According to Koskela (2000), 'surveilled space alters human experience'. Emotions are often denoted as representing a particular type of physiological and cognitive state that is felt consciously and named (for example, anger, disgust, fear, joy, sadness and surprise). Being observed has widely been theorized to induce emotions or 'cultures of emotion', creating a sense of anxiety, fear (Minton 2009) and suspicion (Chan 2008). One example of this is video surveillance, with CCTV cameras being seen as producing an 'emotional space' and a 'paradoxical space' (Rose 1993). Koskela (2000) describes video surveillance/biometric forms of IM as evoking both positive and negative emotions simultaneously, 'to the extent that one may feel both threat and security'. Koskela uses the example of a CCTV camera in the subway, late at night, and how a female can feel at the same time a borderline emotion of security and threat – although she knows she is being observed, she does not know by whom.

This shift in emphasis in relation to the nature of identity and its apparent paradox – both fixed and fluid, constantly changing depending on context and the different technologies employed – contributes to the almost constant low level of fear and anxiety associated with IM within the city in terms of Grusin's (2010: 2) notion of premediation. Consequently, the negative features associated with Grusin's premediation, such as low-level anxiety and general acceptance of future practices and technologies, are currently being experienced within the city. We are now living in environments where we move within a never-ending cycle between premediated scenarios; where media constantly delivers the future to us through films, books, videos, the Internet of Things, etc., thereby creating a constant level of low-stress situations (tension) that we have learned to smoothly accept within our daily lives. Through the lens of identity management, then, we can observe that the city is increasingly 'premediated'.

References

Armpriester, C. (2011), 'Interview: Adam Harvey and The Anti-Face', http://www.theartblog.org/2011/04/interview-adam-harvey-and-the-anti-face/. Accessed 31 December 2011.

Bauman, Z. (2006), *Liquid Fear*, Cambridge: Polity Press.

Blas, Z. (2014) 'Facial WeaponiZation Suite (2011–2014)', http://www.zachblas.info/projects/facial-weaponization-suite/. Accessed 14 June 2014.

Chan, J. (2008), 'The new lateral surveillance and a culture of suspicion', *Sociology of Crime, Law and Deviance*, 10, pp. 223–39.

Cochrane, Greg (2012), 'Microchipped ID wristbands heading for UK festivals', *BBC Newsbeat*, 12 January, http://www.bbc.co.uk/newsbeat/16548000\. Accessed 14 June 2014.

Ellis, D., Tucker, I. and Harper, D. (2013), 'The affective atmospheres of surveillance', *Theory and Psychology*, 23, pp. 716–31.

Foucault, M. (1977), *Discipline and Punish: The Birth of a Prison*, London: Penguin.

Freeman, K. (2012), 'Are brain waves and heartbeats the future of passwords?', *Mashable*, 24 April, http://mashable.com/2012/04/24/brain-waves-passwords/. Accessed 14 June 2014.

Ganeva, T. (2011), 'Biometrics at Pizza Hut and KFC? How face recognition and digital fingerprinting are creeping into the U.S. workplace', *Alternet*, 26 September, http://www.alternet.org/story/152539/biometrics_at_pizza_hut_and_kfc_how_face_recognition_and_digital_fingerprinting_are_creeping_into_the_u.s._workplace. Accessed 14 June 2014.

Golbeck, J. (2014), 'What a toilet hoax can tell us about the future of surveillance', *The Atlantic*, 29 April, http://www.theatlantic.com/technology/archive/2014/04/what-a-toilet-hoax-can-tell-us-about-the-future-of-surveillance/361408/. Accessed 14 September 2014.

Grusin, R. (2010), *Premediation: Affect and Mediality After 9/11*, London: Palgrave Macmillan.

Harvey, A. (2014), 'Camouflage from face detection', http://cvdazzle.com/. Accessed 14 June 2014.

Hicks, J. (2012), 'Bringing the stories home: Wafaa Bilal's war on the public narrative of war', *Caracteres*, http://revistacaracteres.net/revista/vol1n2noviembre2012/bringing-the-stories-home-wafaa-bilals-war-on-the-public-narrative-of-war/. Accessed 14 June 2014.

IMPRINTS (2014), 'Do you ever wonder…', http://www.imprintsfutures.org/. Accessed 14 June 2014.

Kaplan, A. N. and Haenlein, M. (2010), 'Users of the world, unite! The challenges and opportunities of Social Media', *Business Horizons*, 53, pp. 59–68.

Koskela, H. (2000), 'The gaze without eyes: Video-surveillance and the changing nature of urban space', *Progress in Human Geography*, 24, pp. 243–65.

Lyon, D. (2010), 'Liquid surveillance: The contribution of Zygmunt Bauman to surveillance studies', *International Political Sociology*, 4, pp. 325–38.

Mann, S. (2004), 'Sousveillance: Inverse surveillance in multimedia imaging', in *Proceedings of the 12th Annual ACM International Conference on Multimedia*, New York, USA, 10–16 October, ACM: New York, pp. 620–27.

Mann, S., Fung. J. and Lo, R. (2006), 'Cyborglogging with camera phones: Steps toward equiveillance', in *Proceedings of the 14th Annual ACM International Conference on Multimedia*, Santa Barbara, USA, 23–27 October, ACM: New York, pp. 177–80.

Minton, A. (2009), *Ground Control: Fear and Happiness in the Twenty-First-Century City*, London: Penguin.

Mistry, P. (2012), 'SixthSense: Integrating information with real world', http://www.pranavmistry.com/projects/sixthsense/. Accessed 14 November 2012.

Murph, D. (2010), 'Walmart to add RFID tags to individual items, freak out privacy advocates', *Endgadget*, 26 July, http://www.engadget.com/2010/07/26/walmart-to-add-rfid-tags-to-individual-items-freak-out-privacy/. Accessed 14 June 2014.

Nguyen, T (2012), 'School uniform alerts parents when students skip class', *ZDNet*, 28 March, http://www.zdnet.com/article/school-uniform-alerts-parents-when-students-skip-class/. Accessed 12 June 2014.

OECD (2007), *Participative Web and User-Created Content: Web 2.0, Wikis, and Social Networking*, Paris: Organisation for Economic Co-operation and Development.

OMRON Global (2012), 'OMRON develops hand gesture recognition technology', http://www.omron.com/media/press/2012/05/e0528.html. Accessed 14 June 2014.

Poole, C. M. (2010), 'Christopher "moot" Poole: The case for anonymity', *TED*, http://www.ted.com/talks/christopher_m00t_poole_the_case_for_anonymity_online.html. Accessed 10 January 2012.

Price, E. (2011), 'RumbaTime Go Watch lets you carry medical and payment information on your wrist', *GIZMAG*, 1 December, http://www.gizmag.com/rumbatime-go-watch/20698/. Accessed 14 June 2014.

RFID Journal (2005), 'Scottish bar joins Barcelona club in RFID tagging customers', *RFID Journal*, 21 January, http://www.rfidjournal.com/articles/view?6117#sthash.Nzds6WwC.dpuf. Accessed 14 June 2014.

Rose, G. (1993), 'A politics of paradoxical space', *Feminism and Geography: The Limits of Geographical Knowledge*, 137: 60, pp. 184–202.

Safety Dynamics (2014), 'SENTRI gunshot recognition: The future of crime prevention', http://www.safetydynamics.net. Accessed 14 June 2014.

Smartlife (2014), 'Welcome to SmartLife', http://www.smartlifetech.com/. Accessed 14 June 2014.

Turner, G., van Zoonen, L. and Harvey, J. (2013), 'Confusion, control and comfort: Premediating identity management in film and television', *Information, Communication & Society*, 17: 9, pp. 986–1000.

Wayman, J. L. (2008), 'Biometrics in identity management systems', *Security & Privacy, IEEE*, 6: 2, pp. 30–37.

Whitby, J. (2012), 'Urban wizard', http://vimeo.com/27832247. Accessed 14 June 2014.

Wimmer, R. D. and Dominick, J. R. (2013), *Mass Media Research*, Boston: Wadsworth Publishing Co.

YouTube (2008), 'Children pay with fingerprint scan', https://www.youtube.com/watch?v=3765T2rGqXw. Accessed 14 June 2014.

—— —— (2011), 'Tesco Homeplus virtual subway store in South Korea', https://www.youtube.com/watch?v=fGaVFRzTTP4&feature=player_embedded. Accessed: 14 June 2014.

Chapter 6

Urban utopics: The politics of the digital city view

Gavin Perin and Linda Matthews

Introduction

The proliferation of images in the contemporary information economy poses a unique problem for civic authorities whose job it is to control the image of the city. The politics underwriting both representational democracy and capitalism make it tactically difficult and economically inefficient to police image production. This means Foucault's model of a 'vigilant architecture' has less traction than Georges Bataille's 'convex, frontal, extrovert' architecture (Hollier 1989: 3–13). As such, any control of the city image requires a persuasive manipulation of digital imaging technologies. In this respect, the promotional Internet Protocol (IP) webcam image is one significant example of how the digital technologies of image production and dissemination mediate power and influence.

The institutional use of the promotional IP webcam instigates a distinctive urban condition. While Washington's 'L'Enfant Plan' (1791) is one of the most complete examples of an extroverted axial urbanism, its potency is based on the corporeal presence of the architecture, not its 'imageability'. Any subsequent image is subservient to this logic: the image is a formal after-effect. By contrast, the webcam functions through a disembodied aerial viewpoint. The digital technologies underpinning this view establish an image-based formal logic that sits outside established urban theories. The unique questions raised by the webcam are as much a representational issue as they are formal, meaning that their politics are best understood by interrogating how these images say what they say. Louis Marin's (1984) deconstruction of city maps is particularly relevant because their form and content tacitly expose the identity of the privileged subject sitting behind these 'portraits'. Methodologically, Marin's comparison of El Greco's 'Painting of Toledo' (1609) with Merian's (1615) and Gomboust's (1647) Paris city maps demonstrates how the distinction between narrative and descriptive images can help identify the idealized subject of the 'utopic' IP webcam view. Moreover, an important extension of Marin's work suggests that any disruption in the transmission of the image can potentially alter the political operation of these emblematic, descriptive images. Therefore, the identification of the subject of the IP webcam image cannot be divorced from an understanding of the technological basis by which these digital images mediate form.

The lie of the truthful image

For a discipline heavily reliant on images, architecture is both deeply suspicious of the semiotic reading of form and generally disdainful of the commercialization of its objects. The architectural image is given authenticity by the belief that even if the plan, paraline, diagram and perspective seduce the viewer, they nonetheless provide a true index of form. The reasons for this mistrust of the image is lost somewhere in the murky discursive ruptures separating Brunelleschi's 'invention' of perspective, Adolf Loos' criminalization of ornament, Debord's critique of the 'society of the spectacle', and the semiotic excessiveness of almost every postmodern architect. What can be said with some confidence is that in the contemporary context this murky history has resulted in pathologizing any form that has been figured according 'to a prior imaging' (Corner 1999: 8).

The disciplinary rejection of the image as both procedurally and intellectually bankrupt comes at a price. This price is that the belief in the drawing as an index ignores the politics of the image, which in many ways is now the base currency of the information economy (Lyon 2002). The believed authenticity of architecture's established representational modes effectively denies the propagandizing potential of all images. The net result of this denial of the image is that the discipline fails to adequately question the images it rejects or supports.

Of the handful of architects and urbanists willing to challenge the functioning of the image in the information economy, there are few willing to challenge the economic system driving its production. For example, prominent Australian architect Carey Lyon (2002) sees the marketed image as a formal template, while for Anna Klingmann (2007), branding is an undeniable condition 'in which architecture can play a critical role as a catalyst to generate an authentic identity for people and places'. Both Lyon and Klingmann see the problem of the marketed image as a failure to offer communities palatable brands and images that ultimately accord with an externally constructed self-image. To the politics of the information economy, these types of solutions focus only on making built form deliver on the promises made by the image. The notion of a successful design becomes linked to being able to impart formal truth to the marketed image. It is here that the issue of authenticity returns, only to be resolved, yet again, by attaining some sort of formal fidelity between image and object. It is of some significance then that Klingmann and Lyon have no ambition to modify architecture's established representational forms or contest the economic basis of the information economy. Any capacity of the marketed image or branded architecture to form 'an interactive consumer experience' does not convincingly address Klingmann's (2007: 4) own critique of contemporary architecture and urbanism, which she believes 'simultaneously represent[s] and support[s] the ideology of capitalism'. The larger political problem posed by such an acceptance of the marketed image is well summarized by James Corner (1999: 158), who writes that imaged-based scenography 'retard[s] […] authentic public life' by not 'confronting the problems of contemporary life'.

Corner's essay 'Eidetic operations and new landscapes' (1999) attempts to resolve the politics of image production without resorting to the fabrication of truthful images. Obviously, the primary aim of his broad survey of alternative drawing practices is to move landscape design practice beyond the representational and formal limits of scenography. In this sense, Corner (1999: 158) agrees with the commonly held criticism that postmodern signification limits built form 'to simply expressing or commenting on [the human] condition'. What underscores his determination to differentiate between the picture and the image is the fact that it locates drawing as the method by which to exceed the representational politics of the indexical picture. This advocacy of open drawing practices makes a great deal of sense in light of Robin Evans' canonical essay 'Translations from drawing to building' (1997). In fact, Corner's thesis – that for the limits of drawing images to be exceeded one must actively embrace the mediating effects of the drawing on form – is completely aligned with that of Evans'. Yet what Corner misses is Evans' observation that the act of translation inevitably privileges things of interest to the author. Corner's faith in an eidetic imagining does not necessarily enable a strategic engagement with the politics behind the image. This is not simply a problem wherein every drawing involves a selective and reductive extraction of information. The capacity of a drawing to be instrumental and representational does not in itself mean that it is devoid of ideological projection. True agency is not guaranteed simply 'by framing the issues differently' (Corner 1999). In the end, Corner wants drawings that are interpretively open and yet instrumentally authored. The belief that the eidetic drawing has a positive outcome also, in the end, idealizes the drawing space as a site of authentic action. Irrespective of Corner's advocacy for new drawing techniques, he is unable to avoid the postmodern problem whereby the drawing inscribes a projected meaning of things into the world.

Corner's advocacy of the drawing is problematic for two important reasons. First, the valorization of the drawing aims to use techniques that are instrumentally disconnected from the explicit design task. The aim of the drawing is to produce creative slippages that circumvent authorship. Secondly, he does not ever question the belief in anthropomorphic control over the technologies of production. The technique might create productive slippages, but ultimately the designer brings the drawing back under control. Nevertheless, architecture's societal agency always exceeds the intent behind the authored construction of mediated images. This point is inferred by Friedrich Kittler and Matthew Griffin (1996) when they write that 'no system […] is self-governing'. If Heidegger's (1977) anthropomorphism believes in the capacity of humanity to control the 'enframing' aspect of modern technology, then Kittler argues that it is technology that disciplines humanity. Moreover, technology's disciplining capacity actually operates without any immediate interest in humanity. If the city itself is outside its own control, then any capacity for anthropomorphic control must be absolutely discarded. Herein lies the fundamental problem in Lyon's, Klingmann's and Corner's approach to the production of meaningful images. If Lyon and Klingmann overinvest in the message and not the medium, Corner overinvests in a medium divorced from addressing how the type of technologies and their operation shape the city. In a direct counter to Marshall McLuhan's (1995) oft-repeated mantra 'the medium is the message', Kittler's radical post-humanism ensures that our relationship to technology is at best opportunistic, and at worst parasitic. In this radical reframing of McLuhan's work, Kittler actually suggests that the technologies constructing the city image create a city that is neither an assemblage of meaningful objects, nor a product of authentic disciplinary drawings and techniques. Instead, agency involves an opportunistic manipulation of the mediating technologies that effectively construct the city portrait. Here, action involves intervening in the material and immaterial systems operating across the 'complex knot of networks [that] surpass the planning ability of the engineers' (Kittler 1996). This ensures that the exploitation of the system is less a question of controlled effect, and more a consequence of a range of somewhat indirect and unknowable effects.

In the chapter 'The city's portrait in its utopics', Louis Marin (1984: 202) argues that the descriptive image 'must totally reveal its object'. Developed 'against the grain of narrative', description must conceal 'its successive nature and present it as a redundant repetition, as if *all* were present at the same time' (1984: 202). According to this definition, the promotional city image fashioned through IP webcam systems results in a purely emblematic type of descriptive image; the obvious parallel between the IP webcam view

Figure 1. Map of Paris by Matthäus Merian (1615)

Figure 2. Map of Paris by Jacques Gomboust (1652).

and Merian (Figure 1) and Gomboust's (Figure 2) Paris maps being that they are all aerial images whose viewpoint is situated in what Marin (1984) terms a 'utopic', nowhere space. Like the two Paris maps, the focus on iconic urban elements creates a visual hierarchy that is orchestrated to present an image that 'stands in for' the total experience of the whole city. So while the webcam can zoom and scan the selected view, this operability does not alter the visual staging of the city's image or the political function of that image.

The important differentiation between the IP webcam view and Merian and Gomboust's city portraits arises from the mode of production used to frame and disseminate the image. In fact, the technical mediation of the digital image results in a fundamentally different type of 'utopic' subject. As implied in Marin's (1984) diagrammatic analysis of Merian's, Gomboust's and El Greco's city portraits, both the content and the drawing technique together establish different utopic subjects. The utopic subject in Marin's case studies alters through the unique way in which each combines narrative and descriptive forms of image and text. Using this approach, Marin concludes that Merian's framing of the central perspectival aerial view of Paris with pictorial images depicting daily life in the city makes the city itself the utopic subject of the image. In contrast, Gomboust's framing of the city plan using a series of aerial views of the king's rural estates makes the king's palace the utopic subject (Marin 1984). El Greco's portrait of Toledo is different still. Using a range of painterly techniques and associated representational contrivances, 'El Greco points out the neutralizing work of the utopic practice within the representation of the city' (Marin 1984: 230) Clearly, all three city maps are intended for a limited audience. Like Giambattista Nolli's (1748) map of Rome, the expense of producing these maps guaranteed that they were produced for a limited audience. This limitation in the technologies behind image dissemination meant that the central mechanism in differentiating the utopic subject was more reliant on the selection and combination of available representational forms. By extension, it is reasonable to argue that the different representational techniques can be opportunistically co-opted to subvert or support the political agendas of those who sponsor the image. The beauty of El Greco's portrait is that he adapts the medium to expose how the map is always political.

The subject of the promotional webcam is different again because it is first and foremost a descriptive image whose success relies on it being widely distributed. By disposing with narrative, the emblematic quality of the IP webcam view clearly provides a city portrait that speaks directly to the image's civic sponsors. The utopic subject is not so much a place, but a branded representation of a valorized part of the city that speaks for the rest of the city beyond the camera frame. The virtual aspect of this viewpoint means that it also has a second viewpoint: namely the domestic environment of the virtual tourist. As soon as the utopic subject becomes a branded image, the civic authorities must permit the viewpoint to extend and bleed into multiple personal spaces. The extension of the view into these multiple spaces is risky, as demonstrated by the facility to pan and zoom the camera. Unlike the Paris maps (where the viewpoint is fixed), the viewpoint of the virtual tourist allows private individuals to construct their own narrative journeys into the captured site. Thus, the camera's manoeuvrability relocates narrative within descriptive form. This important technological difference extends the webcam's 'utopic' subject to include both the idealized image of civic authorities *and* the adaptable view of the virtual tourist. By extension, the release of the webcam view into multiple domestic spaces institutes a new political agency. Here, the virtual tourist can challenge the stability of the fixed 'utopic' subject through the capacity to disrupt the image's technical means of production.

The opportunities to disrupt the intended utopic subject of the IP webcam image arise from the reality that the digital image is highly reproducible and easily disseminated. Unlike Merian's and Gomboust's maps of Paris, the potency of the webcam lies with its means of production. By contrast, the 'affordability' of the digital image foregrounds the pixel's capacity to layer and process highly specific qualitative data. As the base unit of the contemporary image, the pixel ensures that colour and contrast become the primary compositional elements of image-making. The 'trick' of the pixel is that it appears to present the world according to the projective geometry of linear perspective. However, the discrete packaging of visual data in the pixel means that lines exist only when aligned pixels share the same colour and contrast. As Klette and Rosenfeld (2004) illustrate, lines do not actually exist: geometrically, there is no common connecting or intersecting pixel. In the digital image, spatial depth is determined through shifts in colour and contrast adjacencies, rather than by a set of lines receding to a shared vanishing point on the horizon. With qualitative urban conditions represented by an array of pixels distributed in a specific numerical relationship to each other, the demarcation of form through values associated with colour and brightness (rather than through the line) opens up a new opportunity to influence the effect of the image through the construction of its 'viewed' material surfaces.

The importance of the IP webcam view is that it establishes new modes of possible urban engagement. The ability to subvert the ambition of civic site ownership and sponsorship of the city through this view is demonstrated in websites such as the New York-based Institute for Applied Autonomy.[1] Using 'guerrilla' tactics to map the location of CCTV surveillance cameras, this group has developed a web-based application[2] that allows the Internet user to construct a surveillance-free passage through Manhattan. The accessibility to tools like Google Street View is another example in which further supplementary information can be used to construct alternative narratives about the city. The imposition of the Internet user's personal narrative upon the sanctioned city view extends the emblematic webcam image beyond the enactment of a singular 'utopic' image of the city. Moreover the ability of individuals to develop their own unorthodox routes across the urban landscape subverts any desire to construct and preserve an emblematic, stable urban image.

The hidden politics of the digital view

The digital re-presentation of colour and contrast involves numerous interpretative steps, spanning both hardware and software platforms. The primary aim of these procedures is to deliver a smooth, moving image with a visual hierarchy that enhances the status of proprietary systems and protocols (Cantoni, Levialdi & Zavidovique 2011). The performance of these representational systems is governed by the technological imitation of the key procedures associated with human vision (HVS): colour, brightness and shape recognition. Aligning the IP webcam 'pipeline' to these procedures not only facilitates a curation of colour composition, but also removes visual anomalies and develops the formation of orderly image hierarchies.

The first technology in the image production pipeline requires a piece of hardware known as a colour filter array (CFA). Located directly above the pixel sensors, the CFA identifies how the colour in each pixel accords to the additive RGB model of colour mixing. The derivation of colour is achieved through a mapping function operating between the colour model and a colour space. This mapping process is constructed to the specifications of the software producer and is therefore always exclusively product-driven (Barneva & Brimkov 2009: 79). The proprietorial aspect governing these systems means that the subpixel sensor patterns of the CFA always constrain the re-presentation of colour to the RGB spectrum.

The second procedure is a software-based algorithmic process that attempts to remove all visual anomalies that arise in the hardware, with diffraction being the most persistent anomaly that camera manufacturers wish to avoid. The most significant of these visual anomalies are the countless permutations found in the Fraünhofer diffraction pattern. While digital camera lenses are explicitly designed to minimize luminance overload, certain aspects of the camera function, acting in conjunction with the performance of light, remain outside the control of hardware. Interestingly, McCann and Rizzi (2007) assert that the glare produced when light exceeds the range of luminance that can be accurately measured by a camera cannot be rigorously removed by calculation. This means that, despite attempts to the contrary, manufacturers are unable either to completely eliminate this 'problem' or to control the full extent of the effects of these patterns on the image-making process. Contemporary image-making technologies continue to develop scanpath trajectories that attempt to mimic the HVS as a way of maximizing image saliency, as well as to reduce the discrepancy between robotic and human vision.

The third procedure involves another algorithm that interprets the data applied to the webcam's image sensor. The role of the various image sensor architectures is to convert the analogue electrical light charge into a digital value. The algorithms associated with this hardware encode, decompress and subdivide this data into sequences of 'scan lines' or raster scans (Foley et al. 1997). The procedure of ordering and reading pixels is highly strategic. Algorithms control and vary the direction and vertical retrace action in a way that prioritizes the production of a smooth moving image, isolating and highlighting regions of specific interest within the image (Cantoni et al. 2011). The webcam's sensitivity patterns are extrapolations of the HVS saliency factors that relate directly to the coarse or low-resolution peripheral vision – any anomalous motion patterns are detected through the selective application of a scan pattern that yields maximum information. The ambitions behind the application of these patterns do not always reflect a neutral agenda. It is worth remembering that '[webcam] viewers must be wary that maps, photographs, and webcams, particularly in combination, can present a purposefully selective, highly rhetorical landscape narrative' (Monmonier 2000: 57).

Collectively, the operation of hardware and software aims to deliver the best possible likeness of reality. This is a sentiment amply demonstrated by Lukac and Konstantinos (2005) in their evaluation of different CFA arrangements. Importantly, the organization and distribution of the pixel within the CFA aims to provide the highest level of image colour optimization for camera hardware producers. The underlying desire for image synthesis results in the use of interpolation algorithms that fill in or estimate absent or incongruent data (Poynton 2012: 347). At the same time, camera manufacturers rely on a small number of third party proprietors to develop the performative standards that set out how these systems represent reality. As with the dictates of the RGB spectrum, these industry standards establish a set of hidden aesthetic assumptions about what constitutes a good image. In noting the thinness of research into the industry standards governing different CFA patterns, Lukac and Konstantinos (2005: 1260) argue that the selections governing colour curation advance particular proprietary interests. A case in point is the sRGB (standard RGB) colour space, which is a variation of the RGB colour space model that was created cooperatively by the Hewlett-Packard and Microsoft to standardize the use of colour for the Internet. The Adobe RGB colour space is yet another variant, but irrespective of the proprietary model, each sub-sampling filtering procedure erases the very presence of the technology itself. The problem the image-processing 'pipeline' poses for the production and dissemination of the city image is that each system produces images that simultaneously embed and conceal a set of deeper proprietary interests. These are highly orchestrated visual experiences of the city, wherein the politics of the view encourage the digital manipulation of the primary compositional and structural elements as a way to 'cleanse' the view of disruptive visual effects. The desire to maintain the integrity of the promotional city image ensures that disruptive phenomena are minimized across the webcam network, despite the fact that they register both the presence of a mediating technology and the activity of the city. If the pixel marks the divergence between traditional and contemporary image-making procedures, then the digital mediation of architectural form in the urban context reveals these proprietorial authors as a third, hidden, 'utopic' subject of the IP webcam view.

Disruptive techniques for smooth-running technologies

A series of tests undertaken by one of the authors reveals that the duplication of CFA, scan-order and diffraction patterns within a material façade arrangement directly interferes with the internal processing functions of the camera. Importantly, this disruption of the image requires an upscaled mirroring of the micropatterns within the camera to an urban scale. In such scenarios, the architect can draw upon the geometry of a diverse range of proprietary designed pixel arrangements on the viewed surface to predict, override and control the reception of the urban context over the Internet. In the same way as El Greco used representational form and technique against itself, the duplication of these micro-geometric patterns disrupts the politics of the privileged 'utopic' subject. The disruption of the politics of the view occurs in one of two ways: the built surface can either shift the viewing hierarchy of the image by reorganizing the visual prominence of its content; or it can disrupt the camera's production of a smooth, legible representation of the city. Depending on the technical protocols, these surfaces can initiate effects – either by repeating or varying these patterns, or through the effect of their respective adjacency. Notably, the success of these formal interventions is intrinsically linked to the webcam's pan and zoom function. In an odd inversion of time-motion studies, knowledge is gained through the movement of a recording tool rather than through the body.

The application of the CFA pattern on an architectural surface shifts the image's visual hierarchy to a point where the architect can recalibrate the colour rendering of an entire site. Variations to the 'tried-and-tested' proprietary patterns – such as the Bayer filter array – allow the architect to modify the colour and luminosity of the image. Such variations can be achieved by applying non-traditional red, blue and green patterns to a building façade (Figure 3). In this type of deliberately contrived scenario, the patterning establishes new design hierarchies according to a building's physical surface. The capacity to play with levels of brightness institutes a way of informing the evolution of the building's programme through both colour and texture. For example, a building might be required to stand in high contrast to its context, in which case the architect could design a façade with a pattern, colour and brightness that works in opposition to that of its neighbours.

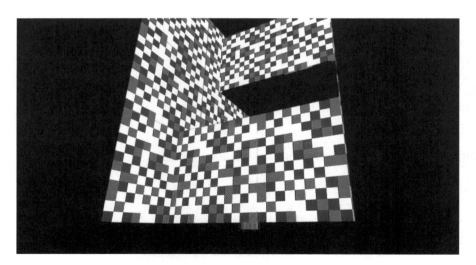

Figure 3. A HVS-based CFA pattern used as a building façade in Times Square, New York. This patter demonstrates a high level of brightness emission competing with context.

By contrast, the requirement for low visibility would mean that the design of the façade complements the surrounding context.

The second category of visual disruptions that enable one to contest the politics of the image involves interrupting the camera's capacity to produce a smooth, legible representation of the city. This act of interruption operates by subverting an algorithmic process. The algorithm is charged with removing various visual anomalies from the image as the camera mechanism moves in and out. Diffraction patterns are just one set of visual anomalies that are algorithmically removed from the image. By extension, simply duplicating the Fraünhofer (or far-field) diffraction pattern onto a façade reverses the camera's capacity to read the surface when operating in its non-diffraction mode. The behaviour of certain Fraünhofer patterns produces two notable visual effects. First, they provide much brighter visual effects than their non-diffracted counterparts. Second, as the camera lens zooms in towards the façade, the initial clear and distinct pattern transforms into a glary and blurred image (Figure 4). Significantly, the degree of visual disruption caused by the mirroring of the diffraction pattern is absolutely predictable. Given that the derivation of the digital image is innately computational and therefore data-based, this predictability is understandable. The benefit of this degree of predictability in the behaviour of the tool provides a metric by which to control the degree of visual disruption caused to the image.

Further disruptive visual effects can be obtained when transposing rescaled scan-order sequence patterns onto façades. It is important to note that the purpose of the scan-order pattern is to enable the webcam's zoom function to interact with HVS perception so as

Figure 4. A Fraünhofer diffraction pattern derived from the traditional raster scan pattern used as a building façade skin in Times Square, New York. The left-hand image shows the pattern's clarity from a distance, while the right-hand image shows its disruptive visual effect as the camera zooms in.

to maximize the replication of reality. During the scanning process of the HVS – where additional attentional scanpaths are being continually generated – the visual saliency of the viewed object needs to be somehow disabled before the viewer's attention so that the scanpath can shift (Itti & Koch 2001). In a viewer-operated camera system such as a webcam, the generative potential of HVS perceptual pathways must be mediated through the manoeuvrability of the zoom lens. The webcam's pan-tilt-zoom mechanism (PTZ) actively contributes to image continuity by mimicking the observed 'planned perceptual actions' found in the saccadic movement of the human eye (Hochberg 2007: 400). The replication of saccadic eye movement requires a solution, found in this case in the flexibility of the camera mechanism, which disables the most recent salient location in favour of the next. The multiplication of viewing trajectories fostered by the movement of the camera is therefore akin to a series of movie cuts, which collectively combine to increase image continuity and thus reinforce the narrative structure of the image (Hochberg 2007). In effect, this system reinforces smooth visual narratives, which are ultimately based on pre-established internal cognitive models derived from observing the viewer's coarse visual pathway.

Figure 5. A traditional raster scan pattern used as a building façade diffraction grating in Times Square, New York. This shows the highly disruptive effect of the pattern as the camera zooms in.

Interestingly, the design of a visually disruptive façade based on scan-order patterns requires a variation of the camera pattern and its orientation, rather than simply a duplication of it. As in the case of the Fraünhofer diffraction patterns, modified scan-order patterns can be applied at a vastly increased scale to a building façade, either as a fenestration pattern or as a second surface 'skin'. As demonstrated in the duplication of CFA and diffraction patterns, the image is disrupted when the camera zooms in and out (Figure 4). In the case of the traditional raster scan pattern, the pattern becomes not only glary and indistinct as the webcam lens moves, but at a close-up aperture, the visual effect is one of continual fluctuation because the camera is unable to resolve the pattern algorithmically and, by extension, mechanically. Again, the nature of the process ensures that the production of disruptive visual effects occurs at different, predictive moments in the webcam's trajectory (Figure 5). The ability to orchestrate the point at which this disruption occurs allows the designer to interfere strategically with the viewer's presumption of a smooth self-directed image.

Conclusion

As Marin shows, the visual conceit in the early cartographic representations of the city reveals deeper ideological certainties. For Marin (1984: 230), the beauty of El Greco's 'View of Toledo' (1600) is that its visual axis effectively 'figures the deconstruction of the representation'. The genius of El Greco lies with his capacity to compose an image that disrupts the smooth running of the conventions of narrative and descriptive image-forms. Marin sees this as an opening up of a representational discrepancy, exposing the difference between the real and the represented. In fact, El Greco's 'View of Toledo' 'shows the shift and spacing between the map and the landscape [and] signifies the substitution between the orders of painting and nature' (1984: 243). Of course, the city portraits discussed by Marin are in a sense fixed images; their political potency is limited to critique. The politics of the promotional IP webcam image is of another order. Their potency comes from being active images that must be widely disseminated in order to achieve their goal. The dilemma civic authorities face with the webcam image is that in order for them to truly function as persuasive representational vehicles, their content must be released back into the world. The inherent openness of the webcam content means these images can be contested. In questioning the structure of the sanctioned city image, action now extends into the design of urban surfaces that 'hijack' the predetermined viewing hierarchies of the image.

The IP webcam view mediates the image of the city to open three possible utopic subjects: the first is the ideal city as seen and promoted by the civic authorities; the second is the desirable itinerary seen by the virtual tourist; and the third is the utopic of the city activated by a disruptive design practice. Without this third utopic subject, the image is left uncontested, allowing the civic authorities and proprietors of image technology to remain as the true purveyors of the city image. The designerly exploitation of the qualitative properties of pixel arrangement and connectivity rejects the politics of promotion and concealment. The inclusion of colour and brightness, as an addition to the canon of image artefacts and city views, alters the political conditions by which urban space is understood. The capacity to disrupt the image ensures that the representation of the city is a heterogeneous and complex trace of multiple spaces. Positioning the pixel as the pivotal generative unit of the urban surface directly initiates a series of procedural strategies that subverts the politics of the branded city image from within the very visioning devices that are designed to normalize image reception and disable its affective properties. The technical disruption of the image tips the balance back towards the viewer without resorting to redemptive messages associated with the branded image or eidetic drawing. Rather, the disruptive image contests the stultifying effects of the urban spectacle, or what Marin (1984: 102) refers to as 'the neutralizing work of utopic practice within the representation of the city'. The ensuing co-opting of the digital image opens up a new type of space between sign and signified that provides a mechanism for opportunistic intervention in the material and immaterial systems that mediate our experience of the city. To achieve this utopic urban condition, architecture and urbanism must not only redraw its own disciplinary boundaries, but must also reform its own formal, spatial and material expectations.

References

Barneva, R. P. and Brimkov, V. E. (2009), 'Digital geometry and its applications to medical imaging', *Advances in Computational Vision and Medical Image Processing*, 13, pp. 77–92.

Cantoni, V., Levialdi, S. and Zavidovique, B. (2011), *3C Vision: Cues, Context and Channels*, Philadelphia: Elsevier.

Corner, J. (1999), 'Eidetic operations and new landscapes', in J. Corner (ed.), *Recovering Landscape: Essays in Contemporary Landscape Architecture*, New York: Princeton Architectural Press, pp. 153–69.

Evans, R. (1997), 'Translations from drawing to building', in *Translations from Drawing to Building and Other Essays*, London: Architectural Association.

Foley, J. D., van Dam, A., Feiner, S. K. and Hughes, J. F. (1997), *Computer Graphics: Principles and Practice*, Cornell, NY: Addison-Wesley.

Heidegger, M. (1977), *The Question Concerning Technology, and Other Essays*, New York: Garland.

Hochberg, J. (2007), 'Looking ahead (one glance at a time)', in *In the Mind's Eye: Julian Hochberg on the Perception of Pictures, Films, and the World*, Oxford: Oxford University Press.

Hollier, D. (1989), *Against Architecture: The Writings of Georges Bataille*, Cambridge, MA: MIT Press.

Itti, L. and Koch, C. (2001), 'Computational modelling of visual attention', *Nature Reviews Neuroscience*, 2, pp. 194–203.

Kittler, F. A. and Griffin, M. (1996), 'The city is a medium', *New Literary History*, 27: 4, pp. 717–29.

Klette, R. and Rosenfeld, A. (2004), *Digital Geometry: Geometric Methods for Digital Picture Analysis*, Amsterdam and Boston: Elsevier.

Klingmann, A. (2007), *Brandscapes: Architecture in the Experience Economy*, Cambridge, MA: MIT Press.

Lukac, R. A. P. and Konstantinos, N. (2005), 'Colour filter arrays: Design and performance analysis', *IEEE Transactions on Consumer Electronics*, 51, pp. 1260–267.

Lyon, C. (2002), 'Unreal estate', in R. McGauran (ed.), *Take 1 – Urban Solutions: Propositions for the Future Australian City*, Canberra: Royal Australian Institute of Architects.

Marin, L. (1984), *Utopics: Spatial Play* (trans. R. A. Vollrath), Atlantic Highlands, NJ: Humanities Press.

McCann, J. J. and Rizzi, A. (2007), 'Spatial comparisons: The antidote to veiling glare limitations in image capture and display', in *Proceedings of IMQA-International Workshop on Image Media Quality and Its Applications*, Chiba, Japan, 9–10 March.

McLuhan, M. (1995), *Understanding Media: The Extensions of Man*, Cambridge, MA and London: MIT Press.

Monmonier, M. (2000), 'Webcams, interactive index maps, and our brave new world's brave new globe', *Cartographic Perspectives*, 37, pp. 51–64.

Poynton, C. A. (2012), *Digital Video and HD: Algorithms and Interfaces*, Waltham, MA: Morgan Kaufmann.

Notes

1. See http://www.appliedautonomy.com/.
2. See http://www.appliedautonomy.com/isee.html.

Chapter 7

Place, play and privacy: Exploring location-based applications and spatial experience

Melanie Chan

Introduction

Location-based applications are a growing category of digital tools that gather information about the geographical position of a communication device, such as a smartphone or tablet, as part of its functionality. In this chapter we will illustrate how the increasing ubiquity of location-based applications create a situation in which the technological mediation of everyday life is becoming ever more pervasive and persistent. It is critically important to gain insight into the ways in which location-based applications intersect with the social relations, spatial encounters and the practices of everyday life. Following the analytical schema presented by Leah Lievrouw and Sonia Livingstone (2005), this chapter will examine artefacts – such as smartphones or tablets, human activities or behaviour – and the panoply of social arrangements, all engendered in some way by these location-based applications.

To weave together the various strands of argument surrounding the technological mediation of spatial experience, we will explore three key themes: place, play and privacy. First, we will investigate the ways in which location-based applications map the geographical terrain according to lifestyle and consumption categories. Second, we link the use of location-based applications in the urban environment to computer-game play. Third, we try to identify the many ways in which location-based applications can be used to collect and mine personal data. Location-based applications are at the heart of contemporary concerns relating to privacy, monitoring and surveillance, and this three-pronged approach provides enough perspective to successfully analyse their ideological dimensions. In doing so, it will be argued that the pleasurable ludic aspects of these technologies are offset by the ways in which they commercialize urban experiences, and are implicated in surveillance and data mining.

Any analysis of location-based applications involves an examination of the discourses that surround them, paying particular attention to the relationships between these new technologies and physical spaces. As Hall, Evans and Nixon (2013: xix) observe, 'it is by our use of things, and what we say, think and feel about them – how we represent them – that we give them a meaning'. Furthermore, Terry Flew (2014) claims that there are often celebratory discourses surrounding new technologies that detail how they will enhance our daily lives. Once that technology starts to become mainstream and familiar, these optimistic expectations start to flounder. Certainly in recent years, there has been a significant growth in the use of mobile media technology, especially smartphones. For instance, in the United Kingdom, the OFCOM (2014: 19) report *Adults' Media Use and Attitudes* indicates that 'use of a mobile phone of any kind among all adults' stands at 92%'. Along with the growing use of smartphones, the report indicates that 'six in ten (61%) say they have between one and 20 apps installed on them' (2014: 19). Similar findings are revealed in the Pew Center Research report *U.S. Smartphone Use in 2015* (Smith et al. 2015), which states that 64 per cent of American adults now own a smartphone.

As a result of the growth of smartphone devices and applications, the space between online and offline presence is becoming blurred. Public spaces with wireless connections now enable us to engage in private mediated consumption (such as conversations, sending text messages and conducting Internet searches). Sherry Turkle (2008) points out that we have become intimately tethered to technological devices such as smartphones and tablets. In the early days of mobile technology, using a mobile phone in public places or whilst with others was not socially acceptable. This is no longer the case. Sociologist Michael Bull (2005) in fact coined the phrase 'no dead air' to refer to the ways in which mobile music devices enabled listeners to create their own cocoons of media consumption through customization of their environments (e.g. personalized playlists) and the personalized management of time (such as listening to music to fill time during commuting).

Bull's argument about mobile music devices could also be applied to smartphone applications. For instance, Larissa Hjorth and Ingrid Richardson (2009) describe how location-based gaming can be used to offset the frustration or boredom of waiting for public transport or standing in queues. As mobile devices such as music players and smartphones have become commonplace, transportation hubs such as train and bus terminals have become places where people communicate with others who are not co-present, whilst ignoring those in the same physical space around them. Sherry Turkle (2008: 122) emphasizes that 'the presence of our tethering media signal that we do not want to be disturbed by conventional sociality with physically proximate individuals'. Taking Turkle's argument into consideration, this chapter explores the ways in which location-based applications impact upon both our physical spaces and consequent social interaction.

There is not currently a great deal of academic literature that focuses specifically upon smartphone and tablet applications in communication studies, and the study of location-based applications is particularly underdeveloped. Gerard Goggin and Larissa Hjorth (2014) investigate mobile media in relation issues and debates such as political economy, ecology and creativity. Meanwhile, Jennie Germann Molz (2012) has studied the relationships between mobile devices, social networks and tourism. The work of Rich Ling and Jonathan Donner (2009) also provides an analysis of the mobile phone as a social, cultural and technological artefact. What is presented here then is an attempt to contribute to the study of technologically mediated encounters, and thereby stimulate further debate about location-based applications.

Space/place

In order to prepare the groundwork for our subsequent discussion, it is useful to begin with some preliminary remarks about the conceptualization of space and place. Phil Hubbard (2007) remarks that space is often considered an abstract concept, whereas place refers to a specific location. Extending Hubbard's discussion, space can be studied at the macro level, whereas place can be studied at the micro level. At the macro socio-economic level, Henri Lefebvre (1991) illuminates the ways in which space can be a mechanism that supports the interests of the dominant power within society. Other writers, such as Manuel Castells (2000) and Zygmunt Bauman (2000), also provide insightful arguments about space in relation to technology, information and global capitalism. In contrast to macro studies of space, place can be examined at the micro level to elucidate specific communities of interest and the practices within them.

Cartography is a practice that relates to the construction of knowledge, power and legitimation. Ordnance Survey maps, for instance, transform physical space into information through the use of conventional symbols that represent roads, railways, mountains, hills, rivers, pathways and gradients. Once we learn what these conventional symbols represent, we can use an Ordnance Survey map to orient ourselves as we move through space or to find a specific location. In his analysis of space, knowledge and power, Leighton Evans (2014: 74) reminds us that 'cartographers are affected by the ideological and cultural influences placed upon them in their role in society, and maps as products and artefacts generate specific territorial knowledge'. From this perspective, cartography is linked to the ordering and management of spatial relations. Hakim Bey (1991), for example, critiques the ways in which cartography has been used for political purposes and what he terms 'psychic imperialism'. In an attempt to counter the control of places, Bey proposes the creation of Temporary Autonomous Zones for areas that are more transitory and emergent. Cartography has traditionally relied on the mapping of physical space through the use of conventional symbols. However, to gain further insight into location-based applications, we also need to consider how digital spaces have evolved, as well as the mechanisms by which they are mapped and controlled.

Location-based applications transform the spatial terrain into digital information that can be acquired and possessed. Cartography historically created a formal abstraction of the physical world through the use of conventional signs and symbols. Digital technology, on the other hand, transforms physical space through mathematical code into data. Spatial relationships become malleable when they are transformed into data, and can be manipulated and circulated to a greater degree than traditional Ordnance Survey maps printed on paper. One of the distinctive features of location-based applications is that computer-generated and physical space become intertwined in a new mode of representation. As William J. Mitchell (2005: 19) remarks, 'the social and cultural functions of built spaces have become inseparable from the simultaneous operation of multiple communication systems within and among them'. Going further, Mitchell claims that with the development of digital communication systems, we are no longer constrained by time or physical space. Instead we have become *homo electronicus*, defined by our 'endless shifts of attention and engagement throughout the reaches of space and time' (2005: 185). Drawing upon the arguments presented by Tutt and Mitchell, this chapter highlights technologically mediated experiences by focusing on the location-based application Foursquare.

Foursquare

Foursquare is a socially and culturally significant location-based application that, according to the company's website,[1] has 50 million registered users as of 2015. Foursquare was created by Internet entrepreneurs Dennis Crowley and Naveen Selvadurai and launched in 2009. Crowley studied Interactive Telecommunications at New York University (NYU), and one of his tutors was media and communication scholar Clay Shirky. During an interview with Tim Adams in the British newspaper The Observer, Shirky discusses the Interactive Telecommunications curriculum in relation to the development of Foursquare. In particular, Shirky (cited in Adams 2010) states that students considered the ways in which 'the grid of Manhattan was like a grid in a game scenario'. Indeed, the name Foursquare evokes the grid plan of New York City, with its numerical street names like First, Second and Fifth Avenue. The rectangular grid of Manhattan, which was outlined in the Commissioners Plan of 1811, involved the shaping of urban space into grid-like, standardized units (Lindner 2015). Moreover, this geometrical aesthetic can be placed in the wider context of the architectural style of modernism. The geometry of the modernist aesthetic emerged during the industrial era, when it became possible to mass-produce standardized objects. As Stanislaw van Moos (1979) points out, modernist architects such as Ludwig Mies van de Rohe (1886–1969) and Le Corbusier (1887–1965) presented new forms of urban spaces based on grid-like, standardized structures, and buildings made from concrete, glass and steel. Instead of producing grids from physical materials, global positioning technology constructs information grids using base stations that divide space into defined segments.

Michel de Certeau (1988) also describes the ways in which toponymy (the naming of city spaces) maps our spatial experiences within specific historical, social and cultural contexts. For example, the East End or West End of London, uptown/downtown, or Harlem or the East Village in New York are each associated with different inhabitants, buildings, sounds, symbols and lifestyles. Place names may also recall historical figures, such as Avenue Victor Hugo in Paris; or a place may be named as an act of remembrance, recalling certain events (for instance, Trafalgar Square in London). In contrast to the practice of toponymy, Foursquare maps spatial relationships according to informational content based on lifestyle categories, including arts, best nearby, food, nightlife and trending. In this way, Foursquare falls into the same genre as tourist guide books (such as the *Lonely Planet* series) and magazine publications (such as *Time Out*), all of which provide information about leisure and sites of consumption.

Locations on Foursquare are allocated a numerical rating using data mining of likes/dislikes and positive or negative comments generated by those who use the application. The practice of allocating ratings to locations has increased in recent years through online platforms such as Google Reviews and Trip Advisor. Weiguo Fan and Michael D. Gordon (2014) outline a range of practices that are now used to influence consumer behaviour through brand engagement or information about particular locations. These practices include social media analytics, sentiment and trend analysis, polarity lexicons and opinion mining. Fan and Gordon explain that what these practices have in common is that they extract data from online sources and analyse them for marketing purposes.

There is a mass of information in contemporary culture, yet our attention span is limited. We may attempt to deal with this situation by seeking out information that matches our interest and is relevant to us. However, we may then miss out on information relating to unexpected ideas, people or places that are outside of our existing range of tastes and interests. The work of Robert B. Cialdini (2007) indicates that we are influenced by degrees of popularity wherein choices are validated by social proof. More people may visit a particular place if it appears to be popular on a location-based application. Additionally, Cialdini (2007: 140) states that 'the principle of social proof operates most powerfully when we are observing the behaviour of people just like us'. Internet activist Eli Pariser (2011) contends that what has tended to happen with the growth of social networks is that people connect with those they already know, and who have similar interests and opinions. Consequently, the behaviour of those who use location-based applications is strongly influenced by what their friends like, or the places their friends and peers visit. Richard H. Thaler and legal scholar Cass R. Sunstein (2008) have also investigated the ways in which people can be nudged into changing their behaviour through choice architecture. In other words, the choices that are made available to people and how those choices are presented can influence their behaviour. Thus, the sites that are listed as the most popular on location-based applications are more likely to nudge people into visiting them. We also need to think critically about how places are included or excluded in the choice architecture of location-based applications. For instance, the choice architecture of location-based applications could be influenced by organizations that are willing to pay for places that support their economic interests.

Play

In the 1960s, developments in computing and computer graphics led to the creation of a new form of space and spatial relationships (Woolley 1993). The North American writer William Gibson encapsulated the concept of this new form of space through his use of the term 'cyberspace' in his novel Neuromancer (1986). In Gibson's novel, cyberspace refers to an abstract environment generated by computer code. This new form of computer-generated space provided the platform for the development of virtual environments and computer games. During the late 1970s and 1980s, computer games were played in amusement arcades, shopping centres or bars. From the mid-1980s onwards, gaming consoles and personal computers opened up the possibility of using computer games within the domestic sphere. Notably during this period, there was an emphasis on the boundaries between the virtual space of the game and real-world environments. During the mid-1990s, there were a range of critical studies about cyberspace and virtual environments (cf. Carter 2005; Franck 2002; Turkle 1994, 1997). However, in agreement with Dylan Tutt (2008), these studies of cyberspace and virtual reality were often framed according to disembodiment and disconnection from the world around us. Yet the development and popularity of location-based applications has produced a situation whereby 'mediated interaction cannot simply be disembedded from everyday life' (Tutt 2008: 1158).

Instead of having a clear demarcation between the space of a game and the physical environment, location-based applications incorporate features of our physical environment into a gaming experience. Game scholar Ingrid Richardson (2010) speculates that the blurring of boundaries between the virtual and the real in the context of mobile gaming also has implications for the concept of the magic circle or dedicated game world. What is noteworthy about location-based applications is that the urban environment becomes the site of game-playing experiences. A case in point is provided by the location-based application Ingress (2012) created by Niantic Labs. It is an augmented reality game that blends real-world locations with game-playing activities. The game is based on the premise that a global event has occurred during which the Earth has been seeded with a new form of exotic matter by an alien race. Players are divided into two factions, namely the Enlightened Faction (which believes that this global event will catapult mankind to a higher state of consciousness) and the Resistance (who holds a more dubious view about the impact of exotic matter upon mankind). What Ingress does is transform the physical environment of monuments, public buildings, public spaces and transport hubs into portals that can be fought over and acquired by the competing factions. In this way, the physical infrastructure of the world becomes part of a game-playing experience.

The incorporation of the ludic qualities of gaming into everyday experience is also evident in the application Zombies Run!, created by Naomi Alderman and Rebecca Levene of the company Six to Start. Zombies Run! provides a technologically mediated approach to running, in which exercise is framed as an epic adventure through storytelling, characterization and music. Players of the game are given missions that form the basis of running logs and status reports to share with others via social networking. By linking to social networking sites, location-based applications like this facilitate friendships and a sense of competition amongst different users. Another location-based application that combines ludic and social elements is Sacracy. It embeds medieval iconography and game-world quests into real-world environments through the use of GPS technology. Players can move through physical space and also move a virtual character through the game to solve puzzles. Finally, Tourality is a location-based application that allows players to compete with others to get to a particular location in the shortest possible time.

Location-based game applications provide a series of enticements such as points, badges and 'levelling up'. For instance, Sacracy features an achievement screen listing players with the highest scores. Players can increase their scores by improving their skill in using weapons and moving up to different levels. In the case of Tourality, users compete for virtual gold and trophies that are acquired by reaching specific locations. The game-playing features of location-based applications also involve a degree of performing for an imagined audience. For instance, some players feel compelled to manage their online status through in-game chat or the continual updating of their profile to reflect their latest achievements. As game designer Jane McGonigal (2012) points out, players of location-based games are able to generate a sense of achievement by overcoming obstacles and improving their skills. In the context of our working lives, people generally work towards that accomplishment of goals that are corporate driven rather than personal. In contrast, location-based games enable the player to exercise a more liberating agency within the structural limitations of the programming and software.

Privacy

The modes of surveillance that are made possible by location-based applications are historically, socially and culturally specific. The movements of those who use location-based applications can be tracked, observed and shared with others through GPS and social networks. Movement through physical space can be curtailed through visible boundaries such as walls, gates and sentry points that maintain privacy by preventing others from observing or interacting with us. In the case of computer-based technology, it is possible to construct what Marc Andrejevic (2007) terms 'digital enclosures', such as information grids and geo-fences, raising concerns in relation to privacy, data mining and surveillance. Andrejevic explains digital enclosure as a concept that refers to the trails we leave while using the Internet to send e-mails, conduct Google searches or engage in online shopping. Smartphones can be continually tracked and recorded in a similar way using satellite GPS. Orbiting the Earth, these satellites triangulate the position of the user to a set of spatial coordinates held in a database. Although smartphones and location-based applications seem to offer us many benefits, less visible is the extent to which they can be used to mine personal data:

> [U]sing a cell phone or credit card these days is deceptively simple: communicating and purchasing are streamlined and simplified, but we have very little access to the forms of information collection and circulation that are taking place behind the scenes and screens.

> (Andrejevic 2007: 4)

The application Life 360[2] – founded by Chris Hulls and Alex Haro – simultaneously tracks and connects a range of family members. By April 2015, Life 360 claims that 50 million families are using the application to map the location of family members and friends. The developers of Life 360 promote the application as a way of solving problems based on different family members having different schedules and activities across multiple locations. Life 360 also draws upon parents' desire to keep their children safe by knowing where they are, who they are with and what they are doing. Those who use Life 360 can set up automatic notifications for places they frequent the most, and then share this information within their inner circle. These features of Life 360 position surveillance as something that people will willingly accept because it satisfies their need to feel safe.

Although it may be free to open an account with companies such as Foursquare and Life 360, their business model is predicated upon the collection of data from users so that it may be used for commercial gain. The use of personal data by these companies and third-party affiliates is set out in their terms and conditions. Yet these terms and conditions are written in complicated legal language that can be difficult to comprehend. Moreover, Foursquare and Life 360 are in a powerful position in respect to their users because accounts can only be set up with these companies by accepting their terms and conditions in their entirety. Users are forced to accept the terms and conditions offered to them if they want to use these applications to find information and communicate with family, friends and colleagues.

To set up an account with Foursquare or Life 360, users must provide sensitive personal data such as their name, e-mail address and date of birth. After the user's personal data is collected, an individual profile is created, enabling them to upload user-generated content such as photographic images and text before connecting with others. In the case of Foursquare, users can create a basic profile that displays their photographic image, social connections and a history of the reviews they have created about any locations they have visited. Meanwhile, users of Life 360 are encouraged to provide data about their social connections in order to create particular groupings – or 'circles' – that may also include caregivers and other extended family members.

Whilst users may find it easy to open an account with Foursquare or Life 360, it is difficult to ascertain how the data generated by the account will be handled over time. When a person is placed under surveillance, their activities are monitored, but they may not be aware of who is watching them or for what purpose. From this perspective, it can be contended that Foursquare or Life 360 are in a position of power in the customer relationship because they can oversee the data that is provided by users. In contrast, those users are powerless in terms of determining exactly how those companies collect and share their data. For instance, the Foursquare privacy policy states that:

> We may work with advertisers or other partners and advertising service providers to serve ads or services that may be relevant to you based on your inferred interests or

location (or both) to computers, mobile phones or other devices, which may use a device ID, cookie, pixel or other similar technology placed by Foursquare or the third party.

(Foursquare 2015)

The privacy policy provides no detailed information about the third party affiliations that exist between Foursquare and other companies, or how they will use the data that they obtain. Foursquare also uses cookies – small pieces of data that are sent from their website and stored on a user's browser whilst they visit that site. One of the functions of cookies is to compile the browsing history of users. Foursquare compiles data on the locations a user has visited, along with the locations their friends have visited, in order to provide information to them about special offers and recommended places (e.g. bars, restaurants and other retail outlets).

The content that is provided by users of applications can also be used for commercial purposes. For instance, the Life 360 application website states that by posting content a user gives the organization:

[…] a royalty-free, sublicensable, transferable, perpetual, irrevocable, non-exclusive, worldwide license to use, reproduce, modify, publish, list information regarding, edit, translate, distribute, syndicate, publicly perform, publicly display, and make derivative works of all such User Content.

(Life 360 2015)

In his critical assessment of the Internet and social networks, Andrew Keen (2015) refers back to the Stasi's (the East German secret police) mission to collect information about every member of East German society. According to Keen, the Stasi surveillance system was based on a network of informants who sought to scrutinize the daily lives of all citizens. This project to amass information on all East German citizens now seems parochial compared to the global operations and surveillance capabilities of companies such as Google and Facebook. Furthermore, citizens now disclose personal data themselves via their voluntary use of social networking sites.

Michel de Certeau's (1988) study regarding the subversion of institutionalized forms of power is useful in terms of our understanding of the privacy and surveillance implications accompanying location-based applications. To explain how subversive tactics operate, de Certeau makes analogies between the linguistic system as a whole and the creativity of individual speech. Although individual speakers are required to draw upon the conventions of language to make meaningful utterances, he contends there is also an opportunity for them to exercise a degree of agency through improvised speech acts. From this vantage point, language use and the practices surrounding the exploration of the urban environment can be considered as symbolic systems of signification that generate meaning in specific historical, social and cultural contexts. Elucidating this position, de Certeau (1988: 97) writes: 'The act of walking is to the urban system what the speech act is to language or the statements uttered'. Drawing analogies from language, de Certeau (1988: 98) defines walking as 'a space of enunciation in which walking becomes a personal statement, or form of expression'. There is a subjective element to our walking practices as we drift through the city or take detours to explore new places. These aspects of our movement through the city cannot be fully mapped, measured and monitored. For instance, our footsteps 'cannot be counted because each unit has a qualitative character: a style of tactile apprehension and kinaesthetic appropriation' (1988: 97). Even the ways in which we walk have a subjective qualitative aspect that eludes systems of measurement and quantification. Taking de Certeau's arguments about creativity, subjectivity and agency into account, it is worthwhile to consider the terminology that surrounds location-based applications. For instance, are people who engage with these applications positioned as users, players or consumers – or a combination of all three? In addition, how much agency or creativity can be exercised when engaging with these applications?

In his study of everyday life, de Certeau concentrates on the key distinctions between strategies and tactics. Strategies refer to the dominance of space through institutionalized forms of ownership, as in the privatization of places or controlled movement through those places. The integration of GPS into smartphone devices offers a clear example of strategic deployment through its creation of electronic tagging devices that can track our movements while they take place. Data can also be collected on mobile communication and our location through base transceiver stations (BTS) and call detail records (CDR), which give details of the location of a caller and the duration of their call (Poole 2006). In de Certeau's schema, tactics provide a set of unofficial, marginal and improvisational practices that can be used to subvert dominant ideological strategies and practices. Gary T. Marx (2002) similarly outlines a series of specific practices that can be used to subvert surveillance mechanisms; for instance, masking moves could be used to create false accounts or profiles when using location-based applications.

Gary T. Marx also asserts that we may be sometimes compliant with surveillance systems by providing information to authorities or companies when it is advantageous or necessary. One example of this would be where the disadvantages of providing personal data may be offset by commercial discounts in stores or other forms of reward. The data that is generated by location-based gaming applications could also be acquired and utilized by governments, law-enforcement agencies or commercial interests. Computer science researchers at Cambridge University even obtained data sets from Foursquare users via publicly available information on Twitter. These data sets were then analysed to investigate levels of activity in different cities (Noulas et al. 2012). In an article in the *New Scientist*, journalist Chris Baraniuk (2013) detailed the ways in which companies such as McDonalds, Starbucks and Dunkin Donuts used mobility information from Foursquare data sets to figure out where to open new outlets.

Conclusion

This chapter has outlined the ways in which power and control relate to the mapping of physical space. Maps only become legible through a certain degree of literacy, since we must learn to recognize a conventional set of symbols. In a similar fashion, location-based applications map and control space mathematically through our shared computer code. Location-based applications such as Foursquare are shown to map places according to lifestyle and popularity levels, as opposed to more topographical qualities. Capturing and displaying information about places allows Foursquare and similar applications to nudge people to visit certain places while leaving other parts of the urban environment completely unexplored.

Significantly, location-based applications can be used to transform the urban environment into a game environment. Whilst location-based applications such as Ingress, Zombies Run!, Sacracy or Tourality may be promoted as enjoyable ludic experiences, they are also a primary mechanism of surveillance and data mining. In some cases, users of location-based applications may openly disclose personal data as they communicate with others via social networks. However, the data which is captured from these location-based applications may also be sold by the site of activity for marketing and advertising. Crucially, the ludic discourses surrounding these applications can be regarded as a mechanism that supports institutional power and the status quo. The reinforcement of corporate dominance in the commercial relationship with consumers is maintained by the fact that the precise mechanisms of data mining remain somewhat opaque to those who use them.

The surveillance and privacy implications of personal data in relation to location-based applications are part of a broader set of concerns about the impact of technological developments. As devices become increasing networked and incorporated into everyday life, it will soon be possible to continually trace the movements, behavioural practices and social networks of individuals in even greater detail. For instance, the Internet of Things (Burrus 2014) refers to the ways in which the physical infrastructure of the urban environment will soon be replete with information captured from a wide swathe of sources, including street lights, traffic signals, closed-circuit television and other smart networked objects. We can imagine a scenario whereby a user leaves digital footprints through the use of their smartphone, location-based applications and the myriad objects they use in daily life within an urban environment.

The introduction of such comprehensive forms of communication and information-gathering is likely to generate further debate from individuals and consumer advocacy groups, as well as legal and government institutions. In May 2014, The European Court of Justice ruled that an individual has the right to request that online information about them be removed if it can be considered irrelevant, outdated or excessive. This ruling is known as 'the right to be forgotten', and is already reverberating in a multitude of requests made to Google and Facebook. In the future, it may be possible that individuals will request that information relating to bars or restaurants that they frequented years ago be removed because it is no longer relevant. It may be objected that information about where they had a coffee or lunch using location-based applications is not sensitive personal data, and is somewhat insignificant in terms of privacy and surveillance. However, as this chapter elucidates, it can be maintained that these micro-moments of our everyday lives become increasingly significant when they are tracked continually, forming a perpetual web of technological surveillance. The practical informational function and ludic qualities of location-based applications are thus significantly offset by their clear and pervasive surveillance dimensions.

References

Adams, T. (2010), 'Will Foursquare be the new Twitter', *The Observer*, 25 April, http://www.theguardian.com/technology/2010/apr25. Accessed 9 May 2015.

Andrejevic, M. (2007), *iSpy – Surveillance and Power in the Interactive Era*, Lawrence, KA: University of Kansas.

Baraniuk, C. (2013), 'Foursquare check-ins tell stores where to set up shop', *New Scientist*, 16 August, http://www.newscientist.com/article/mg21929304.600-foursquare-checkins-tell-stores-where-to-set-up-shop.html#.VVCsRo5VhHw. Accessed 11 May 2015.

Bauman, Z. (2000), *Liquid Modernity*, Cambridge: Polity Press.

Bey, H. (1991), *Temporary Autonomous Zones*, Brooklyn: Autonomedia.

Bull, M. (2005), 'No dead air! The iPod and the culture of mobile listening', *Leisure Studies*, 24: 4, pp. 343–55.

Burrus, D. (2014), 'The Internet of Things is far bigger than anyone realizes', *Wired*, November, http://www.wired.com/2014/11/the-internet-of-things-bigger/. Accessed 8 July 2015.

Carter, D. (2005), 'Living in virtual communities – An ethnography of human relationships in cyberspace', *Information, Communication and Society*, 8: 2, pp. 148–67.

Castells, M. (2000), *The Rise of the Network Society*, Oxford: Blackwell.

Certeau, M. de (1988), *The Practice of Everyday Life*, Berkeley: University of California Press.

Cialdini, R. (2007), *Influence: The Psychology of Persuasion*, New York: HarperCollins.

Evans, L. (2014), 'Maps as deep: Reading the code of location-based social networks', *IEEE Technology and Society*, Spring, pp. 73–80.

Fan, W. and Gordon, M. D. (2014), 'The power of social media analytics', *Communications of the ACM*, 57: 6, pp. 74–81.

Flew, T. (2014), *New Media*, Oxford: Oxford University Press.

Foursquare (2015), 'Foursquare Labs, Inc. privacy policy', https://foursquare.com/legal/privacy. Accessed 13 November 2015.

Franck, K. (2002), 'When I enter virtual reality, what body will I leave behind?', in N. Spiller (ed.), *Cyber_Reader: Critical Writings for the Digital Era*, London and New York: Phaidon, pp. 238–45.

Germann Molz, J. (2012), *Travel Connections: Tourism, Technology and Togetherness in a Mobile World*, Oxford: Routledge.

Gibson, W. (1986), *Neuromancer*, London: Grafton.

Goggin, G. and Hjorth, L. (eds) (2014), *The Routledge Companion to Mobile Media*, New York: Routledge.

Hall, S., Evans, J. and Nixon, S. (eds) (2013), *Representation*, London: Sage and Open University.

Hjorth, L. and Richardson, I. (2009), 'The waiting game: Complicating notions of (tele) presence and gendered distraction in casual mobile gaming', *Australian Journal of Communication*, 36: 1, pp. 23–35.

Hubbard, P. (2007), 'Space/place', in D. Atkinson et al. (eds), *Cultural Geography: A Critical Dictionary of Key Ideas*, London: IB Tauris, pp. 41–48.

Keen, A. (2015), *The Internet is Not the Answer*, London: Atlantic Books.

Lefebvre, H. (1991), *The Production of Space*, Oxford: Blackwell.

Lievrouw, L. and Livingstone, S. (2005), *The Handbook of New Media: Social Shaping and Consequences of ICTs*, London: Sage.

Life 360 (2015), 'Terms of service', https://www.life360.com/terms_of_use/. Accessed 13 November 2015.

Lindner, C. (2015), *Imagining New York City: Literature, Urbanism and The Visual Arts 1890–1940*, Oxford: Oxford University Press.

Ling, R. and Donner, J. (2009), *Mobile Communication*, Cambridge: Polity Press.

Marx, G. (2002), 'A tack in the shoe: Neutralizing and resisting the new surveillance', *Journal of Social Issues*, 59, pp. 369–90.

McGonigal, J. (2012), *Reality is Broken – Why Games Make us Better and How They Can Change the World*, London: Vintage.

Mitchell, W. J. (2005), *Placing Words: Symbols, Space and the City*, Cambridge MA: MIT Press.

von Moos, S. (1979), *Le Corbusier: Elements of a Synthesis*, Cambridge, MA: MIT Press.

Noulas, A., Scellato, S., Lathia, N. and Mascolo, C. (2012), 'A random walk around the city: New venue recommendations in location-based social networks', Paper presented to *IEEE International Conference on Social Computing*, Amsterdam, Netherlands, 3 September.

OFCOM (2014), *Adults' Media Use and Attitudes Report*, London: OFCOM.

Pariser, E. (2011), *The Filter Bubble – What the Internet is Hiding from You*, London: Viking.

Poole, I. (2006), *Cellular Communications Explained: From Basics to 3G*, Oxford: Newnes.

Richardson, I. (2010), 'Ludic mobilities: The corporealities of mobile gaming', *Mobilities*, 5: 4, pp. 431–47.

Smith, A., McGeeney, K., Duggan, M., Rainie, L. and Keeter, S. (2015), *U.S. Smartphone Use in 2015*, Washington: Pew Research Center.

Thaler, R. T. and Sunstein, C. R. (2008), *Nudge: Improving Decisions About Health, Wealth and Happiness*, New Haven, CT: Yale University Press.

Turkle, S. (1994), 'Constructions and reconstructions of self in virtual reality: Playing in the MUDS', *Mind, Culture and Activity*, 1: 3, pp. 158–67.

—— —— (1997), *Life on the Screen: Identity in the Age of the Internet*, New York: Simon and Schuster.

—— —— (2008), 'Always on/Always-on-you: The tethered self', in J. E. Katz (ed.), *Handbook of Mobile Communication Studies*, Cambridge, MA: MIT Press, pp. 121–37.

Tutt, D. (2008), 'Where the interaction is – Collisions of the situated and mediated living room interactions', *Qualitative Inquiry*, 14: 7, pp. 1157–179.

Woolley, B. (1993), *Virtual Worlds,* London: Penguin.

Notes

1. https://foursquare.com.
2. www.life360.com.

Chapter 8

Post-digital approaches to mapping memory, heritage and identity in the city

Georgios Artopoulos and Nikolas Bakirtzis

Introduction

Over the past decades, a continuously increasing trans-regional population movement from the countryside to cities has transformed urban landscapes and cultural experience. This development is expected to further fragment large metropolitan areas with contemporary or historic territorial, social and cultural divisions, thus resulting in further gentrification and decomposition of the cities' territorial cohesion (Burdett & Wagstaff 2011). In this context, historic cities facing cohesion challenges due to physical, sociopolitical and/or cultural division offer a particularly intriguing framework to analyse and map the relation between identity, collective memory and spatial experience. Divided historic cities like Jerusalem, Mostar, Berlin, Belfast and Nicosia, to name some key examples, provide complex layered canvases where heritage retains a key role in the spatial experience of their urban environments. The changing demographics of these cities present important new challenges that call for actions that will strengthen territorial and social cohesion. Monuments of cultural heritage can be a catalyst in redefining the spatial experience of historic cities for citizens and outsiders alike. Although this relation has been addressed in scholarship, advanced technologies can offer vast new possibilities for transdisciplinary research that effectively responds to the challenged cohesion of contemporary urban societies.

This chapter presents the concepts, challenges and constraints of a transdisciplinary study that foregrounds the use of technology to critically understand the role of heritage monuments in mapping the experience and social memory of the spatially distributed multiplicity of public space, involving architects, historians, archaeologists, computer engineers, visualization specialists, etc. The historic city of Nicosia, which remains physically divided between Greek and Turkish Cypriots, is the study's primary pilot application – a complex historic space where, under the typical multiplicities of contemporary urban landscape, both the political issue of division and the memory of a shared past lie (Michaelides 2012; Bakshi 2011, 2012). This chapter presents the development of a virtual living laboratory of urban exploration that studies how the interaction with, and use of, cultural heritage monuments can affect the perception, appropriation and transformation of social and cultural identity. In the long term, the proposed research will contribute, through the analysis of the data collected, insights and tacit knowledge regarding possible planning strategies and the impact of future interventions on the urbanscape of historic city centres. In the case of the walled Nicosia, it is a reality that it has not only been divided but also fragmented in its preservation and development over the last 40 years. Unlike studies focusing on the politics of division, this research starts with the impact the enforced separation of the urban terrain has had on the experience and understanding of the city.

The concept of this study revolves around the dynamic relations between historic urban environments, and the complex interactions between users, identities, communities and memories associated with particular areas of a city (Sack 1986). The complexity of contemporary cities – especially historically layered cities – has grown to unprecedented degrees (Burdett & Sudjic 2011; Hall 2012; Browning 2000), and it is acknowledged that there are different ways of studying and approaching their challenges (Cilliers 1998; Mitleton 2006). Common resources, shared space in multicultural environments and public space are all considered in this chapter as constituting parts of the archipelagos of spaces in the contemporary city. In these complex urban realities, monuments can play the role of 'cultural lighthouses' – condensers that punctuate flows of movement, and trigger social interaction, exchange of information and engagement with history, ultimately shaping the character of the city. Chapters in the long, layered history of these monuments can be used as stages of the ever-transforming urban territory that 'unhide' critical moments in the palimpsest of the city's history (Artopoulos & Bakirtzis 2014).

The disrupted experience of historic cities' contemporary civic space

In the case of the Cypriot capital Nicosia (Michaelides 2012), whose historic core remains enclosed behind the iconic sixteenth-century Venetian fortifications, the historical transformations of the Paphos Gate demonstrate the spatial complexity of the city's cultural landscape (Figure 1). As part of the city's medieval fortifications, which for centuries defined the experience of urban space, the Paphos Gate was one of the city's 'thresholds' separating urban from rural, outside from inside, safe from hostile, known from unknown, etc. (Bakirtzis 2010). The Gate also served as barracks for the Ottoman and the British rulers of the island, aimed at controlling this sensitive entryway. At the start of the twentieth century, part of the walls adjacent to the Gate were demolished to effectively free the city and allow its development beyond its fortified limits.

Since the 1974 war and the physical separation of Nicosia, the Paphos Gate has become an iconic symbol of division, located as it is on the infamous 'Green Line' that divides the city into two halves (Figure 2). The Gate's history mirrors the city's transformations from the late medieval era through to early modern period. The ambitious yet futile efforts of the Venetians to defend the city provided the new Ottoman rulers (1571–1878) with a clearly defined urban entity. The Gate continued to be used under British rule (1878–1960) until the early twentieth century, when part of the defensive wall north of the Gate was demolished to allow vehicles and better communication between the historic core and the newly developed neighbourhoods beyond its walls. Continuous use and

Figure 1.1. View of Paphos Gate from inside the walls. Notice the two ramps on either side of the walkway (screen-grab of the raw point cloud 3D model generated via a laser scanning of the site.

Figure 1.2. Setting up and testing the first-generation of interaction hardware at the Visualization Lab (Cyprus Institute).

Figures 1.3 and 1.4. Four historical phases of the Paphos Gate, with diagrams of the circulation in and around it. The contemporary reality of the studied public space, a popular tourist destination, as formed by the coexistence of parallel 'dimensions' of alternative realities, e.g. a construction completed as it used to be, or as it is planned to become, allows researchers and professionals to experiment, test and explore hidden conditions of the built environment. It also invites visitors – both citizens and tourists – to learn from past stories, imagine their place in the new conditions presented for the city, and immerse themselves in staged places.

maintenance have left their mark on the Gate, offering intriguing glimpses into various chapters of its history (Figure 1).

Historical actions – such as the accumulative building of auxiliary structures, change of use, transformation enforced by cultural, political or religious reasons, renovation, rehabilitation or partial demolition of cultural monuments or parts of a historic

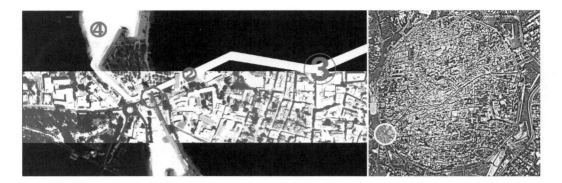

Figure 2.1. Paphos Gate.

Figure 2.2. Similarly to the Gate, Nicosia's Holy Cross Catholic Church lies atop the thinnest part of the buffer zone that divides the city.

Figure 2.3. The 'Green Line'.

Figure 2.4. The moat around the walls.

Figure 2.5. Aerial view of the historic centre of Nicosia and its medieval fortifications (the location of the Paphos Gate is highlighted).

city – produce a different, unplanned image (and therefore cognition) of space. These transformations of the built environment provoke changes in the perception of social and cultural identity.[1] Going beyond the typical challenges[2] of social space in cities (including competition, privatization and gentrification), this research uses technology to study public space through the analysis of the emergent relationships between the cultural characteristics of communities and the spatial conditions of heritage sites. Monuments of cultural heritage can be approached not as built artefacts that state the presence of the 'other' community, but rather as reminders of a shared past that can facilitate the vision of a common future (Smith 1991). Distinct from the sociopolitical discussion of the destruction of buildings and monuments associated with the 'other's' spatial presence, the proposed methodology focuses on the process of the recognition of heritage by the inhabitants of a place through everyday use (Bevan 2012). In this framework, choosing or learning to ignore particular sites during daily occupation patterns and habits is a political act that forms a selective understanding of shared histories and identities.

The case of Nicosia offers an instructive example of this selective process. Following the hostilities between Greek and Turkish Cypriots in the 1960s, and the consolidation of the physical division of the city of Nicosia after the 1974 war, the once shared urban landscape of the historic core of the city became a contested frontline between two polarized communities. This divided reality filtered into the daily experience of the city, directly influencing the ways heritage has been perceived and interpreted (Gumpert & Drucker 1998; Papadakis 1998). Churches, monasteries, mosques and Ottoman public fountains were abandoned, while streets and neighbourhoods changed names in an effort to rewrite the city's history and topography. At the site of the Paphos Gate, the monumental Venetian structure amalgamated with the actual dividing line (Atun & Doratli 2009).

Responding to this problem, bi-communal initiatives like the Nicosia Master Plan (Demetriades 1998) and trust-building efforts sponsored by the international community invested in the restoration and preservation of shared heritage. Among these efforts, it is important to note the awarded documentation and study the architectural heritage within the buffer zone in imminent danger of irreversible deterioration (Petropoulou 2008). However, these efforts have not produced the expected results in the context of Cyprus' layered histories and identities (Canefe 2001). Most restored buildings remain in an awkward historical limbo, being sporadically used for cultural events but having in effect lost their role and position in Nicosia's traumatized civic identity (Zesimou 1998). Studying how and what users of Nicosia choose to neglect enables the technologically more advanced methodology of this study to develop and test spatial strategies; these can then be used study and contribute to the re-association of these built historical sites with the everyday lives and habits of its citizens.

Continuous bodily movement between contested narratives of urban space

Nicosia's division is not only physical, but can also be invisible. This is evident in the ways in which different communities occupy the public space, as well as incorporeal language barriers, political or religious identities, etc. It is thus clear that although the topography of a borderline (i.e. its physical presence) can be ephemeral, the topology of separation (i.e. spatial configuration and the apparent relations between distributed enclaves of occupation) can last longer and may also be permanent. Alan Cohl (1999: 31) remarked that 'wandering through a city, a spatial text is written, which, if read, emanates with chance and memory'. The theoretical aspirations of the presented hypothesis focus on how users understand their physical body's location in relation to the border, and what that border means to them in terms of their everyday use of public space. Societies develop identities and reproduce (among other processes) memories via inscriptions onto cultural artefacts (monuments, books, etc.) and participatory rituals that engage members of each community in social activities and bodily experiences (Connerton 1989; Sorkin 1992). Through the use of digital media techniques that trace bodily movement, the presented transdisciplinary methodology attempts to generate of a collaborative stage capable of sustaining interaction and mapping, as well as representing social memory and its relation to cultural heritage.

Post-digital methods have the capacity to support an alternative study of public space and monuments of cultural heritage as part of an urban renewal strategy of compliance that benefits the lived experience of using public space and walking in the city. The simulation of possible scenarios of intervention (e.g. exploring the potential for the implementation of landscape design proposals involving cycling routes and linear parks) can offer a test bed and starting point for collaboration between the two sides of the division line towards the transformation of the moat into a belt of events that unites the two divided sides of the historic city (Bakshi 2012). The presence of the moat is considered an asset for the city and part of its identity. However, its current state is problematic: following the city's division, it has been treated as a discontinuous leftover

Figure 3. The exterior façade (top) of the Paphos Fate area and plan view (bottom) of the excavation area of the moat by the Gate (screen grab of the raw point cloud 3D model generated via the laser scanning of the site).

space servicing the walled city, hosting parking spaces, ephemeral sports amenities, etc. Distinct from other studies that focus on the representational power of the Venetian walls as a symbol of the city – and the way this was used by both communities as a cognitive mechanism of memory – the present research is occupied with viewing the moat as an 'interface location' (i.e. a shared resource of the city). A 3D reconstruction of the various phases that the public space and heritage site of the Paphos Gate went through will be spatially contextualized with the moat of the Venetian fortifications (Figure 3). As the moat is currently an empty, open-air zone around both parts of the divided capital, this extension of the digitally simulated terrain beyond the Paphos Gate exemplifies how the presented digital methods can contribute to the study of the physical space of the city via the use of a hybrid interactive environment. Incorporating larger parts of the city assists the formation of detailed research inquiries about the symbiotic and complementary participation of old and new interventions in the development of the non-symbolic (re)presentation of the city, as well as the impact that political and cultural changes have on the everyday use of transitional spaces by different communities and groups.[3]

The presented research is based on transdisciplinary collaborations between simulated environments, computer science, archaeology, architecture, urban studies and cultural heritage (Figure 4), and focuses on knowledge sharing and communicating experience. It suggests a new experience-centred method of cultural heritage site explorations that enables data collection of misappropriated territories and challenged historical sites. This methodology supports the emergence of a spontaneous narrative flow between the new (i.e. projected future interventions in the urbanscape), the old and the absent (i.e. unbuilt, demolished or transformed), as the techniques presented hereafter offer a parallel understanding of alternative urban conditions and capture uncertainties in spatial experience – including in movement, in choice, in stasis, etc. The originality of this approach lies in the way improvements in existing digital interactive solutions are combined for the first time to enable researchers to translate the citizen's expectations and reactions to specific points of interest.

This simulated urban stage enables the study of occupation patterns: namely how the position, scale, organization, form, proportions and experiential aspects (i.e. light, material textures, etc.) of space, transfigured in time, impact the bodily movement of users of the particular space to provoke changes in walking pace, direction, points of stasis, points of interest, etc. The visitor has a highly personal and unique educational experience, and people with learning and other disabilities are also able to take advantage of this experience. This approach differs from digital methods for the simulation of urban terrain via agent-based modelling, wherein individuals are grouped in collective identities, abstract generalities stripped of singularities and the unique characteristics of citizens belonging to different communities. These techniques leave no room for indeterminism, nor the breadth of uncertain behaviours that constitute the everyday life of the city.

Figure 4.1. Applying textures on the tessellated model of the Paphos Gate via photogrammetric techniques. This was generated using a raw 3D point cloud.

Figure 4.2. Example of the use of advanced visualization techniques. In this image, reflectance transformation imaging[4] is used to study the Ottoman emblem located over the Gate.

Figure 4.3. Remains of Nicosia's medieval sewage system.

The concept behind the data acquisition tools that complement this new methodological approach relies on the association of bodily movement with spatially distributed presentation of historical and future narratives. The real-time exploration of a projected space extends participants' experience of street walking into a journey of exploration, discovery and understanding spatial relations. Through exploration, the users engage with a narrative; with this strategy, the presented research aims to place them inside digital and physical spaces (Figure 5). Digital methods of urban analysis have been criticized for not integrating notions of bodily movement into space, since computational environments are often considered to be scale-less and bodiless (Dyson 1998). Introducing exploration incentives and narrative inquiries in virtual spaces adds a new level of engagement with the tools of spatial analysis, which will hopefully contribute to the long-standing discussion about new technologies of representation, and their role in understanding and constructing built environments (Batty 2013).

The virtual environment that supports this methodology can enable collaborating stakeholders to explore the chosen public space/heritage site, learn about its history and inquire about issues of accessibility (i.e. ease of access and anticipated behaviour). Choosing routes inside, over and around the reconstructed monument – as well as during different phases of its long history, paths to approach it from the neighbourhood, points of stasis to gaze over the other side of the wall and to possibly examine the various spoliated material, reliefs, inscriptions and other artefacts that were found embedded in the façades of the monument – allows researchers a more informed study of how members of different communities perceive the particular public space. Overlaying circulation paths, as well as mapping the characteristics of user visits, will benefit the visualization

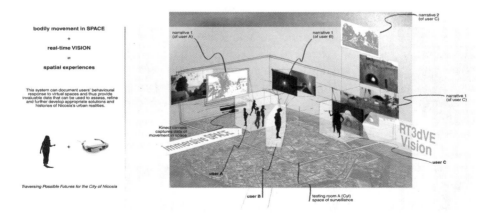

Figure 5. Staging the virtual environment with the use of Oculus Rift™ goggles and Virtuix Omni.

and in-depth survey of the way people make sense of the spatially distributed complexity of historic cities. Immersed in this environment, visitors can act as spontaneous agents that explore and interact with each other on the virtual stage (Mandeville 2014). The purpose of this journey is twofold: while users educate themselves about the history of the monument, operators of the environment are able to collect data on movement and spatial behaviour.

This virtual space is also populated by ambiguous constructions – for example, found objects, remains and leftovers of demolished buildings, historical artefacts – that invite users to explore and intervene in (and therefore engage with) the digitally simulated environment so as to understand and learn. In this context, the research presented envisions the creation of a platform that can contribute not only to the study of the past, but also to serve as a test bed for future urban interventions and projective experimentations, such as the Nicosia SOPAZ Educational Campus Strategy. Beyond the incorporation of reconstructions of historical buildings, the staging of future interventions that are at the stage of procurement or under public discussion is one strategy that will offer insights for the degree of integration and public acceptance that the planned works may have with the rest of the existing urban space.

A common (play)ground: Prototype interfaces for staging virtual civic space

The challenges of this transdisciplinary study lie in two areas: (1) the degree of realism that the virtual construction of the simulated spaces exhibits; and (2) the implementation of a natural and intuitive user interface that will enable the immersion of users in the virtual environment. Previous experiences of digital and hybrid environments underlined the importance of embedding practical activities in the virtual space that will motivate individuals and communities to share its spatially-organized resources (Artopoulos 2012). The combination of dedicated interaction hardware and advanced computer simulations brings particular interest to the field of digital cultural heritage, especially when this system of hardware and software enables the expressive potential of bodily movement. Relying on the stereoscopic vision of Oculus Rift™ goggles and the Virtuix Omni walking device for interaction in the real-time virtual environment of the Paphos Gate (Figures 1.1, 1.2, 2 and 5) allows the collection of bodily movement data that is more descriptive of the users' spatial behaviour than data collected through typical input devices in digital worlds (e.g. keyboard, mouse, joystick).

Producing data of virtual visits by users of different age, education, cultural background and ethnic origin can offer a broader spectrum of responses, which can further the understanding of the qualitative variances of their city-walking experience. Capturing the multiplicity of a historic city is of paramount importance for the affectivity of the staged public space. In addition, the number of users is of key importance: higher number of players covers a broader spectrum of unique behaviours, and therefore offers a more representative and clear understanding of citizens' preferences. This prototypical interface enables the staging of a responsive narrative experience and, in doing so, provides a method of investigating human actions in knowledge-based environments (Artopoulos & Condorcet 2006).

The lack of historic data for the accurate development of the simulated terrain by means of maps, drawings, textual descriptions, etc., can severely limit the faithful representation of the complexity of the reconstructed space. The more articulated the reconstruction of the space is, the more accurate the understanding of how and why people behave the way they do in the virtual environment. Information from historical sources and archaeological research regarding the simulated spaces' articulation, material, dimensions and usage (e.g. the ephemeral operations that take place in the moat; social habits of the inhabitants of the area within the timeframe of the study; and the topography and organization of the urbanscape) are important for the recreation of the structure and social qualities of public open space (Wu & Plantinga 2003).

The application of this methodology to other historical cities will enable the creation of a network of nodes of staged virtual civic space that can facilitate the collection of data and exchange of information between the areas studied. Binnie et al. (2006) discussed how the diversity and multiplicities of contemporary urban life are increasingly becoming a major challenge for metropolises. In the case of the research presented here, the visualization of this data would highlight patterns of occupation alongside a map of the different kinds of complexity exhibited by the contested areas of the studied cities. The contradistinction of behavioural patterns and circulation data with user-generated metadata (e.g. tags, sound recordings and textual descriptions) can offer researchers new opportunities for the analysis of this complexity via explorable three-dimensional cross-media maps. User information and traced paths are displayed over a three-dimensional immersive environment. Researchers can then revisit and replay the subjects' activities recorded by the system in order to formulate observation hypotheses. In this way, the platform functions as a time machine.

Conclusion

According to Gaffikin et al. (2010: 493), 'social conflict has spatial expression, and that spatial form in turn helps shape the conflict'. As such, the reactivation of public space in challenged urban environments necessitates new ways of studying this spatial form. Preliminary studies in Nicosia show that the identification of heritage monuments in the daily spatial experience of refugee families remains partial and selective. Buildings and public spaces originally created with the purpose of becoming urban condensers and vessels of social life are no longer recognized as such, but left in decay by the Greek-Cypriot or Turkish-Cypriot community. However, the historic context of urban environments offers a higher level of complexity beyond simple reduction to dipoles and oppositions.

This intricate framework is generated by layered symbiosis: the centuries-long coexistence and interactions of communities; the impact of conquerors and colonizers; the new with the old. This social, procedural organization is an essential characteristic of the very structure of public space. Being able to extensively study this process with digital tools can potentially provide the means to stitch together the hard borders of contested space in segregated cities.

The synergy of virtual environment technologies with urban studies and architectural history can contribute to the development of transdisciplinary projects that will enable holistic studies of contested urban space, particularly historic cities and their future forms. Distinct from practices that work at the 'bird's-eye view' level of urban dynamics, the methodology presented in this essay focuses on the micro-scale of the moving body on the performative stage of civic space. Citizens inhabit pockets of a city's event stage and, during their everyday repetitive rituals and habits, experience moments of uncertain scenarios and unexpected (creative) accidents (Broeckmann 1998). Distinct from a flattened, instantaneous perception of an entire city in its totality (as happens when viewed from a satellite), it is the short everyday sequences of these settings that construct the experience of inhabiting a city. Building on previous research of performative spaces for presentation and collaboration purposes (Nitsche & Richens 2005; Artopoulos & Condorcet 2006), this chapter examined the role of: (1) data visualization techniques – a factor which involves vision, and therefore brings to the fore issues of representation and aesthetics (a qualitative parameter); (2) levels of interaction, which elaborated programming skills (a quantitative parameter); and (3) the dynamic associations between the kinetic aspects of the human-computer interface and the architectonic qualities of projected space. This third role involves articulated cognitive and kinaesthetic parameters in the cross-media, transdisciplinary study of tangible and invisible areas of division in the historic core of contemporary cities.

The study's field of operation was analysed in this chapter as a quasi-physical environment; a performative stage[5] that is suspended between the city's real-world materiality and the virtuality of digitally simulated terrains of its historical and projective phase. The users of this simulated environment are taking cues from the spatial organization and geometry of physical space, as projected in the digital one. This digitally staged stimulus in turn motivates the spatial behaviour of the visitors, and triggers their response by means of bodily movement; this is both physical (via the Oculus Rift™) and digital, projected in the simulated terrain of the studied city. Mapping the spatial experience of historically layered monuments and spaces can provide a model methodology for transdisciplinary approaches that inform the discourse between digital heritage and more traditional humanities research. For the study of contested urban environments, such efforts offer a neutral virtual canvas upon which researchers can engage urban planners and policy-makers towards a better understanding of the past, a closer analysis of contemporary challenges and informed planning for the future.

Acknowledgments

This chapter draws from research[6] conducted at the Cyprus Institute (Cyprus) in collaboration with the National Center for Supercomputing Applications at the University of Illinois at Urbana-Champaign. The authors also want to acknowledge the close collaboration of the Cyprus Department of Antiquities, particularly its director, Dr Marina Solomidou-Ieronymidou, and archaeological officer Polina Christophi, as well as the support of Agni Petridou and Athina Papadopoulou from the Municipality of Nicosia.

References

Amin, A. (2008), 'Collective culture and urban public space', *City Journal*, 12: 1, pp. 5–24.

Artopoulos, G. (2012), 'Prototype spatial models of interaction', *International Journal of Visual Design*, 6: 3, pp. 39–56.

Artopoulos, G. and Bakirtzis, N. (2014), 'Virtual narratives for complex urban realities: Historic Nicosia as museum', in *Electronic Media and Visual Arts (EVA) Berlin 2014 Book of Proceedings*, Berlin, Germany, 25 November, Berlin: Staatliche Museen zu Berlin, the Fraunhofer IGD and EVA Conferences International, pp. 190–99.

Artopoulos, G., Bakirtzis, N. and Hermon, S. (2014), 'Spatially-organized virtual narratives of contested urban space: Digital methods of mapping the spatial experience of shared heritage', in *Proceedings of the Digital Research in Humanities and the Arts Conference, DRHA2014*, London, UK, 31 August–3 September.

Artopoulos, G. and Condorcet, E. (2006), 'House of affects – Time, immersion and play in digital design for spatially experienced interactive narrative', *Digital Creativity Journal*, 17: 4, pp. 213–20.

Atun, R. and Doratli, N. (2009), 'Walls in cities: A conceptual approach to the walls of Nicosia', *Geopolitics*, 14, pp. 108–34.

Bakirtzis, N. (2010), 'The practice, perception and experience of Byzantine fortification', in Paul Stephenson (ed.), *The Byzantine World*, London and New York: Routledge, pp. 352–70.

Bakshi, A. (2011), 'Memory and place in divided Nicosia', *Spectrum Journal of Global Studies*, 3: 4, pp. 27–40.

—— —— (2012), 'A shell of memory: The Cyprus conflict and Nicosia's walled city', *Memory Studies*, 5: 4, pp. 479–96.

Batty, M. (2013), *The New Science of Cities*, Cambridge, MA: MIT Press.

Bevan, R., (2012), 'Attack on townscapes: The role of heritage in protecting common grounds', D. Chipperfield (ed.), *Common Ground: A Critical Reader: Venice Biennale of Architecture 2012*, Venice: Marsilio, p. 220.

Binnie, J., Holloway, J., Millington, S. and Young, C. (2006), 'Conclusion: The paradoxes of cosmopolitan urbanism', in J. Binnie, J. Holloway, S. Millington, and C. Young (eds), *Cosmopolitan Urbanism*, London: Routledge, pp. 246–53.

Bollens, S. (1999), *Urban Peace-building in Divided Societies: Belfast and Johannesburg*, Boulder, CO: Westview Press.

Broeckmann, A. (1998), *The Art of the Accident*, Netherlands: Distributed Art Pub (DAP).

Browning, G. (2000), *Understanding Contemporary Society: Theories of the Present*, London and Thousand Oaks: Sage.

Burdett, R. and Sudjic, D. (eds) (2011), *Living in the Endless City*, London: Phaidon.

Burdett, R. and Wagstaff, S. (2011), *Global Cities*, London: Tate Modern.

Calame, J. and Charlesworth. E. (2009), *Divided Cities: Belfast, Beirut, Jerusalem, Mostar and Nicosia*, Pennsylvania: University of Pennsylvania Press.

Canefe, N. (2001), 'One Cyprus or many? Turkish Cypriot history in Nicosia', in S. Gunn and B. Morris (eds), *Identities in Space: Contested Terrains in the Western City since 1850*, Aldershot: Ashgate, pp. 60–78.

Cilliers, P. (1998), *Complexity and Postmodernism: Understanding Complex Systems*, London: Routledge.

Cohl, A. (1999), *Mutating Cities*, Nicosia: Architectural Press.

Connerton, P. (1989), *How Societies Remember*, Cambridge: Cambridge University Press.

Demetriades, L. (1998), 'The Nicosia Master Plan', *Journal of Mediterranean Studies*, 8: 2, pp. 169–76.

Demi, D. (1997), *The Walled City of Nicosia: Typology Study*, Nicosia: United Nations Development Programme

Dyson, F. (1998), '"Space," "being," and other fictions in the domain of the virtual', in J. Beckmann (ed.), *The Virtual Dimension*, New York: Princeton Architectural Press, p. 38.

Fainstein, S., Gordon, I. and Harloe, M. (eds) (1992), *Divided Cities: New York and London in the Contemporary World*, Oxford: Blackwell.

Frenay, R. (2006), *Pulse: How Nature Is Inspiring the Technology of the 21st Century*, London: Little, Brown.

Gaffikin, F., Mceldowney, M. and Sterrett, K. (2010), 'Creating shared public space in the contested city: The role of urban design', *Journal of Urban Design*, 15: 4, pp. 493–513.

Gaffikin, F. and Morrissey, M. (2011), *Planning in Divided Cities: Collaborative Shaping of Contested Space*, Oxford: Wiley-Blackwell.

Gibson, J. J. (1979), *The Ecological Approach to Visual Perception*, Boston: Houghton Mifflin.

Gumpert, G. and Drucker, S. (1998), 'The Green Line: Impact and change in Nicosia', *Journal of Mediterranean Studies*, 8: 2, pp. 205–22.

Hall, S. (2012), *City, Street and Citizen*, London: Routledge.

Haseman, B. (2006), 'A manifesto for performative research', *Media International Australia incorporating Culture and Policy*, 118, pp. 98–106.

Laville, F. (2000), 'Foundations of procedural rationality: Cognitive limits and decision processes', *Economics and Philosophy*, 16, pp. 117–38.

Malone, K. (2002), 'Street life: Youth, culture and competing uses of public space', *Environment and Urbanization*, 14, p. 157.

Mandeville, B. (2014), *The Fable of the Bees or Private Vices, Publick Benefits*, vol. 1, http://oll.libertyfund.org/titles/mandeville-the-fable-of-the-bees-or-private-vices-publick-benefits-vol-1. Accessed 10 September 2014.

Michaelides, D. (ed.) (2012), *Historic Nicosia*, Nicosia: Rimal Publications.

Mitleton-Kelly, E. (2006), 'A complexity approach to co-creating an innovative environment', *World Futures: The Journal of General Evolution*, 62: 3, pp. 223–39.

Neill, W. J. V. (2004), *Urban Planning and Cultural Identity*, London: Routledge.

Nitsche, M. and Richens, P. (2005), 'Mindstage: Towards a functional virtual architecture', in B. Martens and A. Brown (eds), *Computer Aided Architectural Design Futures 2005*, Netherlands: Springer, pp. 331–40.

Papadakis, Y. (1998), 'Walking in the *hora*: Place and "non-place" in divided Nicosia', *Journal of Mediterranean Studies*, 8: 2, pp. 302–27.

Papadopoulou, A. (2007), 'Restoration and re-use of Omeriye Ottoman baths, Nicosia, Cyprus', in *First Euro-Mediterranean Regional Conference, Traditional Mediterranean Architecture Present and Future*, Barcelona, Spain, 12–15 July, Barcelona: RehabiMed, pp. 571–73.

—— —— (2008), 'The Nicosia Master Plan, 26 years of bi-communal cooperation', in *Proceedings of the Scientific Symposium of the International Scientific Committee of Historic Towns and Villages of ICOMOS*, Athens, Greece, 9–12 March 2006, International Council on Monuments and Sites (ICOMOS), pp. 184–87.

Perbelini, G. M. (1994), *The Fortress of Nicosia: Prototype of European Renaissance Military Architecture*, Nicosia: Zavallis Litho.

Petridou, A. (2011), 'Nicosia: Perspectives for urban rehabilitation', *Journal of Mediterranean Studies*, 8: 2, pp. 350–64.

Petropoulou, E. (2008), *The Unknown Heritage along the Buffer Zone*, Nicosia: European Heritage Days.

Pullan, W. and Gwiazda, M. (2009), 'Designing the biblical present in Jerusalem's City of David', in U. Staiger and H. Steiner (eds), *Memory Culture and the Contemporary City: Building Sites*, London: Palgrave Macmillan, pp. 106–25.

Sack, R. (1986), *Human Territoriality: Its Theory and History*, Cambridge: Cambridge University Press.

Smith, Anthony D. (1991), *National Identity*, New York: Penguin.

Sorkin, M., (ed.) (1992), *Variations on a Theme Park*, New York: Noonday.

Wu, Jun Jie and Plantinga, Andrew J. (2003), 'The influence of public open space on urban spatial structure', *Journal of Environmental Economics and Management*, 46: 2, pp. 288–309.

Zesimou, S. (1998), 'Seeing beyond the walls: Maps, power and ideology in Nicosia', *Journal of Mediterranean Studies*, 8: 2, pp. 252–83.

Notes

1. 'All boundaries, whether national, global or simply street names on a road map are socially constructed. They are as much the products of society as are other social relations that mark the landscape. For this reason, boundaries matter. They construct our sense of identity in the places we inhabit and they organize our social space through geographies of power' (Malone 2002: 2).
2. 'An important distinction needs to be drawn between cities contested around standard issues of pluralism – disputes about social reproduction around differentials in class, ethnicity, power and status – and those contested around both pluralism and sovereignty – the latter concerning issues of state legitimacy and rival claims of national belonging [...] such cities have not been immune from the main urban narratives over recent decades, e.g the extent to which "fake" anaesthetized public space is replacing the more authentic, if messy, "real" urban spaces' (Gaffikin, Mceldowney & Sterrett 2010: 494).
3. 'The experience of public space remains one of sociability and social recognition and general acceptance of the codes of civic conduct and the benefits of access to collective public resources. It continues to be an experience that supports building awareness of the commons, perhaps one that falls short of fostering active involvement in the life of a city, but still underpins cultures of sociability and civic sensibility' (Amin 2008: 7).
4. See http://vislab.cyi.ac.cy/category/rti/ and http://www.linksceem.eu/ls2/developed-codes-software/medici.html.
5. The virtual environment does not try to be a representational tool for the museum. Rather, its value can be found between the clarity of the digital model and the complex multiplicities of the physical space; between political decisions (top-down control) and the indeterminism of everyday life (bottom-up irregularities).
6. This research was presented at the 43rd Computer Applications and Quantitative Methods in Archaeology "KEEP THE REVOLUTION GOING" Conference (CAA 2015 SIENA) at the University of Siena, Italy (April 2015); the Digital Research in Humanities and the Arts 2014 International Conference at the University of Greenwich, UK (2014); and the Joint Research Centre (JRC) of the European Commission, Brussels (October 2013).

Chapter 9

Responsive transport environments: System thinking as a method to combine media architecture into a digital ecology to improve public transport

M. Hank Haeusler

Background media architecture

We are living an era where media façades and media architecture are no longer a novel feature in our cities, but rather more commonplace. This is exemplified in publications (Haeusler 2009; Haeusler, Tomitsch & Tscherteu 2012), and further evidenced by the Media Architecture Institute's (MAI) project documentation, summits and biennale since 2007 (MAI 2015). Since 2007, research in the field has been presented and discussed in an architectural context at the Media Architecture Biennale and Media Façade Summit (MAI 2015); in addition, research has been presented in a human-computer interaction (HCI) context at the Pervasive Displays (2015) and MediaCity (2015) conferences since 2012. Discourse and research in media architecture is now centred 'at the intersection of physical and digital space and needs a form of understanding that is beyond traditional architecture and media art/design as it brings up entirely genuine challenges and opportunities' (MAI 2015), and encompasses 'interfaces, physical integration, robustness, content, stakeholders, situation, social relations, and emerging use' (Dalsgaard & Halskov 2010: 2277).

Media architecture is a topic of not only increasing focus within architectural and design conferences – including the Media Architecture Biennale and Venice Biennale of 2014 – but has also found growing attention from a range of disciplines at the conferences listed above. Discussion has centred on 'enabling communication and interaction within urban settings', as well as exploring 'social involvement in a specific urban context [through the] use of media and technologies', and, 'interactions between spatial mobility and the formation of communities in urban settings' (European Commission 2012). Furthermore, the Pervasive Displays (2015) conference series has stated its aim to bring together researchers with a 'common interest in the opportunities and challenges raised by the emergence of pervasive display systems as a new communication medium for public and semi-public spaces'. Collectively, these aims reframe the discussion of media architecture as settings for interaction, and give focus to the technological practices people adopt and develop to mediate social experience, potentially influencing changing behaviours in public space (European Commission 2012).

For each of these conferences, arguably the approaches and thinking find origins in the ubiquitous computing paradigm initially proposed by computer scientist Mark Weiser (1991). But what else has propelled such interest in media façades and media architecture projects in HCI and architecture since the early 2000s?

One could argue that an increased interest in the field from both of these perspectives is due to the falling costs of large-screen TVs and LEDs. This has enabled greater research and evaluations not only in lab environments, but also 'in the wild' – as Fatah gen Schiek's research for 'Screens in the wild' (UCL 2015) showcases. Furthermore, one could argue that, due to better accessibility to hardware, research communities in HCI have been able to adapt their research from tabs and pads to boards (Weiser 1991). (This last reason has been discussed in the aforementioned HCI conferences).

The same is true in architecture, where falling costs have propelled the use of LEDs onto building façades. In the case of large format displays, both hardware costs and energy consumption rates continue to fall significantly; between 1999 and 2007, costs fell by 95 per cent, resulting in display costs of only $1000/m^2$. More generally, digital technology is now over 90 per cent more efficient than conventional lighting when used for illumination applications (Collins 2008).

Further still, formal recognition of media architecture in the architectural discipline has been recently evidenced with media façades included as an 'element' of architecture at the 2014 Venice Architecture Biennale, which was curated by Rem Koolhaas (Zaearo-Polo et al. 2014).

With falling costs and the easier integration of large screens or building-size LED façades, one can argue that media façades are here to stay and will become increasingly commonplace. However, there are aspects to media architecture that neither the aforementioned conferences nor recent research have yet discussed. As outlined, both architecture and HCI media architecture is often discussed in the context of design: namely in terms of architectural integration and as a façade element in the former; and media content curating and interaction design in the latter. When situated in the light architecture domain, the discussion is often highly technical (particularly in respect of LED and lighting technology). While significant post-cinematic opportunities for media façades and urban screens remain – particularly through the combination of participatory content with site context – these are often very site-specific design challenges (cf. Dalsgaard & Halskov 2010; Fatah gen. Schiek 2015).

Given this, it is considered timely here to rethink the conceptualization of media architecture from merely a design, technology or content topic for two reasons. Firstly, technology development (i.e. the object) is often out of reach for more design-based disciplines, and more often the purview of science and engineering disciplines. Thus, architects, designers or HCI scientists are not necessarily steering the direction of technological development, but rather apply what is developed in other disciplines.

Secondly, following Cedric Price (cited in Burns 2007), who stated in the 1960s that '[t]echnology is the answer, but what is the question?', a preoccupation with technology can move the discussion away from understanding and addressing the actual problem. There is a greater need to understand the relationship between technologies and how technology operates within a social or physical (or other) context. This idea can be closely linked to the views of Christopher Alexander (cited in Steenson 2014: 93), who stated in an interview with Stephen Grabow in 1983 that '[w]e give names to things but we don't give many names to relationships'. In this way, Alexander also directs the discussion to the relationship or interaction of parts within a system.

This chapter therefore considers how media architecture can be (re)conceptualized through a systems approach, and will explore what role parts and technology play as components of systems. It asks how media architecture can fit into a framework of thinking and theory that shifts the focus from the object towards the design of a system. This sits within the tradition of thinking of scholars like James R. Boyce, who stated in his article 'What is the systems approach?' that:

> [...] as the pace of technological change was felt to quicken, efforts to forecast the next change become more common, and more urgent. What is interesting for the question of technology and architecture is the application of management theories and system thinking to the profession and design process themselves.
>
> (Boyce 1969: 172)

So, what (new) understanding can be gained from analysing media architecture from a system-led perspective?

Observations and defining research

Broadly speaking, when adopting a general system theory perspective, two key observations can be made in regard to the design of media architecture as architecture-led (object-based) or interaction design-led (interaction-based) design. In each case, the tendency is to do exactly what Alexander has previously criticized; that is, focus on the production of an object (façade, screen) or a specific mode of interaction, but neglect consideration of the overall system. Yet, it is argued here that:

1. when networked to ICT infrastructure and augmented by other digital technologies such as sensors and actuators, media architecture can become much more than just a screen: it becomes a system (Haeusler et al. 2012);
2. when equipping building skins with digital technologies, a building can become an autonomous system able to sense and collect data, process this data into information, and then communicate this information to other buildings and people to generate new knowledge. This then influences the performance of buildings and/or the urban context (Haeusler 2010). In many contemporary examples of media architecture, communication occurs mainly from building-to-humans and not yet from building-to-building;
3. in order to communicate information between buildings, each building needs to know what data to collect and how to process this data into information. More

importantly, it needs to know and understand what information is useful to other buildings. To adopt a conversational analogy, this involves 'common interests': in human conversation, a topic of common interest is needed between two people for the conversation to thrive;

4. subsequently, if communication and rules about language and the use of language are relevant to form a civil society, as argued by William Allman (1995), one can argue that rules to manage a system or a 'digital ecology' are essential for buildings to communicate. This is where general system theory comes into play, and more specifically, its subset systems thinking theory.

Systems thinking theory was advanced by Ludwig von Bertalanffy (1969) and later incorporated into architectural theory by notable figures such as Christopher Alexander (1964). In his text Systems generating systems (1968), Alexander asserted that:

A generating system is not a view of a single thing. It is a kit of parts; with rules about the way these parts may be combined and a system as a whole is not an object but a way of looking at an object. It focuses on some holistic properties, which can only be understood as a product of interaction amongst parts.

(Alexander 1968: 91)

One can therefore make the final observation that if media architecture wants to shift away from an object or technology bias towards the design of a system that generates and connects a 'digital ecology', systems thinking theory provides a productive framework for consideration. As a result, the following research hypotheses and context have been proposed to test the application of systems thinking to media architecture:

1. Media façades, large screens and sensors can form unity in a building's skin (ranging in size from large infrastructure to urban furniture) that match a building's computing, sensing and communication capacity to that of a state-of-the-art smartphone.
2. The architectural and urban context in which the research is situated is in one typology only, transport infrastructure, defined as ranging from train stations to interchanges to bus stops.
3. The communication between the transport typologies is limited to transport-related topics, namely wayfinding, timetabling, ticket information and customer information.

Based on the above, the following core research question has been posed: Can system thinking as an approach to conceptualizing media architecture as a digital ecology help to facilitate smart city public transport strategies that support better access to information, thereby providing better access to infrastructure?

Methodology

This chapter sets out to address the core research question posed through the presentation of the results and findings of a three-year ARC (Australian Research Council) Linkage research grant. The research team, Encircle, had a total of eight research partners, spanning architecture, transport planning, HCI, robotics, computer science and design engineering innovation. The 'Bus Stop of the Future' prototype project formed the main research outcome of this investigation.

More broadly, Encircle aimed to investigate the development of a 'digital information layer' to improve the delivery of information in public transport. Drawing on systems thinking (Steenson 2014; Boyce 1969; von Bertalanffy 1969; Alexander 1964), as well as cybernetic approaches (Steenson 2014; Wiener 1948; Pask 1961, 1975), it helped develop a framework for a 'digital information layer' to improve the delivery of information in public transport. It also allowed us to think about and define typology-specific rules with which to describe interactions within the typology so as to establish a digital ecology. Furthermore, action research methods (Burns 2007) and user-centred design (International Organization for Standardization 2010) were adopted by the research team prior to the actual design of the bus stop in order to define the public transport environment and its associated stakeholders (i.e. people, provider, policy, precinct).

Understanding the conditions that influence a system corresponds with treatment approaches that are designed to heal and enhance the performance of the human body. In medicine, syndromes are a collection of signs and symptoms that are observed in, and characteristic of, a single condition. In our research, these conditions (syndromes) were noticed through subjective experiences between stakeholders (symptoms), while objective observation (signs) was conducted through in vitro examinations (studies). In vivo studies[1] were conducted through observations in situ, while ex vivo studies[2] were conducted to test isolated elements. Based on these in vivo and ex vivo studies, the depth and systemic nature of the syndromes could be treated through digital design interventions. The design and development of the 'Bus Stop of the Future' thus became an interchange that functioned as a true hybrid form of digital content and physical space (Tscherteu 2012); an architecture integrated with a media set-up that consists of software, computing and other hardware.

Hypothesis

As outlined in the introduction, a key objective of many media architecture projects to date has been a more site-specific mode of communicating content and generating forms of interactive engagement between the user/observer and the media façade. However, in order to establish a system that combines several media façades and digital technologies to form an 'urban ICT' device necessary for smart and ubiquitous cities, this chapter argues for the application of Alexander's theories relating to systems thinking; and subsequently how the concept of a digital ecology can be applied to achieve responsive public transport systems (Gardner, Haeusler & Tomitsch 2010).

This concerns the concept of 'generating a system'; that is, understanding 'design' not as a single entity or object, but rather as 'a kit of parts'. It also concerns the concept of a 'system as a whole'; in other words, that which is not an object, but rather a way of looking at an object through an organizational logic. According to Alexander (1968), any building can be understood as a generating system with a 'traditional' kit of parts (e.g. columns, beams, panels, windows, doors, etc.). All of these parts are assembled according to certain rules in order to function as a system. While not traditionally considered as part of the architectural kit of parts, it is argued here that urban screens and media façades – as well as sensors, actuators and computing hardware – can be more purposefully integrated within an overall building system (Zaearo-Polo et al. 2014).

Turning now to the concept of 'a system as a whole', Alexander (1968) further describes this as 'holistic phenomena', which can only be understood as a product of interaction among parts. Seen in this way, we can begin to think of interactions between multiple buildings over the scale of a council area, a city, even a region, or perhaps globally. Public transport is a good example of a holistic phenomenon, as it only functions as a whole: the parts can be considered as the physical infrastructure (e.g. train stations or bus stops); while the trains or buses, tracks or routes the vehicle drives along together form the system.

Notably, there has been criticism of Alexander's thinking. Menges and Ahlquist (2011) have previously argued that Alexander's theory only provides a way to characterize a system, but does not extensively describe the process by which a system can be generated. In general support of this criticism, it is argued here that a system with 'interaction amongst parts' requires further means of feedback to control the constrained relationships, to subject the assembly of parts to certain constraints and to ensure interaction of these parts. Significantly, this is where it is envisioned that LED, plasma and LCD screens – as well as sensors, actuators and computing hardware – can play an important role in supporting the 'interaction amongst parts' part of the system by monitoring itself to achieve a holistic phenomenon.

This requires exploring the primary modes of interaction to develop a feedback system to control, enable and maintain the rules. Kirchner et al. (2010) have argued for four primary modes of interaction: (1) human —> system (i.e. the human acts on the system); (2) system —> human (i.e. the system acts on/for the human); (3) human <— system (i.e. the human observes the system); and (4) system —> human (i.e. the system observes the human). Relatedly, Haeusler (2011) has previously argued for a need for a fifth mode of interaction – a system <— —> system mode – whereby the system observes and acts on/ for the other system.

This is useful here because the system needs to understand what kind of system it is in the first place in order to give an indication or rules of what to observe and what to act upon. A system in architecture could be defined through its typology (a taxonomic classification of characteristics specific to a context), a concept not dissimilar to the notion of a 'pattern language' (Alexander 1977).

Thus one could argue for two possible rules for interaction amongst parts (building systems) in a city system: non-typology-specific rules and typology-specific rules. As an example, non-typology-specific rules describe the interaction between an office building and an apartment block, while typology-specific rules describe the interaction within one typology (for example, two bus stops or train stations).

Whereas the first is harder to define, as the rules can be compared with communications between typologies, the second one is clearer. Non-typology-specific rules can be compared with a conversation between a soccer fan (i.e. office building typology) and a fine art lover (i.e. apartment block typology), where both have very clear rules (passion) within their system (hobby); however, one party has to first establish and understand the rules (a common discussion point) amongst both systems in order to achieve a holistic phenomenon (a long-lasting conversation). On the other hand, typology-specific rules are like two gardeners (i.e. bus stops) who both have the same interest (rules of interaction amongst parts), so can talk to each other about flowers and trees (timetable information and bus arrivals). In short, when a common context or 'conversation' topic is established between various buildings of the same typology (or two people), an interaction between them become more possible. Thus through non-typological and topological-specific rules a modus operandi for generating content exists that does not see the content as a site-specific interaction, but as part of a digital ecology where parts (like screens and sensors) are connected: 'rules about the ways these parts may be combined' (Alexander 1968: 91).

The following section of this chapter will further introduce a prototype based on the hypothesis of 'generating a system' (bus stop) out of 'a kit of parts' (sensor, screens, roof, seating elements, etc.). In doing so, it enables a 'system as a whole' to act as a responsive public transport system in which an interaction (content) based on typology-specific rules function as a control on the constrained relationships to one another. This aims to describe the process by which a system (the responsive transport environment) can be generated.

The Bus Stop of the Future – prototyping

Most cities around the globe are experiencing rapid population growth. As Gardner et. al (2010) argued in Infostructure – A Transport Research Project, pressure on public transport systems can be either addressed by improving the proximate access to transport services (physical and contextual), access to service frequency (operational and demand led) or access to information (commuter interface). Access to information in a highly complex metropolitan transport environment needs to be holistic (i.e. all data from all parts of the transport system) rather than just localized data (i.e. information from one train station or bus stop). In this context, the 'Bus Stop of the Future' investigated the development of a 'digital information layer' to improve the delivery of information at and around bus stops by collecting and accessing data from the whole transport network. As such, it needed:

1. to tap into ICT technology (such as mobile phones) with transport data and sensor data from transport assets, such as the GPS on buses – 'a kit of parts';
2. to augment and equip existing bus stops with ICT ('a kit of parts') and combine with the first stage to make them an urban ICT asset – 'generating a system'; and
3. to develop software or apps for an urban interaction – typology-specific rules – that describe the interactions within the typology.

The first point describes personal devices or transport assets owned by individuals and/ or developed by companies and organizations. These are generally out of the reach and control of research teams, architects and designers, but those that are in existence can be accessed. Thus, in contrast to the first point, the second point is within the reach of architects and designers, as both their designs are within the architectural domain. Consequently, the research team concentrated on the development of these when

Figure 1. Bus stop side view with LED panel. © Xavier Ho

designing and developing the 'Bus Stop of the Future'. The third point outlines the content and defines the logic of how different assets can communicate with each other. This was discussed in the hypothesis and tested through developing content.

Figure 2. Interacting with location information. © Xavier Ho

As the scope of this chapter does not allow an extensive outline of the development process, this chapter refers here to the book INTERchanging – Future Designs for Responsive Transport Environments (Gardner 2014), which documents the design concepts developed at the University of New South Wales in January 2014 by the BEIL programme. These were developed for third and fourth-year BA students from the schools of architecture, computational design, interior architecture, landscape architecture, industrial design and construction management. Alongside this, Masters of Design Computing students at the University of Sydney developed a series of apps to be displayed on the full-scale prototype. Ideas and concepts for these apps were based on shifts in the day-to-day engagement with digital technology, and how apps could better influence how we commute and travel. As interaction designers, these students had the expertise to develop apps not dissimilar to mobile phone apps for the bus stop. Their main challenge was to translate interaction design concepts that work on a personal device with a small-scale screen to a public device used by many users concurrently on a larger screen.

Figure 3. Active surveillance content of 60-inch screen. © Xavier Ho

With the design finalized, the team then commenced production using the facilities available at each of the universities. Based on the optimization phase, the team fabricated the bus stop out of 18mm plywood panels using a 3-axis CNC mill. In parallel to the design optimization phase, the design team had to select and specify the computing hardware used in the bus stop. For this, all the elements apart from the LEDs could be purchased at a standard electronics shop. This was an important point for the team, as we aimed to demonstrate to the research partners that urban ICT does not require expensive state-of-the-art technology, but can be achieved with everyday consumer electronics.

As described in the introduction to this chapter, apps and content development are crucial to realize of a 'responsive' and/or 'interactive' bus stop in a responsive public transport environment. The interaction design students at the University of Sydney, under the supervision of Dr Martin Tomitsch, developed three different content proposals for the bus stop's four different screens.[3] These were: real-time bus timetable and seat availability information (displayed on the large LED screen); an active surveillance system (displayed

Figure 4. Exhibition launch bus stop. © Marie Caccamo

on the 60" screen facing inward); and local business information (displayed on the 42" screen facing inwards) (see images).

The design of the hardware and software had a key research constraint worth mentioning here. As there was only one bus stop prototype – and as this mock-up was situated in a museum – it was not possible to test or evaluate how a transport system in which interaction (content) based on typology-specific rules could function as a control of the constrained relationships to one another, nor the process by which a system (the responsive transport environment) can be generated. Consequently, the potential contribution of this project is discussed in the following section on a theoretical level, rather than an applied and tested one.

Discussion and contribution

It has been argued thus far that the prime concern is not necessarily the hardware for enabling typology-specific rules for interactions within a typology, but rather the context (in this case, public transport). The context defines the content displayed on the hardware (and the participation of users via the hardware) to allow a communication and automation control between bus stops, and bus stop and passengers so as to define a regulatory system, its structure, constraints and possibilities. In short, it is argued that context/content create a digital ecology that unlocks urban infrastructure problems via a concentration on 'infostructure' (content) rather than infrastructure (building new buildings).

Further substantiation of this argument is provided here with the example of the real-time bus timetable and seat availability information app. In this example, there are two hardware stakeholders: the bus stop (equipped with the screen and sensors like a webcam and Wi-Fi connection) and the bus (equipped with a GPS sensor, a webcam and/or a smart ticket reader and a Wi-Fi connection). The webcam in the bus would analyse (via an algorithm) if a seat were occupied or not, thereby defining the number of available seats. This could also be achieved and/or support the first data set input (webcam) via the tap in/tap out of a smartcard to pay for the trip, which would define the number of people on the bus. Together with the location information, this could be sent to the bus stop and both sets of information (arrival time and seat availability) would be displayed. The bus stop itself could 'see' how many people are present, and predict and eventually 'learn' how many people are likely to use the next bus, before sending this information to the next bus stop and further down the line. Eventually (again based on a yet-to-be-developed algorithm) bus stops and buses could collect data and gain information about travel patterns that could lead to improved knowledge and understanding of travel usage on certain routes, thereby evolving the system from a fixed timetable (bus comes Monday to Friday every 10 minutes) to a dynamic system (bus route knows when most people travel and constantly alters the dynamic timetable). In this way, it is the content that enables a dynamic system, while the hardware plays only a supporting role.

In conclusion – and to define the contribution – it is argued that the research has 'generated a system' (bus stop) out of 'a kit of parts' (sensor, screens, roof, seating elements, etc.) to enable a 'system as a whole'. This acts as a responsive public transport system in which an interaction (content) based on typology-specific rules function as a control of the constrained relationships to one another.

Conclusion

The chapter has argued that this method of 'system' thinking has the potential to unlock transport problems because it concentrates on the 'infostructure', rather than its infrastructure. Yet, how does this relate back to media architecture, as discussed at the beginning of the chapter?

The 'Bus Stop of the Future' project has demonstrated that a screen can be more than just an advertisement when augmented by additional digital technologies. Furthermore, through equipping the bus stop with ICT, a bus stop can become similar to an autonomous system (e.g. a robot) as it adopts similar principles (Haeusler & Beilharz 2011). The key difference between a bus stop and a building façade is a matter of scale and technology. Yet, the technology is once again not the problem here. As argued in *INTERchanging – Future Designs for Responsive Transport Environments* (Gardner et al. 2014), urban screens and media façades have demonstrated limitations related to content and their poor integration into the built and urban environment. This is typically because they are designed to follow the causality of *technology* (the existence of LED screens) → *space* (applying LED screens in the built environment) → *content* (designing visual imagery). By contrast, the research discussed in this paper reverses this path to begin with *context* (the overarching typological topic, here public transport) → *content* (designing experiences that reflect the needs and interests of citizens) → *space* (reflecting locational, cultural and political parameters) → *technology* (using appropriate technologies to achieve the first two goals). When placing context/content at the forefront of the discussion – and acknowledging that, for example, a media façade needs approximately 8,000 hours of content a year to display an engaging programme (as at Federation Square, Melbourne) – one can see enormous challenges in achieving this for each single media façade in a city, country or globally. This is particularly true given that content is often generated and designed by something *other* than itself, via a team of designers.

Consequently (and in conclusion), the alternate approach suggested here is an allopoietic design of content that takes an autopoietic content[4] approach[5]:

An autopoiesis machine is a machine organized (defined as a unity) as a network of processes of production (transformation and destruction) of components which: (i) through their interactions and transformations continuously regenerate and realize the network of processes (relations) that produced them; and (ii) constitute it (the machine) as a concrete unity in space in which they (the components) exist by specifying the topological domain of its realization as such a network.

(Maturana & Varela 1980: 78)

With a system in place as described in the hypothesis, and with a bus stop prototype functioning as an autopoietic machine – which through an autopoietic content approach can sense data relevant to public transport, process this data into information (through typology-specific rules acting as control of the constrained relationships to one another) and communicate relevant data to other bus stops – the system as a whole becomes responsive and intelligent. Critically, this approach has the potential to be applied to a wider range of contexts than transport alone, thus extending media architecture to other realms of performativity. This goes some way to addressing Alexander's (1964: 130; 1968: 90) vision of subtler kinds of buildings, and of producing buildings guaranteed to function as holistic systems in the social and human sense.

References

Alexander, C. (1964), *Notes on the Synthesis of Form*, Cambridge, MA: Harvard University Press.

———— (1968), 'Systems generating systems', *Architectural Design*, 7/6, pp. 90–91.

Alexander, C., Ishikawa, S. and Silverstein, M. (1977), *A Pattern Language: Towns, Buildings, Construction*, Oxford: Oxford University Press.

Allman, W. (1995), *Stone Age Present: How Evolution has shaped modern life – From Sex, Violence and Language to Emotions, Morals and Communities*, New York: Touchstone Press.

von Bertalanffy, L. (1969), *General Systems Theory: Foundations, Development, Applications*, New York: George Braziller.

Boyce, J. R. (1969), 'What is the systems approach?', in W. W. Braham and J. A. Hale (eds) (2007), *Rethinking Technology: A Reader in Architectural Theory*, Oxford: Routledge.

Burns, D. (2007), *Systemic Action Research: A Strategy for Whole Systems Change*, Bristol: Policy Press.

Canadian Centre for Architecture (n.d.), 'Cedric Price: Fun Palace', http://www.cca.qc.ca/en/collection/283-cedric-price-fun-palace. Accessed 12 January 2015.

Collins, A. (ed.) (2008), *Atlas of Global Development*, Washington, DC: The World Bank.

Dalsgaard, P. and Halskov, K. (2010), 'Designing urban media façades – Cases and challenges', in *Proceedings of the SIGCHI Conference on Human Factors in Computing Systems*, Atlanta, USA, 10–15 April, New York: ACM, pp. 2277–286.

European Commission (2012), 'MediaCity report summary: Final activity report summary of the EU funded project', http://cordis.europa.eu/result/rcn/52120_en.html. Accessed 13 January 2015.

Fatah gen. Schiek, A. (2007), 'Towards an integrated architectural media space', http://firstmonday.org/ojs/index.php/fm/article/view/1550/1465. Accessed 27 March 2007.

Gardner, N., Haeusler, M. and Mahar, B. (2014), *INTERchanging – Future Designs for Responsive Transport Environments*, Baunach: Spurbuch.

Gardner, N., Haeusler, M. and Tomitsch, M. (2010), *Infostructure – A Transport Research Project*, Sydney: Freerange Press.

Haeusler, M. (2009), *Media Facades – History, Technology, Content*, Ludwigsburg: avedition.

Haeusler, M. and Beilharz, K. (2011), '[Architecture = Computer] – from computational to computing environments', in *Proceedings of the 14th International Conference on Computer Aided Architectural Design Futures*, Liege, Belgium, 4–8 July, pp. 217–32.

Haeusler, M., Tomitsch, M. and Tscherteu, G. (2012), *New Media Facades – A Global Survey*, Ludwigsburg: avedition.

International Organization for Standardization (2010), 'Ergonomics of human-system interaction – Part 210: Human-centred design for interactive systems', http://www.iso.org/iso/catalogue_detail. htm?csnumber=52075. Accessed 13 January 2015.

Kirchner, N. et al. (2010), 'Robotassist – A platform for human robot interaction research', in *Proceedings of the Australasian Conference on Robotics and Automation 2010 (ACRA 2010)*, Brisbane, Australia, 1–3 December, pp. 1–10.

Langheinrich, M., Memarovic, N., Elhart, I. and Alt, F. (2011), 'Autopoiesic content: A conceptual model for enabling situated self-generative content for public displays', in *Proceedings of the 10th International Conference on Mobile and Ubiquitous Multimedia, MUM 2011*, Beijing, China, 7–9 December, http://www.uc.inf.usi.ch/sites/all/files/PURBA-7_cr.pdf. Accessed 15 August 2015.

Maturana, H. and Varela, F. (1980), *Autopoiesis and Cognition: The Realization of the Living*, Boston: D. Reidel.

Media Architecture Institute (2014), 'Home page', www.mediaarchitecture.org. Accessed 5 December 2014.

MediaCity (2014), 'About', http://mediacities.net/site/about/. Accessed 5 December 2014.

Memarovic, N., Elhart, I. and Langheinrich, M. (2011), 'FunSquare: First Experiences with Autopoiesic Content, *Proceedings of the 10th International Conference on Mobile and Ubiquitous Multimedia, MUM 2011*, Beijing, China, 7–9 December, http://www.uc.inf.usi.ch/sites/all/files/PURBA-7_cr.pdf., pp. 175–84, Accessed 15 August, 2015.

Menges, A. and Ahlquist, S. (2011), *Computational Design Thinking*, Chichester: John Wiley & Sons.

Pask, G. (1961), *An Approach to Cybernetics*, London: Hutchinson.

—— —— (1975), *The Cybernetics of Human Learning and Performance*, London: Hutchinson.

Pervasive Displays (2012), 'Home page of the 2012 conference', http://www.pervasivedisplays.org/2012/. Accessed 5 December 2014.

—— —— (2015), 'Home page of the 2015 conference', http://www.pervasivedisplays. org/2015/. Accessed 5 December 2014.

Steenson, M. W. (2014). '*Architectures of information: Christopher Alexander, Cedric Price, and Nicholas Negroponte and MIT's Architecture Machine Group*'. PhD dissertation, Princeton, NJ: Princeton University, http://bit.ly/steenson-archofinfo-dissertation. Accessed 8 January 2015.

Tscherteu, G. (2012), 'Media architecture scenes', in G. Tscherteu, M. C. Lervig and M. Brynskov (eds), *Media Architecture Biennale Catalogue 2012*, http://www. mediaarchitecture.org/media-architecture-compendium. Accessed 7 May 2014.

University College London (UCL) (2015), 'Screens in the wild', https://www.bartlett.ucl. ac.uk/space-syntax/screens-in-the-wild. Accessed 8 January 2015.

Weiser, M. (1991), 'The computer for the twenty-first century', *Scientific American*, 265: 3, pp. 94–104.

Wiener, N. (1948), *Cybernetics of Control and Communication in the Animal and the Machine*, Cambridge, MA: MIT Press.

Zaearo-Polo, A., Trüby, S., Koolhaas, R., AMO, Harvard GSD and Boom, I. (2014), *Façade – Elements of Architecture – 14th International Architecture Exhibition, la Biennale di Venezia*, Venice: Marsilio.

Notes

1. Latin for 'within the living'; thus within the public transport environment.
2. Latin for 'out of the living'; thus outside the public transport environment.
3. The fourth 42" screen, which faced outwards from the bus stop, showed information about the project, and credited the project participants. As such, it did not need any developed content.
4. From the Greek *allo-* (meaning 'other'), *auto-* (meaning 'self') and *poiesis* (meaning 'creation' or 'production'). This refers to a system capable of reproducing and maintaining itself.
5. The concept of autopoeisis and autopoiesic content is the subject of two papers by Langheinrich et al. (2011) and Memarovic, Elhart and Langheinrich (2011). However, due to the scope of this chapter and its focus on systems theory and the prototype development of the bus stop, the contributions to the field by the two above-mentioned authors cannot be discussed at this point in greater detail.

Section Three

Studies and trials – Examples of community uses of digital
technologies

Chapter 10

Digital urban health and security: NYC's got an app for that

Kristen Scott

Introduction

Within New York City's Road Map for the Digital City: Achieving New York City's Digital Future, city officials outline their strategy to make NYC the world's 'leading Digital City', and 'create a healthier civil society and stronger democracy through the use of technology' (City of New York 2011a: 5). Exactly what is meant by the use of such terms as 'healthy' or 'healthier' is not altogether clear, but the narrative of urban health provides a strong rhetorical thread for the city's larger digital technological goals. NYC's use of the metaphor of a healthy civic society, however, becomes an ideological narrative that obscures the city's use of many of its digital technologies as subtle examples of contemporary neo-liberal mechanisms of power, in which the government crowdsources responsibility for the city's overall civic health to its population. This chapter examines NYC's use of smartphone applications and short message service (SMS) text services specifically, and argues that such digital initiatives, while functioning to construct healthy and productive social bodies, contradict the city's concomitant claim of building a stronger democracy. By motivating residents to self-regulate, construct and maintain themselves as neo-liberal citizen subjects, such digital applications raise further concerns about the city's role in the administration and regulation of people's activities; the existence of certain regimes of knowledge and intelligibility about residents' everyday practices; the training of the body through subtle mechanisms of biopower; and the interpellation of residents into an increasingly pervasive digital panopticon.

The city's use of digital technologies to meet many of its larger civic goals also raises concerns about what may be one of the latest manifestations of neo-liberal practice: the use of social networks and mobile communication technologies to facilitate new forms of power. New York City officials have been particularly zealous in their use of social media to govern. Open-source governance – sometimes also referred to as Gov 2.0 – is a phenomenon in which governments increasingly use various forms of digital media in an attempt to provide government services to residents more cost-effectively. This can be in order to improve city services, support citizen empowerment through more direct communicative channels with government officials, or interact more efficiently and quickly with its residents in the case of larger public emergencies. Open-source governance relies primarily on social media and mobile communication technologies, because citizens can be more easily reached in the virtual spaces they most often frequent. But while social media and mobile technologies have provided platforms for citizens to voice their concerns, help support the formation of political networks and enabled greater overall public communicative potential, these technologies – and the information produced – have also been increasingly mediated, monitored and regulated by governments.

The 'social', furthermore 'hovers as a paradox, between a space of state coercion governed by law and a space of market spontaneity governed by individual incentives and price' (Davies 2013: para. 4); thus, when being 'social', we are both bound by rules and free at the same time (2013: para. 4). While neo-liberalism might have been initiated as an attack on socialism, and indicative of 'a movement that was partly defined in opposition to the very idea of the "social"' (2013: para. 2), the increased use of social media may also signify that 'neoliberal government no longer places quite so much emphasis on the market, as a mechanism for organizing knowledge, regulating freedom and achieving transparency' (2013: para. 2). We can see this paradox playing out in New York City, as government and neo-liberal interests use social media to continually vie for resident/consumer attention. This 'new mutation' of neo-liberalism furthermore incorporates social media in such a way as to resist critique (2013). As such, a closer examination of the use of such technologies in governance becomes all the more crucial.

Mobile mediations: Urban health and smartphone social management

In a self-assessment of New York City's digital reach, city officials calculated that its government reached over 25 million people a year through its website NYC.gov, NYC 311 and more than 200 social media channels (New York City 2011a: 7). The following year, NYC reported that its initiatives substantially increased its digital engagement to reach more than five million individuals a month through more than 280 social media channels, including Facebook, LinkedIn, YouTube, Twitter, Tumblr, SMS subscriptions and Foursquare, as well as through city-sponsored smartphone applications and the NYC. gov website (City of New York 2012a: 20). Assuming most New Yorkers are accessing their information 'on the go', city officials make use of social media to engage the public on 'their terms and [within] their most comfortable, native digital environment' (2012a: 43). Recognizing the 'ubiquity of mobile technology', NYC officials aim to provide more access to government through popular social media, smartphone apps and mobile-friendly websites so as to increase engagement with its population.

As part of the city's strategy to provide residents with increased access to city services, solicit feedback and reportage, and gather data from mobile users that, when aggregated, will help inform policy decisions, NYC hosts a variety of smartphone apps. Some of these city-sponsored apps are created during the city's yearly BigApps contest, a weekend-long competition designed to challenge software developers to create innovative apps using raw city data made available on the city's public open data platform. The goals of the competition are to design apps that will both 'improve access to information and government transparency, making it easier and more fun to visit, live and work' in NYC and 'to encourage innovation and the creation of new intellectual property with commercial potential' (Challenge Post 2011: para. 1). Other smartphone apps are developed and sponsored by city departments, such as the NYC Department of Mental Health and Hygiene and the city's Department of Information Technology and Telecommunications.

Framed as a necessary service in the interests of the overall 'health' of the city, and building upon former Mayor Bloomberg's broader health initiatives and policies (Moore

DO put the condom on an erect (hard) penis before there is any contact with a partner's genitals.

DO use plenty of lubricant with latex condoms as lubricant reduces friction and minimizes the risk of the condom breaking.

DO change to a new condom if you have prolonged vigorous and/or anal sex to avoid tearing or breakage.

DON'Ts:

DON'T store condoms in a glove compartment, trunk, wallet or back pocket where the temperature and humidity can damage them. And don't use them after the expiration date, as old condoms can be dry, brittle or weakened and can break more easily.

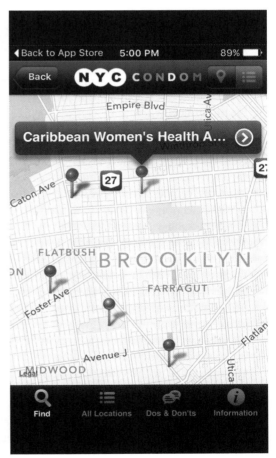

Figure 1. iPhone screenshot – condom advice.

Figure 2. iPhone screenshot – site locator.

2012), NYC's smartphone apps encourage residents to have safe sex, eat healthy, recycle, work, reduce calorie intake, volunteer and exercise (City of New York n.d.). In 2010, for example, in an effort to reduce drunk driving incidents and 'make New York City's streets even safer' (City of New York 2010), the NYC Department of Transportation released the You The Man app, which helps residents score their intoxication level and identify nearby alternative transportation options. The NYC Department of Environmental Protection (2012) advertises the WaterOnTheGo.NYC app as a healthy alternative to sugar-sweetened beverages. CalCutter NYC assists residents in counting their calories, while the ABC Eats app enables diners to check a restaurant's safety record. In the city's first year hosting these smartphone apps on its official city website, NYC reported over 77,000 smartphone application downloads (City of New York 2012a). One of NYC's most popular apps has been the NYC Condom Finder, which was launched on Valentine's Day in 2011. If one is in need of a condom while out in the city, this app can pinpoint the user's location and provide a map of the five closest condom distributors. The app also provides a list of 'dos' and 'don'ts' for proper condom use (Figure 1). In 2013, NYC also released The Teens in NYC Protection+ smartphone app, which helps teenagers to locate sexual health clinics, where they can obtain free condoms, STD and HIV testing, pregnancy testing, emergency contraception and birth control (Figure 2).

Former New York City Health Commissioner Thomas Farley suggested that because New Yorkers are mobile, the city needed to reach residents with sexual health information through these kinds of mobile applications (New York City Department of Health and Mental Hygiene 2012). Through the use of the NYC Condom Finder and The Teens in NYC Protection+ apps, NYC is said to be on the 'cutting-edge of using new technology to promote safer sex', bringing the city 'closer to making safer sex the norm' (2012). New York City officials, however, have been criticized for giving away free condoms on the one hand, while simultaneously using them to target people for prostitution and arrest. As Jim Dwyer (2014: para. 5) points out, 'One arm of the government is giving people condoms', while the other confiscates them 'from the very people who are most vulnerable'.

These kinds of smartphone apps are examples of the more subtle digital mechanisms of biopower that function chiefly to encourage residents to self-regulate and self-manage their behaviours in such a way as to be beneficial to the overall population and social body. Additionally, both disciplinary and security apparatuses of power (Foucault 2004) are embedded within smartphone applications such as these, and further heightened by the contradictory act of giving away free condoms while treating any possession of an excessive number of condoms punitively as justification for determining who can be arrested on prostitution charges (Dwyer 2012). Both applications also engage modes of discipline and population control by socially prescribing an obligatory act (safe sex) in an effort to prevent the spread of communicable diseases and lower rates of unwanted pregnancies. Yet they also engage modes of security, as they involve an effort by the NYC government to contain and order the reality of social experiences while still allowing the natural course of events (sexual activity) to take place. In instances such as these, the law prohibits what the state does not want, and discipline prescribes what it deems desirable. As Foucault (2004) argues:

> [...] the essential function of security, without prohibiting or prescribing, but possibly making use of some instruments of prescription and prohibition, is to respond to a reality [in this case, people having sex] in such a way that this response cancels out the reality to which it responds – nullifies it, or limits, checks, or regulates it.
>
> (Foucault 2004: 69)

When conjoined with New York's HIV Reporting and Partner Notification (HIVRPN) Law, which requires anyone diagnosed with HIV and AIDS to report all sexual and needle-sharing partners to their medical provider (New York State Department of Health 2013), these mechanisms work in tandem to further regulate and deploy regimes of power over the body and population. And, as Foucault reminds us, it is this power over life (or biopower) that appears in both disciplinary and regulatory forms to help control and determine the usefulness of the body to society.

Furthermore, the responsibility for the well-being of the urban population is shifted from the government to the residents through a more diffuse power structure, as well as strategies of governmental control that are increasingly exercised through the digital technological apparatuses of residents' everyday life. The idea of freedom – or freedom of circulation – is a crucial component in this particular mode of power. According to the assistant health commissioner, Monica Sweeney, 'We want New York City to be the safest city in the world to have sex [since] [a] lot of people come here for that' (cited in Huffington Post 2011: para. 3; author italics). As opposed to earlier forms of sovereign rule, where absolute rule over individual subjects entailed saying 'no' to various actions, modern society is posed with the problem of how to say 'yes' to the desires of individuals, but in such a way as to still function towards the management of populations and productive bodies (Foucault 2004). As Foucault (2004: 87–104) argued, the 'conduct of conduct' has become one of the central problems of modern governance, in part because it involves this paradox. On the one hand, liberalism evokes and asserts the freedom and rights of the individual (to have sex and choose whether to use a condom); yet the government attempts to regulate that individual behaviour through smartphone apps such as these, or at least to encourage its population to self-regulate.

As can be discerned from NYC's use of mobile applications that underscore health, the social is 'brought back as a way of providing support, such that individuals can continue to live the self-reliant, risk-aware, healthy lifestyles that neo-liberalism requires of them', and this phenomenon of 'social prescribing' becomes indicative of new neo-liberal techniques of state power (Davies 2013: para. 9). New 'techno-utopian policy visions' and 'digital tracking' of health behaviours, such as we see in New York City, help to create a new kind of neo-liberal government management (2013: para. 12). But these kinds of techniques, Davies (2013: para. 13) adds, are also indicative of a supplement to neo-liberal logic, rather than its replacement; the 'new form of sociality' that emerges, as in the case of NYC with its reliance on social media, does not necessarily represent a buffer between the economic individual and the coercive state, but is indicative instead of how the two are 'firmly cemented together'.

Andrew Barry (2001) has proposed that interactivity, such as we see in peoples' use of social media and smartphone apps, can be a means to counter disciplinary power, and allow for new forms of agency and subjectivity that disrupt the knowledge/power nexus. And we can certainly discern recent examples in support of this perspective, such as the use of smartphone videos of police brutality that raise public awareness and provide evidence needed for investigations and prosecutorial actions. Indeed, the increased number of interactive smartphone and Internet users seem to logically lead to a decrease in Foucauldian disciplinary power. And yet, as Jarrett (2008) argues, while interactivity may provide a solution to the disciplinary state, it also becomes a disciplinary tactic of the neo-liberal state in the twenty-first century. The interactive user in today's society is being shaped and reinforced into an active entrepreneurial citizen of neo-liberalism. As the Internet becomes increasingly characterized by private ownership and control, Mark Andrejevic's (2007a: 297) 'model of digital enclosure' is particularly useful in helping to illuminate how, despite the appearance of greater convenience and access provided by networked interactive environments (such as mobile smartphone apps), we voluntarily enter a space in which our information is recentralized, consolidated, commodified and controlled. Andrejevic (2007a: 297) suggests that the ubiquitous Internet interactivity in which we engage also has the potential to accelerate the commodification of, and centralized control over, public information. Interactive users thus help to further construct the disciplinary force of the neo-liberal state.

Digital technological affects of security and safety

Because media messages – in this case those delivered by the City of New York – are no longer confined to one particular medium, but rather distributed across varying mediums (smartphones and social networks, for instance), these messages combine to construct and maintain affective, mediated relationships between us and technology, becoming mutually constitutive in the process. Given how we interact every day with our devices, we tend to embody a perpetual cyclical and affective relationship that then perpetuates the same feedback loops (Grusin 2010). According to Grusin (2010: 90), contemporary technologies train us to become affective cyborgs, and it is this sort of digital hybridity that is 'one of the defining conditions of contemporary mediality'. Grusin's concept of mediality – which in many ways parallels Foucault's model of governmentality – helps to explain how these digital technological applications employ heterogeneous social and political networks that function as governing apparatuses of citizens through collective affect.

Although the city does not explicitly outline goals of security – not once, in fact, is the word 'security' used in the city's report – many of the city's digital technological programmes nevertheless employ assurances of security, primarily through the rhetoric of safety. Considering the terrorist attacks on the World Trade Center in 2001, it seems at first surprising that *New York City's Digital Roadmap* (City of New York 2012a) is completely devoid of any references to security. But then given the collective trauma and grief of New York City residents, international criticism of the United States' invasion of Iraq and Afghanistan, and widespread concerns over the creation of Homeland Security, the USA Patriot Act and the Terrorist Information Awareness program (Ramage 2007), perhaps becoming digitally social is precisely the international public image boost that New York City needed.

While the city may not explicitly articulate security concerns in its published digital technological initiatives, it is present in various digital programmes and applications. One such example is SMS notification services, which are further underscored discursively through references to public well-being and the overall health of the city. This security affect is analogous to what Grusin (2010) calls systems of 'premediation'. He argues that new modes of technology and the rhetoric about them, particularly since 9/11, represent a contextualized regime of security; a national imperative that attempts to subdue public fear of the unknown (2010: 46). Grusin employs the term 'premediation' to describe a recent shift in a larger cultural logic, a logic that appears to be deployed in some of NYC's technological initiatives – from a remediation of the past to a premediation of the future. Through media reports and narratives that describe potential future disasters and catastrophic events, these premediations work to instil and promote collective insecurity and heighten public fear of what *may* happen, while simultaneously offering an affect of security through the sense of a connection to a larger network (2010). In the case of NYC, this affect of security occurs through the use of social networks and mobile applications, since they connect residents to crucial city services and information. Grusin's (2010: 46) theory of premediation helps to explain how some of these digital technological programmes and smartphone applications function to allay public fear, thereby maintaining 'a low level of anxiety as a kind of affective prophylactic'. Frequent social media updates and emergency notifications that reach people on their mobile phones offer compensatory affects of safety and security. By sending out emergency notifications to people's smartphones, NYC provides the public with a sense of compensatory reassurance that feeds the collective need for protection (Grusin 2009).

New York City initially employed two types of SMS notification systems: Notify NYC and NYC 311, both hosted by the NYC Office of Emergency Management. However, in the event of large-scale, public emergencies, text messages sent out are subject to wireless congestion delays or failures. Recognizing these limitations, the city, in a public-private partnership with the Federal Emergency Management Agency (FEMA), the Federal Communications Commission (FCC), the Cellular Telecommunications Industry Association (CTIA) and major commercial wireless carriers, was the first in the United

States to adopt a geo-targeted mobile emergency notification system called the Personal Localized Alerting Network (PLAN) (Homeland Security Newswire 2011). Standing in front of the World Trade Center site in May 2011, former Mayor Bloomberg publicly announced the city's adoption of PLAN, reiterating the need for this emergency alert system and suggesting that 'given the kinds of threats made against New York City at the World Trade Center, Times Square and other places popular with visitors and tourists, we'll be *even safer* when authorities can broadcast warnings to everyone in a geographic area' (City of New York 2011b: para. 2; author's italics). The NYC alert network – which is part of the national Wireless Emergency Alerts (WEA) system established pursuant to the Warning Alert and Response Network (WARN) Act signed into law in 2006 – is an updated version of the Emergency Alert System (EAS) instituted in the 1950s, when radio and television broadcast alerts were the best ways to warn the public of emergency situations. Nowadays, all mobile users with WEA-capable devices are automatically notified in the case of a public emergency. As of April 2012, three different kinds of alerts can be sent to WEA-capable mobile devices (Civic Impulse 2015) by authorized federal, state and local agencies: presidential, imminent threats and AMBER alerts. Only federally approved state and local officials, FEMA and the president of the United States can issue imminent threat alerts.

In the event of a public emergency and the city's issuance of a PLAN alert, cell towers broadcast the emergency notification to all mobile devices in the threat area. Someone from California visiting NYC, for instance, would receive an alert on their mobile device should that person be in the threat area at the time of the emergency, while a New Yorker visiting Florida at the time would not receive an alert. While they may look similar to text messages, these notifications are not texts, but rather use a different technological interface to push notifications to any mobile phone in the impacted area. New York City first used this emergency notification system in October 2012, when Hurricane Sandy began to flood the streets of Manhattan (Howard 2012).

In fact, Grusin (2012) points to NYC's response to Hurricane Sandy as an example of premediation. Grusin (2012: para. 6) argues that Hurricane Sandy was not in and of itself the 'sole agent or origin or cause of catastrophic disaster', but rather the 'disaster' preceded Sandy's arrival. Prior to the hurricane's landfall, schools were cancelled, offices shut down, roads were closed, people were evacuated and emergency alerts were sent out. Grusin (2012: para. 6) argues that while the hurricane itself had real impact and was certainly an event worth reporting, its premediation – through various social media channels – had similarly powerful effects, producing fear before anything even happened, 'in anticipation of [its] happening'. We saw this occur again with the 2015 winter storm Juno, as NYC broadcast warnings over multiple social and mobile channels about the impending blizzard. But the city's premediation of events such as these also help to structure the event, not just represent it. The intent and significance of premediation is to capitalize on the emotion of fear, emphasize the rhetoric of inevitability, and make the public believe they need such protections and early warnings, which then result in the justification of far more surveillance and less resistant citizens (Grusin 2010). The logic of surveillance thus becomes inscribed into the politics of open-source governance through principles of security and safety.

It is argued here, however, that such digital technological applications and services, while certainly working to create a pervasive security, are less focused on surveillance and more on the construction of the ideal autonomous, self-regulating and self-reliant neo-liberal subject. Not only do such emergency preparedness strategies rely on a certain level of crowdsourcing – given that the effectiveness of emergency messages often occur through the multiplication of warnings via numerous social media channels – they also encourage residents to fend for themselves by stocking up on supplies and then taking cover until the emergency event is over. The ideal citizen that is being interpellated here, while perhaps to some degree disciplined through these kinds of digital technological apparatuses, is not a docile one, but rather one who is rational and self-reliant; someone who does not depend upon the government to come to his/her rescue, thereby providing an example of how neo-liberal governmentality functions.

The New York City government further interpellates residents into this ambiguously articulated regime of security by soliciting residents to provide feedback through its various media channels and tools, from smartphone apps and SMS to a variety of other social media platforms. NYC, for instance, urges residents to upload text-messaged inquiries, questions and service reports to its NYC 311 smartphone app; and both 311 and 911 are able to receive pictures and video as text messages from mobile phones and computers (City of New York 2008). In the first year of the launch of the NYC 311 smartphone app, over 3,000 reports were submitted (Beck 2013). Former New York State Senator Eric Adams, in collaboration with app designer Garth Narr, also created the Brooklyn Quality of Life app, which allows Brooklyn residents to report and upload photos of suspected criminal activity anonymously. These reports are sent to a team of retired police officers, who then share the information with local investigators through a private Facebook page (Durkin 2012). The idea behind this app was to help encourage those afraid of contacting NYC police directly a way of anonymously reporting crimes. Former Mayor Bloomberg (cited in City of New York 2008: para. 2) boasted that these kinds of digital mobile services were 'bringing government accountability – and crime-fighting – to a whole new level'. According to John Feinblatt, the former Mayor's Criminal Justice Coordinator, the gathering and uploading of information by the public was even a necessary component of effective law enforcement. The city's digital upgrades to both 911 and 311 give the 'public the power', allowing it the means to be 'the City's eyes and ears' (Feinblatt cited in City of New York 2008: para. 4).

But becoming the 'eyes and ears' of the city is also suggestive of a form of sousveillance, a term coined by Mann, Nolan and Wellman (2003) to describe surveillance from below. While sousveillance can help hold city officials and law enforcement accountable – such as we have seen recently with a number of video recordings by citizens of police brutality made public – this kind of surveillance also functions as a crowdsourced neo-panopticon (Mann et al. 2003). Encouraged through the rhetoric of open government, access, citizen-centric engagement and making city government accountable, these city-sponsored technological tools and applications solicit residents to become surveyors of one another. As such, they are yet another example of how some of NYC's digital programmes function in such a way as to put the responsibility of the government's work on its residents. As residents walk about the city or perform their normal daily tasks, they are encouraged to record and report incidents – from a rat seen in a restaurant to disorderly conduct and suspected criminal activity. Not only are citizens encouraged to simply report these issues, they are solicited to upload images, meaning their specific locations can be easily tagged and captured by locating one's geographical position via the smartphone they use to report.

Concluding remarks

While Mark Andrejevic (2004, 2007b) and Alexander Galloway and Eugene Thacker (2007) point to the productive aspects of sousveillance offered by citizen digital interactivity and monitoring, and Steve Mann, Jason Nolan and Barr Wellman (2003) argue that sousveillance has the ability to flatten power relationships, it can be argued that the average mobile smartphone user is not as decisively or politically motivated while reporting a broken parking meter, making a noise complaint to NYC 311 or uploading photos to an app that rates local restaurants. While sousveillance may be an active, purposeful method of monitoring by engaged and technologically-equipped citizen reporters (Zuckerman 2007), the kind of sousveillance that most often occurs with the use of these city-sponsored apps is non-organized, fairly individuated and unintentional. Framed as tools to make residents' lives easier and leading to the collaborative betterment of the city, these applications are instead examples of the seemingly subtler or inconsequential 'instruments' or technologies of neo-liberal governmentality (Foucault 1978).

Furthermore, considering Foucault's (1990) assertion that a 'veritable explosion' of discourse tends to provoke further discourse (such that sex becomes a thing to be confessed), we can argue that the use of these kinds of mobile digital programmes and applications lead to a similar phenomenon. As SMS, smartphone apps and other mobile methods of recording and reporting proliferate, the will to confess, or in this case report – be it one's location on Foursquare every hour or a neighbour's disruptive party – results in a veritable explosion of data. Data produces knowledge, which is then linked to power; and whoever determines methods of reporting and data collection also determines what can be known. As the information collected increases exponentially, and new data is created through users' input and feedback, this information is constantly being collected, distributed back into the system, aggregated and analysed, and thus can inform major public policy decisions. As a result, the power of the state is intensified and reproduced through this constant incitement to report, and everyone in the city with a smartphone is interpellated into this system.

Scholars such as Henry Jenkins (2006), Yochai Benkler (2006) and Clay Shirky (2008) have promoted the politically transformative possibilities of enhanced autonomy provided by digital technologies, such as collective intelligence and participatory democracy. Indeed these and similar claims abound in *New York City's Digital Roadmap* (2012a). However, as Armand Mattelart (1996: xvi) points out, along with media's increased potential for democratic participation also comes the increased potential of those who control the information, processes and platforms to use them for 'social and productive order'. Through its digital initiatives, NYC claims to provide a better quality of life to its residents through unprecedented governmental transparency and open government. These propositions convey a particular set of democratic ideals and practices that in turn rely heavily on the characterization of digital technologies as liberatory and egalitarian. Digital technological tools can also be understood within a larger framework: as social mechanisms of biopower and neo-liberal governmentality that encourage residents to self-monitor and self-regulate themselves to produce, for New York at least, desirable citizen-subjects.

References

Andrejevic, M. (2004), *Reality TV: The Work of Being Watched*, Maryland: Rowman & Littlefield Publishers.

—— —— (2007a), 'Surveillance in the digital enclosure', *The Communication Review*, 10, pp. 295–317.

—— —— (2007b), *iSpy: Surveillance and Power in Interactive Era*, Kansas: University of Kansas Press.

Barry, A. (2001), *Political Machines*, New York: Continuum.

Beck, K. (2013), '311: "The Agency That Never Sleeps"', *Destination CRM.com*, http://www.destinationcrm.com/articles/Editorial/Magazine-Features/311-The-Agency-That-Never-Sleeps-72864.aspx. Accessed 19 May 2015.

Benkler, Y. (2006), *The Wealth of Networks: How Social Productions Transforms Markets and Freedom*, New Haven, CT: Yale University Press.

Challenge Post (2011), *NYC BigApps 3.0.*, https://nycbigapps2011.challengepost.com/rules, Accessed 24 May 2015.

City of New York (n.d.), 'All of NYC's official applications', http://www1.nyc.gov/connect/applications.page. Accessed 24 May 2015.

—— —— (2008), 'Mayor Bloomberg, Commissioner Kelly, Commissioner Cosgrave, and Criminal Justice Coordinator Feinblatt announce that 911 and 311 can now receive pictures and video from cell phones and computers', 9 September, http://tinyurl.com/6nd3yj. Accessed 19 May 2015.

—— —— (2010), 'NYC DOT launches "You The Man" iPhone app to reduce drunk driving in New York City', 8 September, http://www.nyc.gov/html/dot/html/pr2010/pr10_039.shtml. Accessed 19 May 2015.

———— (2011a), *Road Map for the Digital City: Achieving New York City's Digital Future*, http://www.nyc.gov/html/media/media/PDF/90dayreport.pdf. Accessed 20 May 2015.

———— (2011b), 'Mayor Bloomberg, the Federal Communications Commission, the Federal Emergency Management Agency and wireless provider executives unveil new, first-in-the-nation emergency notification service that will reach mobile devices located in affected areas', 10 May, http://tinyurl.com/akn524b. Accessed 19 May 2015.

———— (2012a), *New York City's Digital Roadmap: Progress & Innovation*, http://www.mikebloomberg.com/files/2012NYCDigitalRoadmap.pdf. Accessed 19 May 2015.

———— (2012b), *Mayor's Management Report*, http://www.nyc.gov/html/ops/downloads/pdf/mmr0912/0912_mmr.pdf. Accessed 19 May 2015.

Civic Impulse (2015), *H.R. 5785 – 109th Congress: Warning, Alert, and Response Network Act*, https://www.govtrack.us/congress/bills/109/hr5785http://www.govtrack.us/congress/bills/109/hr5785. Accessed 20 May 2015.

Davies, W. (2013), 'Neoliberalism and the revenge of the "social"', *Open Democracy*, 16 July, https://www.opendemocracy.net/william-davies/neoliberalism-and-revenge-of-%E2%80%9Csocial%E2%80%9D. Accessed 19 May 2015.

Durkin, E. (2012), 'Want to report a crime? Well, politician says, there's an app for that', *Daily News*, 12 August, http://www.nydailynews.com/new-york/brooklyn/report-crime-nypd-politician-app-article-1.1134736. Accessed 22 May 2015.

Dwyer, J. (2014), 'Giving away and then seizing, condoms', *New York Times*, 24 April, http://www.nytimes.com/2012/04/25/nyregion/in-new-york-city-giving-away-and-taking-away-condoms.html?_r=0. Accessed 19 May 2015.

Federal Communications Commission (2013), 'Commercial mobile telephone alerts (CMAS)', http://transition.fcc.gov/pshs/services/cmas.htm. Accessed 19 May 2015.

Federal Emergency Management Agency (n.d.), 'Frequently asked questions: Wireless emergency alerts', http://www.fema.gov/commercial-mobile-alert-system#1. Accessed 20 May 2015.

Foucault, M. (1978). 'Governmentality', in G. Burchell, C. Gordon and P. Miller (eds) (1991), *The Foucault Effect: Studies in Governmentality*, Hemel Hempstead: Harvester Wheatsheaf, pp. 87–104.

———— (1990), *The History of Sexuality: An Introduction*, vol. 1, New York: Vintage/Random House.

———— (2004), *Security, Territory, Population: Lectures at the Collége De France 1977-1978*, New York: Palgrave Macmillan.

Galloway, A. and Thacker, E. (2007), *The Exploit: A Theory of Networks*, Minnesota: Minnesota Press.

Grusin, R. (2009), 'Premediation, economic crisis and the post-9/11 security bubble', *Premediation*, 10 March, http://premediation.blogspot.com/search?q=premediation+9%2F11. Accessed 19 May 2015.

—— —— (2010), *Premediation: Affect and Mediality After 9/11*, Houndsmill: Palgrave Macmillan.

—— —— (2012), 'Premediating Sandy', *Premediation*, 29 October, http://premediation. blogspot.com/2012/10/premediating-sandy.html. Accessed 19 May 2015.

Homeland Security Newswire (2011), 'New York first in nation to deploy PLAN emergency alert system', 12 May, http://www.homelandsecuritynewswire.com/new-york-first-nation-deploy-plan-emergency-alert-system. Accessed 20 May 2015.

Howard, A. (2012), 'NYC's PLAN to alert citizens to danger during Hurricane Sandy', *O'Reilly Radar*, 30 October, http://radar.oreilly.com/2012/10/hurricane-sandy-mobile-text-alert-plan.html. Accessed 20 May 2015.

Huffington Post (2011), 'New York City launches mobile phone app for free condoms', 14 February, http://www.huffingtonpost.com/2011/02/14/new-york-city-launches-mo_n_823250.html. Accessed 19 May 2015.

Jarrett, K. (2008), 'Interactivity is evil! A critical investigation of Web 2.0', *First Monday*, 13: 3, http://firstmonday.org/ojs/index.php/fm/article/view/2140/1947. Accessed 19 May 2015.

Jefferson, C. (2011), 'New York City launches the world's first condom app', *Good Magazine*, 4 February, http://www.good.is/posts/new-york-city-launches-the-world-s-first-condom-app/. Accessed 19 May 2015.

Jenkins, H. (2006), *Convergence Culture: Where Old and New Media Collide*, New York: New York University Press.

Lessig, L. (1998), 'The laws of cyberspace', *Taiwan Net Conference '98 Conference*, Taipei, Taiwan, March, https://cyber.law.harvard.edu/works/lessig/laws_cyberspace.pdf. Accessed 19 May 2015.

Mann, S., Nolan, J. and Wellman, B. (2003), 'Sousveillance: Inventing and using wearable computing devices for data collection in surveillance environments', *Surveillance & Society*, 1: 3, pp. 331–55, http://www.surveillance-and-society.org/articles1%283%29/sousveillance.pdf. Accessed 19 May 2015.

Mattelart, A. (1996), *The Invention of Communication*, Minneapolis: University of Minnesota Press.

Moore, T. (2012), 'Mayor Bloomberg touts app-y meals for healthier choices in city eating', *New York Daily News*, 6 March, http://www.nydailynews.com/new-york/mayor-bloomberg-touts-app-y-meals-healthier-choices-city-eating-article-1.1034351. Accessed 19 May 2015.

New York City Department of Environmental Protection (2012), 'DEP announces more than 500,000 people visited Water-On-the-Go fountains in 2012', 6 September, http://www.nyc.gov/html/dep/html/press_releases/12-62pr.shtml. Accessed 19 May 2015.

New York City Department of Health and Mental Hygiene (2012), 'Health Department's NYC condom finder available on all smartphones in time for National Condom Awareness Day, Feb. 14', 13 February, http://www.nyc.gov/html/doh/html/pr2012/pr003-12.shtml. Accessed 20 May 2015.

New York City Global Partners (2011), *Best Practice: Call Center for Non-Emergency City Services*, New York: New York City Global Partners, http://www.nyc.gov/html/unccp/gprb/downloads/pdf/NYC_Technology_311.pdf. Accessed 20 May 2015.

New York State Department of Health (2013), 'Five things to know about HIV/AIDS reporting in New York State', http://www.health.ny.gov/diseases/aids/regulations/partner_services/index.htm. Accessed 19 May 2015.

Ramage, S. (2007), *Privacy: Law of Civil Liberties*, iUniverse.

Shirky, C. (2008), *Here Comes Everybody: The Power of Organizing Without Organizations*, New York: Penguin.

Zuckerman, E. (2007), 'Draft paper on mobile phones and activism', 9 April, http://www.ethanzuckerman.com/blog/index.php?s=%22vastly+exceeds+internet+usage%22. Accessed 20 May 2015.

Chapter 11

Explorations of an urban intervention management system:
A reflection on how to deal with urban complex systems and
deliver dynamic change

Marta A. G. Miguel, Richard Laing and Quazi Mahtab Zaman

Introduction

Concerns over how we plan and manage urban development have grown as a result of unpredictable and rapid conditional changes in postmodern cities. This chapter explores the shifting contexts of urban environments, which change in an increasingly frequent and dynamic manner. These changes can be understood through the lens of real-time interactions between citizens, planning processes and designers, supported through the use of ICT. We argue for the recognition that urban change will happen in an unpredictable way, and that such interactions can be regarded as extremely valuable information to any urban manager. The approach suggested by the research concerns the scale of interventions in the building environment, and the exploration of tools to facilitate public engagement and awareness of urban complexity.

Three debates emerge from these considerations. The first reflects on how certain medias have generated a global culture that influences complex contextualized varieties (Cowen 2002) and standardized ideas of beauty (Stephens 2000). The second reflects on the emergence of new ways of experiencing the city, including communication channels that contribute to urban formation and development (Laing et al. 2009), while the third explores the process of urban formation in relation to the human quality of life and appreciation of urban morphology (Marshall 2009, 2012). Today, we have modernism, postmodernism, classical and all architectural styles in between. But an argument can be made that global culture emerges from the flattening and standardization of diverse cultures by the media. Following this perspective, cultural expressions including architecture are also flattened. But are we really becoming the same? Is culture becoming flat? Is the standardization of building forms responding adequately to the way in which humans relate to their environment?

Today, media influences the way we design and perceive our environment, but it also changes human relations and therefore the way people use urban spaces. Modern social life emerges from the intersection between architectural forms, the urban environment, social relations and the media, generating a media environment of its own (Venturi 1966). In this intersection, each domain influences another in a variety of ways, creating not only different perceptions of the environment but new dimensions of the city (Augé 2008).

The process of urban formation and the related scale of building influence human perception of, and adaptation to, the built environment. From the perspective of urban planning, one of the major lessons learned from modernism involved the unpredictability of the future, and the fact that people take time to adjust to large-scale changes in their surroundings (Jacobs 1961; Jencks 1981; Coleman 1985; Panerai et al. 2004). Nothing is altering our current urban condition faster than the development and inclusion of new technologies; these, together with our experience of the misfortunes of top-down creationist approaches to the management of urban systems raise many questions as to how and whether we should design and plan our cities (Alfasi & Portugali 2004; Marshall 2009, 2012).

It is certain that the manner in which the public is able to interact and contribute with planning or urban areas can be supported through the use of ICT, and that these tools will become more prevalent as we move forward. However, for them to be fully useful, the end results they seek and the methods they employ have to be based on an understanding of how we (as user-participants) currently understand participation, as well as how our own creative and social engagement processes actually operate. Examples of how these methods support such interaction have been demonstrated in terms of public participation in planning and design multiple times (cf. Laing et al. 2009).

The research reported in this chapter proposes a model to guide more informed public participation that do not foreground technology, but which does reveal some of the most significant human-centred issues and characteristics that the next generation of technological and social media participatory tools will need to understand them. In addition, this chapter suggests that, whilst useful in terms of informing and guiding specific design processes, participatory design exercises cannot easily be applied to wider and less predictable urban contexts. Consequently, while we can use participation strategies and methodologies to support planned urban 'interventions', the interventions themselves should be regarded as being part of a dynamic system of urban change, part of which will be driven by occupants and communities – whether they engage in traditional ways or through the various new forms of inclusivity offered by emerging technologies.

Strategic intervention in the city

Several researchers have considered dynamic ways to deal with the unpredictability of urban complex systems from a planning perspective (Friedman 1997; Marshall 2012; Portugali 2012), while a similar number have focused on the issues of new medias and technologies. Nevertheless, this chapter draws references from human action rather than planning processes. Moreover, it frames design as one kind of human action, and human actions as the building blocks of urban life, which hold a sociocultural reality within them. It also defines these building blocks as short-term evolutionary steps that lead the way to long-term changes (Marshall 2009). A methodology is devised that gives a deeper meaning not only to design, but to human actions themselves, transforming them into what this chapter defines as 'strategic interventions'. This urban planning philosophy implies the nurturing of self-organizing strategies, which naturally emerge from everyday human actions in the city, and which many new technologies seek to foster through the next wave of distanced interactions. It uses top-down strategic interventions as a tool to intentionally nudge urban development and improve human quality of life, and suggests that this represents a base model that forthcoming digital models and tools need to understand.

Strategic interventions are human actions intentionally designed to be utilized as a tool to nudge change and address urban problems within the modern complex urban environment. These interventions emerge from a deep understanding of a context rather than from mediated architectural solution. Complexity theory suggests that strategic interventions are those that are made of the basic elements from which a complex system emerges, and which therefore have the capacity to change that system as a whole (Portugali 1997, 2000; Batty 1994, 2005; Stedman 2006).

Strategic intervention can either originate from bottom-up or top-down actors or actions. Nevertheless, it is the responsibility of the top-down actors/actions to have an overview of the society and to manage urban change adequately. Strategic interventions embrace characteristics of both top-down and bottom-up approaches (Alexander 1966; Jacobs 1970; Marshall 2009; Lane et al. 2009). These should be:

1. contextual;
2. preferably of a small scale and emergent from an awareness and respect of the complexity of a place. They should therefore aim to disturb consolidated systems as little as possible (Marshall 2009);
3. an expression of the common good (Ostrom 1990; Wilson 2011); and
4. designed and applied to speed up or to change the path of development. Their intention is to break the emergent continuity of development when things are not going in the right direction, and nudge urban change towards a sustainable path (Lane et al. 2009).

Evolutionary theory suggests that design and artificial selection serve as a mediator between the user and the urban environment. As such, they can be interpreted as both a form of adaptation (Wilson 2011) and a reproduction strategy (Marshall 2009). In light of this, 'design' is interpreted here as a tool for innovation (Verganti 2009), as well as a short-term local action that can define longer term changes in the system (Loorbach 2007).

Strategic interventions in the building environment: The relevance of architecture in the urban planning process

In line with Marshall (2009), this research considers buildings, plots and routes as the basic elements of the urban syntax, and therefore as examples of strategic elements to manipulate urban form and character. The research also considers urban building blocks that Alexander (1977) describes as 'patterns of space'. Patterns of space are the elements that translate everyday human activities in the built environment. Examples of these elements could be a bus stop, a bakery or a supermarket. The basic elements of space syntax and Alexander's 'patterns of space' can be used as tools to manipulate urban change as a whole. These elements can influence the way people move in the city and help to coordinate human social interactions (Bourdieu 1989). These changes will in turn influence the character of the people who use the city (Sassen 1999).

The lessons learned from modernism have discredited urban planning and shifted the focus towards the architectural object as a catalyst for urban change (Marshall 2009). Following this, fantastic and exuberant architectural design, nurtured in part by the media, have indeed brought dynamic change to places and improved quality of life. This chapter does not aim to debate the purpose of this kind of 'mediated architecture' and its apparent superficial understanding of the relevance of buildings in shaping human life. It focuses instead on the potential role of the kind of architecture that emerges from within a given context; the kind of architecture that emerges as a reaction to a contextual aim or need. Does the architecture that is a consequence of a deep understanding of the dynamic relations of different layers of complexity in a place reflect both the uniqueness of the problems present and their potential within a given context? Does that kind of architecture and design still have a role to play? Can one guide designers to reflect in such contextual complexities, and give them the tools to combine a holistic understanding of spaces with aesthetics? If so, can these issues be embedded in strategies we use today and that we will use in an evermore mediated and technologically near future?

This chapter suggests that we cannot rigidly plan and design the future form of the city, nor let it grow organically. Instead, complex systems are suggested as a strategy to reflect on a new kind of urban planning and city design; one that would avoid standardizing and simplifying the urban form, and which uses design and architecture to guide, generate and maintain its functional complexity. The authors have designed an exploratory framework to explore ways in which to improve human awareness of the urban fabric as a complex and contextual system. In the future, such a framework could – and it is suggested should – be available to all ICT users. It could be integrated in existing design software and eventually be used as a tool to facilitate urban planning processes.

Research approach: The EIMs basic model

The research reported in this chapter led to the development of exploratory models to support professionals (including both designers and decision-makers) to intervene in the city more adequately. They facilitate the design and selection of strategic interventions by guiding users to reflect on a series of complex relations between key intervention areas of urban systems. These areas are referred to here as the exploratory intervention management system (EIMS). The EIMS is composed of two pragmatic models: the first model refers to an image of what a social/urban system is at a given moment in time; the second adds dynamism to that view by engaging with notions of time and change. Both the EIMS models and the methodology to operate them emerge from the intersection of complexity theory, transition management (Loorbach 2007) and spatial planning (de Roo and Rauws 2012).

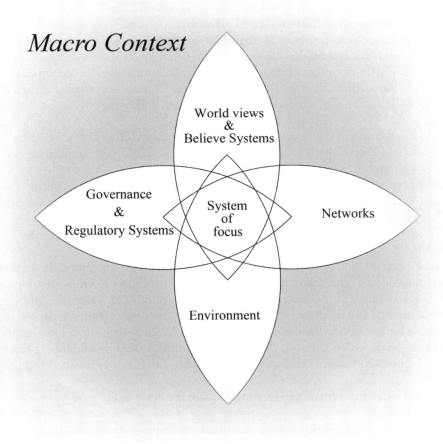

Figure 1. The EIMS basic model and its four intervention areas, which define the system of focus. It relates the system of focus with what is unknown about the system and its macro context.

The EIMS basic model is focused on the characterization of an urban complex system, along with the identification of the system's imbalances, the generation of an intention, and the exploration of strategies to act on the system. The EIMS basic model is characterized by the 'system of focus' and the 'system external' (Loorbach 2007). The 'system of focus' is characterized by four intervention areas, or the aspects of society on which one can intervene in order to improve the system or nudge the direction of urban development.

The four intervention areas consist of the following:

1. World views and belief systems; religion and culture. This area represents innate shared knowledge and memory. It is the lens through which one sees the world and judges what is right or wrong.
2. Physical context or the natural and urban environment.
3. Governance and regulatory systems; politics, economy and regulations. This area represents the system that allows us to exchange goods and services on a fair and ethical basis, from the micro to macro scale (Ostrom 1990; Friedmann 2011).
4. Communication and transportation networks. This area represents the networks that allow us to move and exchange goods, ideas and knowledge.

All that lies around the four intervention areas is considered the 'systems external'. The external area of the model represents that condition which is not controllable (i.e. the unpredictable and the unknown). It also represents the macro-scale of the system during analyses (Loorbach 2007). The EIMS basic model defines interventions categorically by positioning them within the model's four areas of intervention and by relating them to specific subsystems. In other words, the model relates interventions to a specific time and place, to one another, to different hierarchical levels of social systems and to the system as a whole.

At the heart of the system is the intersection of all four intervention areas. The methodology used to characterize it is based on the World System Model, and represents areas of focus relevant to human well-being (Hodgson 2011). Human well-being is contextual and fairly subjective, leading us to address the concept from the perspective of identifiable human needs. We use Hodgson's (2011) World System Model to identify the key human needs which will lead the user to define the system of study: (1) health; (2) wealth; (3) food; (4) water; (5) security and sense of belonging; (6) shelter; (7) education; and (8) energy.

In other words, the human needs represented in the heart of the model are used to:

1. identify the problems of the system and relate those to other aspects of social organization; and
2. define the scale of the system in analysis or the group of individuals on which one aims to reflect.

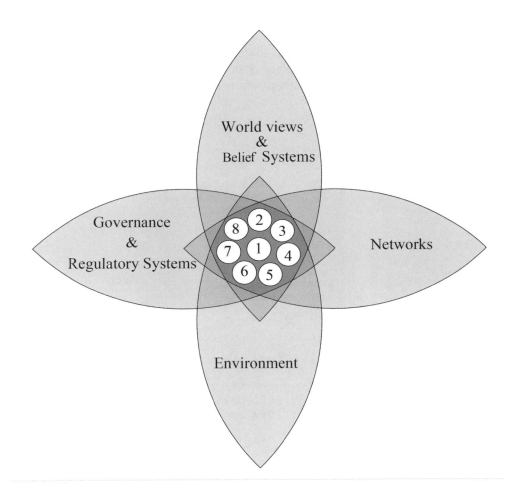

Figure 2. Relationship between the heart of the system and its intervention areas (Hodgson 2011).

This EIMS model is based on the notion of nested hierarchies. Each element of the system (and the system as a whole) are composed of smaller social groups whilst also being part of a bigger one at the same time. The model can therefore be used to relate the system of analysis and intervention areas with both macro and micro levels of social organizations.

Consequently, the EIMS basic model serves to define the social system available for study, and is used to define the needs and possible contributions of that system. This knowledge can be of key relevance to finding a strategy to address a given problem, and to formulate a vision or a common aim for the future (Loorbach 2007). The characterization of the system of focus in relation to the macro levels of the system might help to find the uniqueness of the system in relation to the whole. This can help define kinds of interventions which transform that uniqueness to a contribution that benefits the system as a whole.

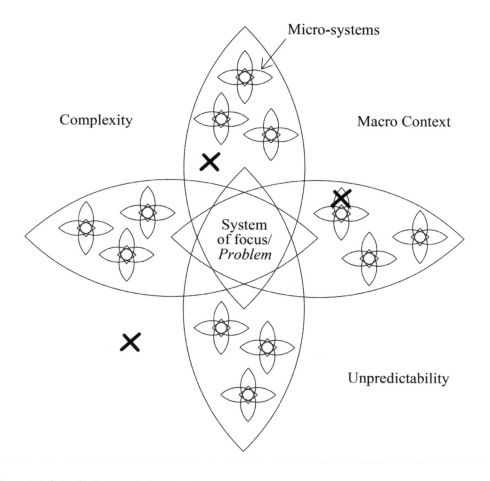

Figure 3. Relationship between the heart of the system, intervention areas and different hierarchies of social organization. In addition, this image exemplifies how to define interventions within these three aspects of social organization.

The EIMS dynamic model

The EIMS dynamic model introduces the notion of time and dynamic change to the basic model, confronting the users with the unpredictability of complex systems.

In the dynamic model, the word 'complexity' refers to unpredictability. It is the domain where everything happens. Meanwhile, 'evolution' refers to time and continuity, and is represented as a background of the system; and 'dynamic change' is related to the self-organization of the system. It relates to the process of natural change and to the new social realities that emerge from it. 'Intervention' refers to a human action, a system of actions or a happening in relation to a specific context in a specific time.

In short, the EIMS dynamic model places both the problems and the solutions of social systems within the contexts of complexity and uncertainty. It leads the user to engage with notions of time and the relationship between cause and unpredictable emergent effects. In combination, the two EIMS models were designed to influence awareness of the complexity of social systems and lead users to reflect on the responsibility implicit in each human action.

Pilot application

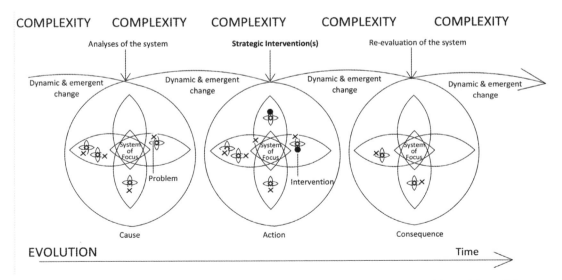

Figure 4. Relates the EIMS basic model with dynamic change. It places the operational phases of the models parallel to the process of urban and social change.

Selected case studies tested the acceptance of the design and management approach, as well as the ability of the EIMS models to serve as a platform to support a multidisciplinary dialogue on urban systems in both academic and professional situations. The first two case studies focused on the selection process of interventions, while the third focused on design as a means to create more adequate interventions in the building environment. The research case study area was the city centre of Aberdeen, Scotland, where two of the studies evolved around a public discussion related to the selection of interventions suggested in 2008 and 2009 (namely 'Union Terrace Gardens: The City Square' and 'Peacock Visual Arts' Centre'). The influence of technology and media in the perception and use of the models was tested by giving the participants different platforms to engage with the models, namely the university ODL platform, different projections of the models and printout versions. Finally, the comparison of different kinds of data led to improvements in the research exploratory tools, the EIMS models, and consequently to a readjustment of the research methodology (Sampson 2004; Cassell & Symon 2004).

Figure 5. Union Terrace Gardens, Aberdeen.

Case study 1

Case study 1 tested the openness of decision-makers to the use of small-scale interventions in the built environment, analysing the applicability of the EIMS models as a selection tool. It also served to develop a deeper understanding of the dynamics in a real-life process of selection. Data was collected over a period of nine months of public and private discussions with key protagonists in the interventions suggested for the Union Terrace Gardens (UTG). To contextualize the role of media in the decision-making process, both the EIMS models and the research design proposal were presented as printout handmade drawings (as opposed to the 3D renderings published on websites and blogs). During these discussions, notes were taken and semi-open interviews were conducted. Using Cullen's (1971) approach, sketches and notes were taken during several walks through Aberdeen city centre. Finally, information available on the Internet regarding the public discussion, especially reports published on the local press website, was systematically analysed.

Case study 2

The second case study tested the acceptance of the EIMS models in an academic context, the difficulties participants had in using them, and the effectiveness of the models in guiding participants to a deeper evaluation and understanding of complex systems and their dynamics. Students participating in the workshop via the Internet were asked to apply the EIMS models in their urban context, and to use the models to investigate the ways in which an intervention of their choice changed their living environment. In addition, data was collected from Internet discussions on Robert Gordon University's ODL platform.

Case study 3

Case study 3 focused on the role of architecture as a potential strategic intervention to nudge urban development, and investigated how aware future architects (final-year MA students) were of the relations between the built environment, human condition (Arendt 1998) and human perception (Ponty 1962), as well as how deeply one influences the other (Wilson 2011). The study was also used to test the participants' awareness of the city as a complex open system (Portugali 2000). From the knowledge gained, we explored the extent to which the EIMS models increased the students' urban and social awareness, and how that shift in awareness influenced the participants' design process.

Summary of the studies' design		Study 1	Study 2	Study 3
Methodology	Qualitative research	*	*	*
	Case studies	*	*	*
Focus groups	People involved with the practice of urban planning	*		
	Academic environment		*	*
Intervention of focus: Strategic Interventions in the built environment.	Micro-intervention	*	*	
	Mid-scale intervention			*
	Macro-interventions	*	*	
Data Collection	Semi-open interviews	*		*
	Questionnaires		*	*
	Observation	*	*	*
	Document analysis	*		
	Analysis of information on the Internet	*		
	Sketches and notes	*	*	*
	Ethnography	*	*	*
Research context	Aberdeen city centre			*
	The Union Terrace Gardens – Aberdeen	*	*	
Research tools	**EIMS:** Exploratory Intervention Management System — Presented visually		*	*
	Aim: Improve the models and test their applicability as a tool to imagine, create and select interventions that can lead to a more sustainable and human friendlier urban environment. — Described orally	*	*	*
	Questions: - Are the EIMS models applicable in real-life scenarios; in what way? - Are they useful? - What are their potentials and weaknesses? - How can we improve them? — Operated by the participants		*	

Table 1. Summary of the research studies' design.

	Research aims	Study 1	Study 2	Study 3
General	Develop a deeper understanding of the dynamics in the design process of interventions in the built environment.			*
	Develop a deeper understanding of the dynamics in a real-life process of selecting interventions in the built environment.	*		
	Develop a deeper understanding of Aberdeen's urban context and its built environment.	*		
	Develop a deeper understanding of the relations and dynamics between top-down and bottom-up forces in Aberdeen; Explore the influence individual participants and organisations have in the decision process and in the decision product.	*		
	Develop an exploratory theory for sustainable urban management. Gather contributions from the participants that might lead to new theoretical approaches.	*	*	*
	Explore the participants' general innate awareness of the city as a complex and unpredictable system.	*	*	*
	Test the awareness of the change an intervention in the building environment can bring to the overall character and dynamics of the city.	*	*	*
EIMS	Test potential of the models to self-educate users and stimulate people to think in complex systems from a holistic perspective.	*	*	*
	Test the capacity of the models to be used as a common language and as a framework to share information between all parties involved in the design and selection of interventions in the built environment.	*		
	Explore to what extent the models are able to help people to be aware of the unpredictable character of complex systems	*	*	*
	Test the applicability of the EIMS models as a framework or a selection tool; Test the capacity of the models to improve the selection process of interventions.	*	*	
	Test the applicability of the EIMS models as a framework or a design tool; Test the capacity of the models to improve the adequacy of design concepts, the quality of the design forms and the design process of interventions.			*
	Test the clarity of the models and identify the difficulties participants would have in operating them.		*	
	Investigate if a more holistic awareness of urban complex systems influence or adds complexity to the design process and their design object.			*

Table 2. Relationship between the research aims and the studies' explorations.

Results and observations from the application

From a comparison of the findings which emerged from case studies 1 and 2, we can conclude that the EIMS models were generally well accepted by the research participants. The models were efficient in leading participants to engage with concepts of complex systems, unpredictability, dynamic change, nested hierarchies and others, which triggered relevant discussions about the problems Aberdeen city is facing today. In addition, they helped participants to define their own intentions and to identify key urban problems. They were efficient in helping to describe the character and current state of urban complex systems, and also helped to identify the relevant subsystems. The models helped the participants to relate their action to micro and macro levels of social organization, to different aspects of urban life and different intervention areas.

One key finding is the fact that the participants who had to use the models to make a visual representation of an urban system engaged with a deeper level of analysis than the participants who were asked to just use the model as a framework for thinking. The challenges encountered by the participants who operated the models were used to improve them, as well as to clearly establish a methodology to operate them. From case studies 1 and 2, we concluded that top-down protagonists perceived big-scale mediated interventions to be more effective. In addition, some argued that the risks related to them were necessary and worth taking (Huxtable 1984). Within the current research, The Union Terrace Gardens Friends' organization defended most of the small-scale interventions suggested by this study.

Case study 1 demonstrated that the EIMS models were inappropriate to help with the selection of interventions. They did not help to establish a common strategy or cooperation between different groups of participants. Moving forward, with newer models in the future, participants should be asked to actively operate the models, and the models should be introduced in the first stages of the selection process. The study showed that ideals and preconceptions are very difficult to change; moreover, they play a key role in the decision-making process (Koprowski 1983). Beliefs and personal convictions influenced both the participants' preferences and actions – issues that will be relevant whatever the digital, analogue or manual platform used. This study demonstrated that ideals and visions are indeed both based on emotional and rational perspectives of the world. They collectively shape decisions and therefore the interventions we make in the environment (Morse 2006); in addition, they become the intentions that shape human interventions.

Case study 1 also indicated that common ideals and visions induce human cooperation and self-organization. As in living systems, people and organizations self-organized within and across groups to form alliances to defend their common beliefs and intentions for the city (Greenleaf 1977; Morgan 1997; Knowles 2002; Sheard & Kakabadse 2007; Polzer & Kwan 2012). Jaina and Tyson (2004) argue that coalitions are formed not only because of similar world-views and meaning systems (Duck 1994), but also according to personal judgments of the competence needed to complete a given task. Interestingly, bottom-down participants formed alliances with organizations because they believed they were more capable of opposing unwanted top-down pressures in that manner; a dynamic witnessed through various social movements in recent years in which online social media has played a fundamental role. The studies suggest that image and media do indeed play a role in the decision-making process, a finding in agreement with previous studies by the authors, which explored the use of ICT and visualization during design participation (Conniff et al. 2010).

All participants, both from top-down and bottom-up perspectives, defended their ideas around the projects' 3D images. These were made available on the Internet and other media, but did not provide any other in-depth information on the projects themselves. This raises the question of whether the basis for the selection of interventions were the design features, the quality of the 3D images presented or the influence of the media in the decision-making process. These represent issues of fundamental import if these participatory exercises are to be carried out on digital platforms in the future. The fact that the system of interventions suggested by this research was presented in the form of sketch plans and sections that did not leave the meeting rooms might have contributed to the fact that it was not considered seriously next to 3D visualizations broadcasted on other proposals (Daft & Lengel 1986; Suh & Lee 2005; Daugherty, Li & Biocca 2008; van der Land et al. 2013).

The context within which discussion and debate take place has been observed in previous studies as being important to the progress of designs, as well as to the interaction between participants. The use of ICT to facilitate such interaction is also vitally important, particularly across disciplines and areas of expertise (Leon et al. 2014). It is important to bring attention to the fact that media was not able to influence the general public's emotional relation with the site. Instead, it misled the perception of space and therefore influenced the selection process. Nevertheless, media did not influence most participants' expectations for the site.

Architecture students participating in case study 3 suggested that the theoretical framework enabled them to relate their design projects to specific contexts and their problems. In addition, it helped them to be more aware of the human aspect of things (Rapoport 1977), rather than focusing exclusively on aesthetics and technical issues. This opens the door for the possible alignment between the mediated architecture (focused on the image of the design object) and the so-called 'social architecture' (focused on the understanding of the relationship between human life and the building environment).

Concluding remarks

Morse (2006) describes how emotional self-awareness provides a way to avoid the 'bounded awareness' phenomena, which causes people to ignore relevant information when making decisions (Bazerman & Chugh 2006). The EIMS models address such problems by encouraging participants to reflect on their emotions and justify what they consider to be a rational choice. They also helped participants to formulate questions and look at problems from different perspectives, significantly reducing the possibility of overlooking important information (Hammond, Keeney & Raiffa 2006). This conclusion encourages further explorations on how to adapt the EIMS models to ICT. If current trends continue, these will provide the basis of the sites and platforms upon which similar exercises in participation and design will take place. EIMS models could then be used to inform the decisions that these platforms offer through real-time interaction between citizens, planning processes and designers. Indeed, we would go one step further and suggest that the EIMS model has to be at the heart of the tools developed on these platforms.

In exploring an interdisciplinary approach based on human action to investigate alternative ways urban systems may be managed, the contribution of this research rests on the challenges in the interactions and interrelationships between disciplines, as well as the underlying lessons it offers in the development of new media platforms for participation and design. It is suggested that future work should aim to further refocus urban theories and disciplines, and to highlight the importance of the interdisciplinary approaches to the study of cities and urban development on these platforms. In addition, it is argued that ICT can build on the human focus of these models to potentially bring more dynamism to urban planning without necessarily compromising the adequacy of human intervention.

References

Alexander, C. (1966), 'The city is not a tree', *Design*, 206, pp. 46–55.
—— —— (1977), *A Pattern Language*, New York: Oxford University.
Alfasi, N. and Portugali, J. (2004), 'Planning just-in-time versus planning just-in-case', *Cities*, 21: 1, pp. 29–39.
Arendt, H. (1998). *The Human Condition*, 2nd ed., Chicago and London: The University of Chicago Press. First published 1973.
Augé, M. (2008), *Non-places: An Introduction to Supermodernity*, London: Verso.
Batty, M. (1994), *Fractal Cities*, London: Academic Press.
—— —— (2005), *Understanding Cities with Cellular Automata, Agent based models, and Fractals*, Cambridge, MA: MIT Press.
Bazerman, M. H. and Chugh, D. (2006), 'Decisions without blinders', *Harvard Business Review*, 84, pp. 88–97.
Blizzard, J. L. and Klotz, L. E. (2012), 'A framework for sustainable whole systems design', *Design Studies*, 33: 5, pp. 456–79.
Bourdieu, P. (1989), 'Social space and symbolic power', *Sociological Theory*, 7: 1, pp. 14–25.

Cassell, C. and Symon, G. (2004). 'Promoting new research practices in organizational research', in C. Cassell and G. Symon (eds), *Essential Guide to Qualitative Methods in Organizational Research*, Thousand Oaks: Sage.

Coleman, A. M. (1985), *Utopia on Trial: Vision and reality on Planned Housing*, London: H. Shipman.

Conniff, A., Craig, T., Laing, R. and Galan-Diaz, C. (2010), 'A comparison of active navigation and passive observation of desktop models of future built environments', *Design Studies*, 31: 5, pp. 419–38.

Cowen, T. (2002), *Creative Destruction – How Globalization is Changing the World's Cultures*, New Jersey: Princeton University Press.

Cullen, G. (1971), *The Concise Townscape*, New York: Architectural Press.

Daft, R. L. and Lengel, R. H. (1986), 'Organizational information requirements, media richness and structural design', *Management Science*, 32: 5, pp. 554–71.

Daugherty, T., Li, H. and Biocca. F. (2008), 'Consumer learning and the effects of virtual experience relative to indirect and direct product experience', *Psychology and Marketing*, 25: 7, pp. 568–86.

Duck, S. (1994), *Meaningful Relationships*, London: Sage.

Friedmann, J. (1997), 'Design for change: Flexible planning strategies for the 1990s and beyond', *Journal of Urban Design*, 2: 3, pp. 277–95.

—— —— (2011), *Insurgencies: Essays in Planning Theory*, London and New York: Routledge and The Royal Town Planning Institute.

Greenleaf, R. K. (1977), *Servant Leadership: A Journey into the Nature of Legitimate Power and Greatness*, New York: Paulist Press.

Hammond, J. S., Keeney, R. L. and Raiffa, H. (2006), 'The hidden traps in decision making', *Harvard Business Review*, 76: 5, pp. 47–48.

Hodgson, A. (2011), *Ready for Anything*, Axminster: Triarchy Press.

Huxtable, A. L. (1984), *The Tall Building Artistically Reconsidered: The Search for a Skyscraper Style*, New York: Pantheon.

Jacobs, Jane (1961), *The Death and Life of Great American Cities*, 2nd ed., London: Penguin.

—— —— (1970), *The Economy of Cities*, New York: Vintage.

Jacob, S. (2011), 'Beyond the flatline', *Architectural Design*, 81: 5, pp. 24–31.

Jaina, J. and Tyson, S. (2004), 'Psychological similarity in work-based relationships and the development of self-efficiency beliefs', *Human Relations*, 57, pp. 275–96.

Jencks, C. (1981), *The Language of Postmodern Architecture*, 3rd ed., London: Academy Editions.

Knowles, R. N. (2002), *The Leadership Dance: Pathways to Extraordinary Organisational Effectiveness*, Niagara Falls, NY: The Centre for Self-Organizing Leadership.

Koprowski, E. (1983), 'Cultural myths: Clues to effective management', *Organizational Dynamics*, 26, pp. 39–51.

Laing, R., Davies, A.-M., Miller, D., Conniff, A., Scott, S. and Morrice, J. (2009), 'The application of visual environmental economics in the study of public preference and urban greenspace', *Environment and Planning B: Planning and Design*, 36, pp. 355–75.

van der Land, S., Schouten, A. P., Feldberg, F., van den Hoof, B. and Huysman, M. (2013), 'Lost in space? Cognitive fit and cognitive load in 3D virtual environments', *Computers in Human Behavior*, 29, pp. 1054–064.

Lane, D., Maxfield, R., Read, D. and van der Leeuw, S. (2009), 'From population to organization thinking', in D. Lane, D. Pumain, S. E. van der Leeuw and G. West (eds), *Complexity Perspectives in Innovation and Social Change*, Netherlands: Springer, 7, pp. 11–42.

van Leeuwen, T. (1992), *The Skyward Trend of Thought*, Cambridge, MA: MIT Press.

Leon, M., Laing, R., Malins, J. and Salman, H. (2014), 'Development and testing of a design protocol for computer mediated multidisciplinary collaboration during the concept stages with application to the built environment', *Procedia Environmental Sciences*, 22, pp. 108–19.

Loorbach, D., (2007), *Transition Management – New Mode of Governance for Sustainable Development*, Utrecht: International Books.

Markus, T. (1993), *Buildings and Power*, London: Routledge.

Marshall, S. (2009), *Cities Design and Evolution*, London and New York: Routledge.

————— (2012), 'Planning, design and the complexity of cities', in J. Portugali, H. Meyer, E. Stolk and E. Tan (eds), *Complexity Theories of Cities Have Come of Age*, London and New York: Springer.

Mikellides, B. (ed.) (1980), *Architecture for People. Explorations in a New Humane Environment*, London: Studio Vista.

Miller, J. G. (1978), *Living Systems*, New York: McGraw-Hill.

Morgan, G. (1997), *Images of Organisations*, London: Sage.

Morse, G. (2006), 'Decisions and desire', *Harvard Business Review*, 84, pp. 42–51.

Ostrom, E., (1990), *Governing the Commons: The Evolution of Institutions for Collective Action*, Cambridge: Cambridge University Press.

Panerai, P., Depaule, J. C., Castex, J. and Samuels, I. (2004), *Urban Forms: The Death and Life of the Urban Block*, Oxford: Architectural Press.

Polzer, J. T. and Kwan, L. B. (2012), 'When identities, interests, and information collide: How subgroups create hidden profiles in teams', in M. Neale and E. Mannix (eds), *Looking Back, Moving Forward: A Review of Group and Team-Based Research: Research on Managing Groups and Teams*, Bingley: Emerald Group Publishing, pp. 359–81.

Ponty, M. M. (1962), *Phenomenology of Perception*, London and New York: Routledge and Kegan Paul.

Portugali, J. (1997), 'Self-organizing cities', *Futures*, 29, pp. 353–80.

————— (2000), *Self-Organization and the City*, Berlin: Springer-Verlag.

—— —— (2012), 'Complexity theories of cities: Implications to urban planning', in J. Portugali, H. Meyer, E. Stolk and E. Tan (eds), *Complexity Theories of Cities Have Come to Age*, London and New York: Springer, pp. 221–44.

Rapoport, A. (1977), *Human Aspects of Urban Form*, Oxford: Pergamon Press.

de Roo, G. and Rauws, W. (2012), 'Positioning planning in the word of order, chaos and complexity: Perspectives, behaviour and interventions in a non-linear environment', in J. Portugali, H. Meyer, E. Stolk and E. Tan (eds), *Complexity Theories of Cities Have Come to Age*, London and New York: Springer, pp. 207–29.

Sampson, H. (2004), 'Navigating the waves: The usefulness of a pilot in qualitative research', *Qualitative Research*, 4: 3, pp. 383–402.

Sassen, S. (1999), *Guests and Aliens*, New York: New Press.

Sheard, A. G. and Kakabadse, A .P. (2007), 'A role-based perspective on leadership decision taking', *Journal of Management Development*, 26: 6, pp. 520–622.

Stedman, J. P. (2006), 'Why are most buildings rectangular?', *Architectural Research Quarterly*, 10: 2, pp. 119–30.

Stephens, S. (2000), 'The difficulty of beauty (aesthetics in architecture)', *Architectural Record*, 11, pp. 95–99.

Suh, K. S. and Lee, Y. E. (2005), 'Effects of virtual reality on consumer learning: An empirical investigation', *MIS Quarterly*, 29: 4, pp. 673–97.

Venturi, R. (1966), *Complexity and Contradiction in Architecture*, New York: Museum of Modern Art.

Verganti, R. (2009), *Design-driven Innovation*, Boston: Harvard Business Press.

Wilson, D. S. (2011), *The Neighbourhood Project*, New York, Boston and London: Little, Brown.

Chapter 12

Innovative urban mobility shaped by users through pervasive
information and communication technologies

Marco Zilvetti, Matteo Conti and Fausto Brevi

Introduction

Developed countries have been experiencing profound changes as networked digital technologies (The Chartered Institute for IT (BCS) 2013; Meikle & Young 2012) have become increasingly prominent in the urban context, supporting innovations in the field of applied sciences and in sociocultural dynamics (Potts et al. 2008). Responsive data and communication spaces are primary factors in creating feedback loops with citizens, local administrations and the environment. Information and communication technologies, as forms of digital media interacting with one another (UNESCO 2002), have become pivotal in this 'age of networked intelligence' (Tapscott 1997). Subsequently, the metropolitan space is gaining growing relevance as a testing ground for the development of innovative solutions, leading to enhanced connectivity opportunities and improved living standards.

In the mid-Nineties, the growth of the Internet led researchers to talk about the 'death of distance', predicting the demise of cities in the foreseeable future as 'leftover baggage of the industrial era' (Gilder 1995, cited in Ratti & Nabian 2010: 383). Despite such forecasts, urban areas have been exploding: since 2008 more than 50 per cent of the world's inhabitants (3.3 billion people) have come to live in cities and this percentage is expected to reach 66 per cent (almost 5 billion people) by 2050 (United Nations 2014). Due to the repercussions of such a rapid growth and increasing motorization, it is therefore advisable to consider traffic issues in the metropolitan environment, where new countermeasures are required to alleviate traffic jams, commuting time and pollution, not to mention the stress and frustration of travellers.

Cities are redefining themselves in the modern age as stages for innovation and user participation. This chapter focuses on the topic of urban mobility and its relationship with the digital world. Due to the amount of intertwined aspects involved, it is necessary to highlight the actual trends and their possible evolution in light of multiple factors, such as physical context, users, new technologies and other transport needs. Presented here are some key reflections that suggest possible directions for addressing tomorrow's urban mobility needs. The intention is to introduce a transdisciplinary overview of current trends and related consequences in the field of urban personal mobility. This will allow this aspect of urban life to be redefined, facilitating the implementation of future intelligent vehicles and transport systems for improved travel conditions in the city.

The responsive city

In the contemporary metropolitan panorama, the phenomenon of the 'smart city' is gaining momentum in so many different fields that it may be losing its meaning (Hemment & Townsend 2013). According to this characterization, the built environment can be viewed as a sort of 'open-air computer', in which physical and digital worlds are intertwined in a complex multi-layered system (Resch et al. 2008).

Cities today represent the ideal environment in which to collect an unprecedented amount of knowledge (i.e. big data), which can be manipulated and potentially turned into solutions that improve quality of life. It follows that technologies become ubiquitous in the built environment: bus stops, CCTV cameras, sensors, information panels, street signs and other urban accessories are now routinely connected to the Web. Urban furniture is now able to 'understand' and even react to the surrounding world by flexibly adjusting according to real-time data (weather, traffic and street conditions, etc.) so that they more efficiently optimize road network use. These features increasingly turn daily urban life and user experience into a set of 'data-clouds of 21st century urban space' (Shepard 2009).

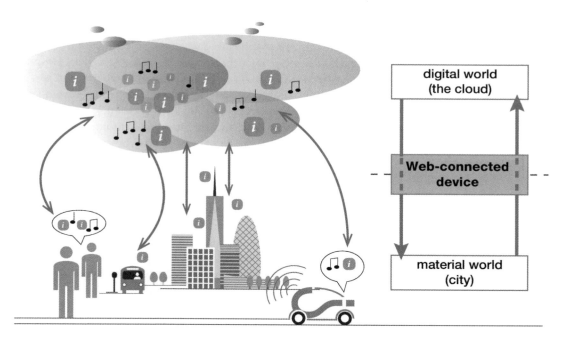

Figure 1. Smart city connections.

The increasing presence of pervasive mobile equipment connected to the Web (e.g. notebooks, smartphones, phablets, tablets and wearable gear) strengthens urban sensing capabilities and gives birth to what Mark Shepard (2011a) describes as 'sentient cities'. This term foregrounds the subjective aspects of the urban capability to feel or perceive data, without necessarily involving the faculty of self-awareness. In these responsive spaces, data-analysis capabilities are embedded throughout urban infrastructures: 'as computing leaves the desktop and spills out onto the sidewalks, streets and public spaces of the city, information processing becomes embedded in and distributed throughout the material fabric of everyday urban space' (Shepard 2009).

According to this framework, the smart environment becomes akin to a responsive body, where it is possible to connect new infrastructural elements or improve existing ones (such as streetlights, platforms, screens, energy distribution systems, etc.) by applying the latest information and communication technologies. The system promises to provide tangible benefits for urban planning, interactions between citizens and spaces, and many other aspects of everyday urban life.

Connected people and collective intelligence

An ongoing sociocultural evolution with origins in the capillary diffusion of the Internet is influencing our communication and collaboration patterns (Jenkins 2006; Levy 1999). From this point of view, the importance of networked connections and relationships must be emphasized and understood according to class, gender, age, ethnicity and other social parameters (Elliott & Urry 2010). The tendency to work together within systems and technological communities results in the evolution of collective intelligence (CI) as an organizing schema to leverage the productive role of group collaborations. Today's technological advancements enable collaborative actions to support a powerful and effective bottom-up approach towards innovative ways of working.

The widespread availability of affordable mobile devices that enable continuous online connection supports a participatory role in the value-generation process (Resch, Britter & Ratti 2012). This phenomenon becomes manifest in context-aware apps, which are designed to create interactive user communities. Some of these encourage the reporting, viewing or discussing of local problems, as in the case of FixMyStreet (MySociety 2015a) and Streetbump (New Urban Mechanics 2015); others, such as Impossible Living (Sesta & Galvani 2013), indicate abandoned places to be brought back to life. Other platforms, such as Foodspotting (2015), may simply suggest the best places for a meal based on dish offerings and location.

In this contemporary scenario, concepts like radical decentralization, crowdsourcing, 'the wisdom of crowds' and peer production represent just some of the available networked models. Pervasive technologies foster efficient tools to involve people in the design process, as well as to analyse feedback and data. Through a comparison of actual design

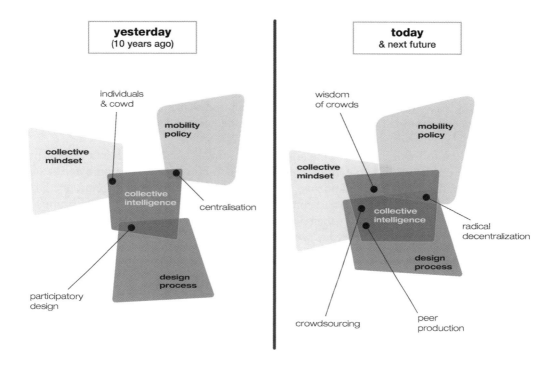

Figure 2. Changes in the networked models.

practices and processes used a decade ago, it is possible to understand how people 'gained relevance' by interacting through social networks, communities, online interactions and collaborative groups.

What emerges is the role of the collective mindset as a meaningful tool, capable of resolving problems at the system level, and of fostering innovation and the development of useful social interactions. In this new operating model, issues that are inherent in the 'bigger picture' are part of the overall system, rather than being single elements or isolated factors (Maher, Paulini & Murty 2010; Midgley et al. 2013). Continuous integration (CI) – the practice of merging all working copies of data based projects to a shared location continuously – is now commonplace. The most inventive outputs may result from a social process involving many individuals (Amabile 1996; Fischer 2004), as collaborative communities support effective improvements to products and services whilst enhancing design practice through collective creativity.

Collective mobility

Cities are no longer just geographical entities: they have become vibrant knowledge network hubs, rich in high-potential connections and cooperating people (Resch, Britter & Ratti 2012), where the urban experience is increasingly mediated through mobile, digital and networked technologies. Individuals now have a different approach to the spaces they traverse in their technologized urban experience, which has consequences for their mental processes. Areas affected include space and mobility perception, interconnecting internal and external factors through diverse social and technological networks (Turcotte & Ball 2013). People can usefully share their unique experiences and data points to provide feedback, potentially leading to more immediate interventions.

In the field of transport, pervasive technologies may prompt initiatives capable of transforming urban mobility in a smart manner that also promotes more sustainable behaviours. Many apps confirm this trend toward the creation of collaborative commuter and traveller communities: FixMyTransport (MySociety 2015b) was created in 2011 and worked until 2015 to report transport issues; Waze (2015) is an efficient navigator with users providing real-time feedback about traffic problems; and iCoyote is a well-known tool for reporting speed cameras.

Even if it is too early to define the future outcomes of current urban trends, it is clear that they will lead to great changes in the way urban vehicles are designed, perceived and used. Automobiles are usually regarded as highly complex, standardized products that provide a solution to the individual need to move comfortably and quickly (traffic permitting). As Urry (2007: 115) states, 'cars are the quintessential produced by the leading industrial sectors and iconic firms within twentieth-century capitalism'. It follows that vehicles are already adapting to changing user lifestyles so as to better assist occupant needs and desires, with the addition of infotainment systems, screens and mobile connectivity. Dashboard design, seating configurations, lighting and the creation of different ambience environments are some of the key aspects which will be required by social trends and user behaviour (as opposed to style).

Limited series and local production

Local peculiarities, traditions and socio-economic backgrounds also play a crucial role in defining local needs, desires and user behaviour. Many recent studies (Fagone 2012; Shaheen & Chirstensen 2015) – from both academics and car manufacturers – highlight the importance of conceiving innovative mobility solutions, relying on IT networks capable of gathering together the best aspects of different means of transport. New designs need to provide effective and flexible answers to commuters who are willing to optimize their urban transfers.

In today's market, it is possible to satisfy a specific niche of customers requiring premium and unique products. As an example, the NIKEiD project, initially launched in 2012, allows Nike customers to customise their online clothing purchases (Nike 2015). Buyers therefore become co-designers, as they personalize the materials and finishes of the selected item. In the car design field, Pagani Automobili (2013) and Mansory Cars (2015) both showcase the finest attention to detail in a traditional sense, whilst simultaneously sporting cutting edge technologies that invite consumer interaction.

As different approaches to design are applied to carefully balance customization and limited editions with industrial production, these products have proved to satisfy consumer desires while enhancing local and flexible production. When applied to car design, this kind of practice may also lead to the production of customized vehicles and solutions for specific urban areas, where a large number of users require personal mobility with some identity and value attached to it. Social agents (including small start-ups and well-framed enterprises) can cooperate as incubators of innovative ideas to build more resilient communities (Greenfield & Shepard 2007). More than ever, car manufacturers rely on the social capital of people interacting and exchanging data on the Web for innovative projects and prototypes. The Fiat Mio project, started in 2009, represents an interesting case study of a 'crowdsourced' car. This futuristic concept car was based on the ideas of thousands of people from around the world: more than 17,000 participants submitted over 11,000 ideas, which Fiat studied and interpreted, creating a detailed design brief to build the Fiat Mio Concept Car (Solon 2010).

Today, some new manufacturers are focusing their efforts on open-source hardware, allowing customers to build their own customized car, as OSVehicle (2013) does with its flexible 'Tabby Evo' chassis. Another low-volume car-maker, Local Motors (LM), is planning to produce a new 3D printed car, and defines itself as 'a free online and physical workspace where creativity, collaboration and design drive vehicle innovations' (Local Motors 2015) as it concentrates on collaborative networks. In this instance, a micro-factory used by LM and its partners is the only physical workspace to design, build and sell vehicles. These examples indicate effective ways to use Web-based technologies, social networks and bottom-up approaches to foster innovation in the context of so-called 'networked individualism' (Wellman 2002). It is therefore possible to reconsider how to actually conceive innovative automobiles, paving the way for more sustainable motoring through user trends, technical know-how, platforms and component-sharing. People can therefore openly collaborate through co-creation to design, build and improve vehicles, customizing them according to specific local needs, as well as to enhance processes and services (IBM Institute for Business Value 2009).

Moving in the responsive urban environment

The starting point to conceive efficient mobility solutions shall be the same: focusing on how to satisfy people, ease their life and improve existing mobility options. In this process, we need to account for more than the relationship between commuting and the traveller's material needs. There is also a wide range of ancillary aspects to consider related to age, sex, ethnicity, self-reported health, relationship status and economic activity. City users move in different ways and patterns according to their everyday needs and personal desires. The experience of commuting affects our sense of personal well-being and may (or may not) justify the traveller's burden during daily commutes. To gather further key user insights, the usual time spent commuting and the mode of transport should be compared to the individual sense of compensation deriving from higher earnings, better career or improved housing conditions (Office for National Statistics 2014). A clever and well-structured use of big data is necessary to unravel much more than simple travelling patterns to create improved mobility in the smart city of the foreseeable future.

A step in the right direction is evident from a consideration of the 2011 IBM Survey. Stockholm obtained the best result in this survey by reducing the sense of frustration related to daily commutes. It instituted a congestion charging system with real-time feedback capable of reducing the time for an ordinary morning commute by an average of 50 per cent (IBM Institute for Business Value 2011). Just a month after its implementation, positive feedback from travellers was reported, making it an exemplar of how new services with real-time assistance can enhance the journey experience.

Towards sustainable transport solutions

Many large cities still experience higher levels of traffic congestion and air pollution, causing added stress for city dwellers. For this reason, there is still much to do in order to tackle those issues, notwithstanding the positive trends towards urban contexts in which 'everything talks'. Capitalism and consumerism often shape people's ideas about prosperity and well-being in terms of both growth and ownership of material goods. As Rifkin (2011) suggests, life in a world of limited natural resources cannot realistically sustain continuous growth. It is crucial to harmonize individual access to material goods with the collective need for a sustainable way of living. This sociological concept is based on a very delicate balance between public acceptance of the theoretical model and its resistance to any practical implementation. As Tim Jackson (2009: 33) points out, 'prosperity means nothing today if it undermines the conditions on which prosperity tomorrow depends. And the single biggest message from the financial meltdown of 2008 is that tomorrow is already here'.

As the right to mobility is a social need, public authorities have a mandatory obligation to grant it (Ramazzotti & Lois 2010). For this reason, policy-makers are called upon to improve the current urban transport system, facing several open issues and requests from the population. As key rings in the mobility chain, local administrators not only plan, control and award transport service, they also link demand (from citizens and policy-makers) with transport tenders (from operators). They also create strategic synergies resulting from the implementation of ICT-like Web platforms, which are run by municipalities themselves (Ramazzotti & Lois 2010). As a result, much of the data gathered about transport, housing, use of space, pollution and other aspects of everyday life is held by government administrations to enhance service quality (Hemment & Townsend 2013).

In a world of finite resources, it is necessary to conceive clever solutions capable of providing optimized products. For this reason, designing high-efficiency vehicles becomes mandatory in order to optimize materials, costs and features to specific contexts and purposes. EU, American and Asian vehicle directives are pushing makers towards designing and manufacturing more sustainable vehicles. Without political support and steady leadership, however, such initiatives are often difficult to achieve, as R&D spending is significant and regarded as a discriminating factor (Rifkin 2011).

The next generation of urban (shared) vehicles

Future scenarios may be the result of intertwined factors such as sustainability, resource exploitation, growing population and pervasive ICT. Even if the car industry has recently gone through tough times, there is a noticeable upswing in both the production of minimalistic cars meant for intermodal commutes and range-extended electric vehicles (Fagone 2012). Shared vehicles may represent the beginnings of a more resilient economy capable of reducing ownership and consumption of goods, ensuring at the same time the right to individual flexible mobility. This vehicle genre may in fact provide better sustainable alternatives for the so-called 'last mile mobility' of daily intermodal commutes. It will soon be possible to consider a suite of options – including personal mobility devices and micro-electric vehicles – to bridge the existing gap between public and private transport modes, so that the overall system becomes more sustainable and flexible.

In this regard, a growing number of urban mobility experts (Melia 2015; Singh 2012) suggest future scenarios in which private car ownership will be pointless, replaced by Web-enabled car club services and other shared solutions. Some municipalities actively support this trend. In Milan, for instance, local administrators have been fostering the introduction of car clubs since 2012, and today free-floating car sharing is growing far beyond expectations (Dell'Amico 2014). It is expected that future urban areas will feature an even wider range of alternatives that make conventional transport either outmoded or less cost-effective. Within this context, Helsinki is working on an ambitious 'mobility on demand' plan, which integrates all forms of sharing and public transport into a single network that aims to make car ownership pointless by 2025 (Greenfield 2014).

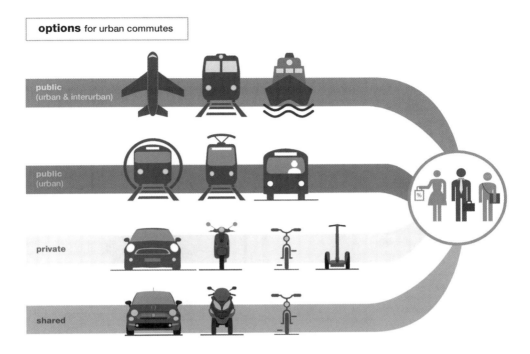

Figure 3. Available alternatives to movement in urban spaces.

The importance of shared information

Cities provide the environment in which the majority of the global population lives and spends most of its time. For this reason, we should first analyse urban behaviours, habits and trends to envision innovative solutions aimed at improving our mobility and transport systems. Metropolitan administrations around the world often struggle to find ways to reduce pollution and traffic. The general conclusion seems to rely on the reduction in the number of cars permitted into a city. Terms like 'multimodal' and 'interconnectivity' have become keywords for urban planners hoping to develop effective solutions for the coming decades. Considering that a car is parked for 96 per cent of its life (Moss 2015), more efficient mobility solutions are obviously required. In this sense, the Carplus 2014 Annual Survey (Steer Davies Gleave 2014) pointed out some positive aspects of car clubs. Whereas the average car in London carries 1.47 people, a shared vehicle serves an average 2.28. The same study also highlighted that almost 13,000 vehicles (corresponding to 5.8 cars for each private one) have been removed from the London's streets as a result of car club members who had sold their cars.

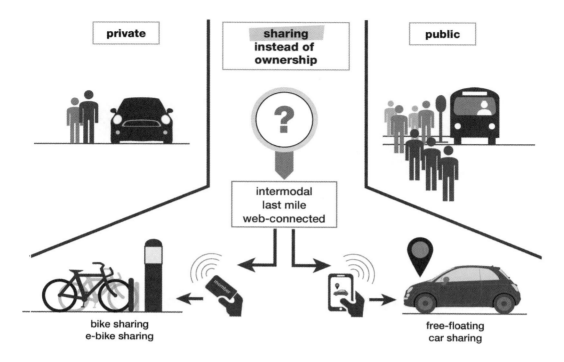

Figure 4. Intermodal 'last mile' transport solutions for a smart city.

Other studies suggest that Web-based technologies should be used to support the way people move and interact with the urban context, making it possible to reinterpret traditional topics of online discussions from a fresh perspective to improve commuters' and citizens' daily conditions. As the politician responsible for sustainable transport in Lyon, Gilles Vesco, has stated, information represents a crucial factor in mobility. In the future, data processing and sharing will account for 50 per cent of transport services, and will allow a better understanding of user points of view (Jambaud 2012). In this regard, it is important to acknowledge the key role of the so-called 'last mile mobility' built on Web-connected mobile products and services suitable for intermodal day-to-day commutes around the city.

Envisioning a future of connected self-driving cars

In urban spaces where embedded technologies become increasingly common, real-time connections and data gathering have assumed growing importance. In other words, 'connected cars will be the ultimate Internet of Things. They will collect and make sense of massive amounts of data from a huge array of sources' (Wollschlaeger, cited in Lawson, McPhail & Lawton 2015: 13). Designers and urban planners often envision future cities in which cars talk to each other, to sensors and to smart street signs. Next-generation vehicles will alert drivers about potential collisions, act as personal assistants, automatically plan the destination route – updating it in real-time by gathering information from the Web – and eventually drive without human intervention.

The impact of smart and driverless technologies on vehicles and services is very significant, as they are conceived to simplify journeys, increase safety and optimize travelling times. This ground-breaking scenario is premised on cloud technologies that make it possible to run apps, networks and real-time connections between individuals and surrounding spaces. Therefore, so-called 'network capital' will become a fundamental aspect of contemporary social processes. Based on communication and information exchange, this will better connect places and people at a distance (Elliott & Urry 2010).

In 2003, the Defense Advanced Research Projects Agency (DARPA) launched the Grand Challenge (Thrun et al. 2006), aimed at spurring innovation in unmanned ground vehicle navigation. Since Stanford University's robot 'Stanley' first won the competition, many efforts have been made in order to advance state-of-the-art autonomous driving. Several ongoing research projects are pushing the technical boundaries to design fully self-driving cars of the future (Buehler, Iagnemma & Singh 2009). Many of them involve stakeholders in the field of ICT, whose presence in the car design field would have been unexpected until few years ago. Driverless cars are expected to reach the market in the foreseeable future, even if it is currently difficult to establish a clear timeline.

Part of this scenario is already reality. After an initial stage of testing using traditional Lexus SUVs and Toyota Priuses with added robotic driving technologies, Google unveiled its first truly driverless electric car prototype in 2014. A second model was presented in 2015, built to test the next stage of its research about self-driving technologies on the streets near the company's Silicon Valley headquarters (Google 2015). This new model is designed to work without a steering wheel or brake pedal, and can ferry two people around without any real-user interaction. According to reports and related articles (Gibbs 2014), there are only two controls in the car interior: the start button and emergency stop button. Pick-up locations and destinations are set through smartphones, while a small screen in front of the passenger displays information about the journey. The same screen even reminds the passenger to take their personal belongings once the journey is completed, suggesting that this car is meant to be more of a replacement for a cab than simply a shared car without a human driver.

Conclusion

Since more than the half of the global population lives in cities, one of the biggest challenges for the coming years is to enhance urban living standards. Politicians have a key role to play in the field of public and private transport. Strictly speaking, it is necessary to develop a resilient society, one in which we can find a balance between individual desires of fulfilment and the collective need for prosperity. This concept is impossible to achieve at our current rate of consumption without new solutions (Jackson 2009).

Mobility represents an open and systemic issue, which requires strong and prolonged cooperation between major private stakeholders, local governments, municipalities and vehicle manufacturers. Pervasive technologies, self-drive capabilities and sharing will constitute the three main pillars upon which to conceive new mobility schemes and infrastructures. Considering the increasing number of people living and moving in urban areas, it is imperative to conceive a suite of efficient, cost-effective and environmentally-conscious solutions to personal and mass mobility. Future urban cars will need to be designed to balance individual needs, desires and expectations on the one hand, and collective needs for efficiency, sustainability and optimization on the other.

The future of mobility seems to be increasingly about converging media; to this end, cars can be seen as a part of a larger ecosystem in which products are connected online (Freudenberg 2015). In this regard, vehicles will probably act as personal assistants, mirroring a user's digital life and eventually becoming an accessory to the smartphone (Moss 2015). The resulting vehicles will be connected, collectively-designed, shareable, intermodal and potentially self-driving. These aspects will enable the conception of a wide range of vehicles ready for the streets of our future smart cities, which should embody real progress for society and its people in tangible terms.

References

Amabile, T. (1996), *Creativity in Context: Update to the Social Psychology of Creativity*, Boulder, CO: Westview Press.

American Society of Mechanical Engineers (ASME) (2015), '3D printing blooms in biomedical', https://www.asme.org/engineering-topics/articles/bioengineering/3d-printing-blooms-in-biomedical. Accessed 14 September 2015.

Anon (2014), 'Car2Go, Crescita Infinita: Dove i Comuni Falliscono, Mercedes Trionfa', *Repubblica Motori*, 29 October, http://www.repubblica.it/motori/sezioni/attualita/2014/10/29/news/cresce_la_flotta_car2go-99173066/. Accessed 6 June 2015.

Argante, E. (2010), *L'Auto Che Sarà: Il Futuro della Mobilità*, Milan: Egea.

Autolib' (2015), 'Autolib' Paris', https://www.autolib.eu/fr/. Accessed 6 June 2015.

Buehler, M., Iagnemma, K. and Singh, S. (eds) (2009), *The DARPA Urban Challenge: Autonomous Vehicles in City Traffic, Springer Tracts in Advanced Robotics (STAR) Series*, Berlin: Springer-Verlang Berlin Heidelberg.

Büscher, M., Coulton, P., Efstratiou, C., Gellersen, H., Hemment, D., Mehmood, R. and Sangiorgi, D. (2009), 'Intelligent mobility systems: Some socio-technical challenges and opportunities', in R. Mehmood, R. Cerqueira, R. Piesiewicz and I. Chlamtac (eds) (2009), *Communications Infrastructure: Systems and Applications in Europe. Lecture Notes of the Institute for Computer Sciences, Social Informatics and Telecommunications Engineering*, New York: Springer, pp. 140–52.

Car2Go (2015a), 'Car2Go. Buongiorno Milano', www.car2go.com. Accessed 6 June 2015.

—— —— (2015b), 'Withdrawal from UK market', https://www.car2go.com/en/london/. Accessed 6 June 2015.

Chartered Institute for IT (BCS) (2013), 'The societal impact of the Internet of Things', http://www.bcs.org/upload/pdf/societal-impact-report-feb13.pdf. Accessed 20 September 2015.

Dell'Amico, M. (2014), 'Car sharing a Milano: Quale scegliere e perché', *Wired Italia*, 9 January, http://www.wired.it/lifestyle/mobilita/2014/01/09/car-sharing-milano-quale-scegliere/. Accessed 6 June 2015.

Egloff, E. (2013), 'Renault s'associe à Bolloré dans l'électrique', *Le Figaro*, 12 September, http://www.lefigaro.fr/societes/2013/09/12/20005-20130912ARTFIG00623-renault-s-associe-a-bollore-dans-l-electrique.php. Accessed 1 June 2015.

Elliott, A. and Urry, J. (2010), *Mobile Lives*, Abingdon: Routledge.

Enjoy (2015), 'Home page', http://enjoy.eni.com/. Accessed 5 June 2015.

Fagone, E. L. (2012), *Car Design: Genesi ed Evoluzione del Design Automobilistico*, Bologna: Editrice Compositori.

Fischer, G. (2004), 'Social creativity: Turning barriers into opportunities for collaborative design', *Proceedings of the Eighth Conference on Participatory Design (PDC 2004)*, Toronto, Canada, 27–31 July, ACM: New York, pp. 152–161, http://l3d.cs.colorado.edu/~gerhard/papers/pd04-final-submit.pdf. Accessed 14 September 2015.

Foodspotting (2015), 'Find dishes', http://www.foodspotting.com/find/in/The-World. Accessed 16 September 2015.

Freudenberg, M. (2015), 'Going mobile: Trends to watch', https://designmind.frogdesign.com/contributors/mark-freudenberg/. Accessed 20 September 2015.

Friends of Earth (2009), 'Overconsumption? Our use of the world's natural resources', http://www.foe.co.uk/sites/default/files/downloads/overconsumption.pdf. Accessed 7 September 2015.

Gerla, M. and Kleinrock, L. (2011), *Vehicular Networks and the Future of the Mobile Internet*, Los Angeles: Computer Science Dept. UCLA, http://nets.cs.ucla.edu/publication/download/702/Vehicular_networks_and_the_future_of_the_mobile_internet_10-jnl_.pdf. Accessed 2 June 2015.

Gibbs, S. (2014), 'Google's self-driving car: How does it work and when can we drive one?', *The Guardian*, 29 May, http://www.theguardian.com/technology/2014/may/28/google-self-driving-car-how-does-it-work. Accessed 14 September 2014.

Google (2015), 'Google self-driving car project', http://www.google.com/selfdrivingcar/. Accessed 15 September 2015.

Gordon, E. and de Souza e Silva, A. (2011), *Net Locality: Why Location Matters in a Networked World*, Chichester: Wiley-Blackwell.

Greenfield, A. (2006), *Everyware: The Dawning Age of Ubiquitous Computing*, San Francisco: New Riders – Peachpit Press.

—— —— (2014), 'Helsinki's ambitious plan to make car ownership pointless in 10 years', *The Guardian*, 10 July, http://www.theguardian.com/cities/2014/jul/10/helsinki-shared-public-transport-plan-car-ownership-pointless. Accessed 5 June 2015.

Greenfield, A. and Shepard, M. (2007), *Ubiquitous Computing and its Discontents*, San Francisco: New Riders – Peachpit Press.

Grupe Renault (2014), 'Renault and Bolloré form a partnership in electric vehicles', http://media.renault.com/global/en-gb/renaultgroup/Media/PressRelease.aspx?mediaid=61455. Accessed 2 June 2015.

Helen Hamlyn Centre for Design (HHCD) (2010), 'Redesigning the ambulance: Improving mobile emergency healthcare', http://www.rca.ac.uk/research-innovation/helen-hamlyn-centre/research-projects/2010-projects/redesigning-ambulance/. Accessed 15 September 2015.

Hemment, D. and Townsend, A. (eds) (2013), *Smart Citizens*, Manchester: Future Everything, http://futureeverything.org/wp-content/uploads/2014/03/smartcitizens1.pdf. Accessed 5 June 2015.

IBM Institute for Business Value (2009), *Collective Intelligence – Capitalizing on the Crowd*, Somers, NY: IBM, http://www-935.ibm.com/services/us/gbs/thoughtleadership/ibv-collective-intelligence.html. Accessed 31 May 2015.

—— —— (2011), *Frustration Rising: IBM 2011 Commuter Pain Survey*, Somers, NY: IBM, http://www-03.ibm.com/press/us/en/pressrelease/35359.wss. Accessed 31 May 2015.

Jackson, T. (2009), *Prosperity without Growth: Economics for a Finite Planet*, Abingdon: Earthscan-Routledge.

Jambaud, A. C. (2012), 'Entretien avec Gilles Vesco', http://www.millenaire3.com/fileadmin/user_upload/Interviews/G.Vesco-mobilite-2012_03.pdf. Accessed 28 May 2015.

Jenkins, H. (2006), *Convergence Culture: Where Old and New Media Collide*, New York: New York University Press.

—— —— (2009), *Confronting the Challenges of Participatory Culture: Media Education for the 21st Century*, Boston: MIT Press.

Lawson, P., McPhail, B. and Lawton, P. (2015), *The Connected Car: Who is in the Driver's Seat? A Study on Privacy and Onboard Vehicle Telematics Technology*, Vancouver:

British Columbia Freedom of Information and Privacy Association, https://fipa. bc.ca/wordpress/wp-content/uploads/2015/03/CC_report_lite.pdf. Accessed 20 September 2015.

Levy, P. (1999), *Collective Intelligence: Mankind's Emerging World in Cyberspace*, New York: Perseus Books.

Local Motors (2015), 'Project redacted – Declassified: Uncover the winning design for the next generation of 3D-printed cars', https://localmotors.com/. Accessed 20 September 2015.

Maher, M. L., Paulini, M. and Murty, P. (2010), 'Scaling up: From individual design to collaborative design to collective design', in J. S. Gero (ed.), *Design Computing and Cognition*, Berlin: Springer-Verlang Berlin Heidelberg, pp. 581–600.

Malone, T. W., Laubacher, R. and Dellarocas, C. (2009), *Harnessing Crowds: Mapping the Genome of Collective Intelligence*, Working Paper No. 2009-001, Cambridge, MA: MIT Center for Collective.

Mansory Cars (2015), 'Mansory Cars – Make your dream come true', http://www. mansorycars.com/. Accessed 15 September 2015.

Meikle, G. and Young, S. (2012), *Media Convergence: Networked Digital Media in Everyday Life*, New York: Palgrave Macmillan.

Melia, S. (2015), *Urban Transport Without the Hot Air*, Cambridge: UIT Cambridge.

Meticulous Research (2015), 'Global medical 3D printing market outlook: 2014–2020', http://www.meticulousresearch.com/research/global-medical-3d-printing-market-outlook-2014-2020/. Accessed 15 September 2015.

Midgley, G., Cavana, R. Y., Brocklesby, J., Foote, J. L., Wood, D. R. R. and Ahuriri-Driscoli, A. (2013), 'Towards a new framework for evaluating systemic problem structuring methods', *European Journal of Operational Research*, 229, pp. 143–54, http://www. sciencedirect.com/science/article/pii/S0377221713000945. Accessed 14 September 2015.

Moss, S. (2015), 'End of the car age: How cities are outgrowing the automobile', *The Guardian*, 28 April, http://www.theguardian.com/cities/2015/apr/28/end-of-the-car-age-how-cities-outgrew-the-automobile?CMP=share_btn_tw. Accessed 27 May 2015.

MySociety (2015a), 'FixMyStreet', https://www.mysociety.org/projects/fixmystreet/. Accessed 15 September 2015.

———— (2015b), 'FixMyTransport', http://www.fixmytransport.com/. Accessed 15 September 2015.

New Urban Mechanics (2015), 'Where's Street Bump being used?' http://www.streetbump. org/. Accessed 15 September 2015.

Nike (2015), 'Customise with NIKEiD', http://store.nike.com/gb/en_gb/pw/nikeid/1k9. Accessed 14 September 2015.

Office for National Statistics (2014), 'Commuting and personal well-being', http://www. ons.gov.uk/ons/dcp171766_351954.pdf. Accessed 6 June 2015.

O'Reilly, T. (2005), 'What is Web 2.0? Design patterns and business models for the next generation of software', http://www.oreilly.com/pub/a/web2/archive/what-is-web-20. html. Accessed 14 September 2015.

OSVehicle (2013), 'Say hello to Tabby Evo', https://www.osvehicle.com/osv-platform/. Accessed 31 May 2015.

Our Future Mobility Now (OFMN) (2011), 'About Our Future Mobility Now', http://www.futuremobilitynow.com/about/. Accessed 15 September 2015.

Pagani Automobili (2013), 'Il Signore delle Supercar', http://www.pagani.com/en/news/2013_1/pagani_signore_delle_supercar.aspx/. Accessed 15 September 2015.

Potts, J. D., Hartley, J., Banks, J. A., Burgess, J. E., Cobcroft, R. S., Cunningham, S. D. and Montgomery, L. (2008), 'Consumer co-creation and situated creativity', *Industry and Innovation*, 15: 5, pp. 459–74.

Ramazzotti, D. and Lois, A. (2010), 'Sustainable flexible transport services: A solution against social exclusion', http://www.sietitalia.org/siet2010/09-Ramazzotti_Lois_paper.pdf. Accessed 31 May 2015.

Ratti, C. and Nabian, N. (2010), 'Virtual space: The city to come', *Innovation: Perspectives for 21st Century*, pp. 383–97, https://www.bbvaopenmind.com/en/article/the-city-to-come/?fullscreen=true. Accessed 15 September 2015.

Resch, B., Britter, R. and Ratti, C. (2012), 'Live urbanism: Towards senseable cities and beyond', in S. Rassia and P. M. Pardalos (eds), *Sustainable Environmental Design in Architecture: Impacts on Health, Springer Optimization and its Applications*, New York: Springer, pp. 175–84.

Resch, B., Calabrese, F., Ratti, C. and Biederman, A. (2008). 'An approach towards a real-time data exchange platform system architecture', *Proceedings of the 6th Annual IEEE International Conference on Pervasive Computing and Communications*, Hong Kong, 17–21 March, New York: IEEE, pp. 153–59.

Rifkin, J. (2011), *The Third Industrial Revolution: How Lateral Power is Transforming Energy, the Economy, and the World*, New York: Palgrave Macmillan.

Riversimple (2015), 'Redesigning cars, redefining business', http://riversimple.com/. Accessed 6 June 2015.

Sesta, A. and Galvani, D. (2013), 'Impossible living', http://www.impossibleliving.com/. Accessed 20 September 2015.

Shaheen, S. and Christensen, M. (2015), 'Shared-use mobility: What does the future hold?', http://innovativemobility.org/wp-content/uploads/2015/03/Shared-Use-Workshop-Summary-v5.pdf. Accessed 10 September 2015.

Shepard, M. (2009), 'Curatorial statement', http://www.sentientcity.net/exhibit/?p=3. Accessed 31 May 2015.

—— —— (2011a), *Sentient City: Ubiquitous Computing, Architecture and the Future of Urban Space*, New York: Architectural League of New York.

—— —— (2011b), 'Near-future urban archaeology: The sentient city survival kit', http://www.onlineopen.org/download.php?id=27. Accessed 10 August 2015.

Singh, S. (2012), *New Mega Trends: Implications for our Future Lives*, New York: Palgrave Macmillan.

Solon, O. (2010), 'Fiat releases details of first-ever crowdsourced car', *Wired UK*, 18 October, http://www.wired.co.uk/news/archive/2010-08/18/fiat-mio. Accessed 20 September 2015.

Steer Davies Gleave (2014), 'Carplus Annual Survey of Car Clubs 2013/14', http://www.carplus.org.uk/wp-content/uploads/2014/04/England-and-Wales_Final-with-cover_2.pdf/. Accessed 15 September 2015.

Tapscott, D. (1997), *Digital Economy: Promise and Peril in the Age of Networked Intelligence*, New York: McGraw Hill.

Taylor, T. (1801), 'The metaphysics of Aristotle', http://warburg.sas.ac.uk/pdf/akh237b32590817.pdf. Accessed 15 September 2015.

Thrun, S., Montemerlo, M., Dahlkamp, H., Staverns, D., Aron, A., Diebel, J., Fong, P., Gale, J., Halpenny, M., Hoffmann, G., Lau, K., Oakley, C., Palatucci, M., Pratt, V., Stang, P., Strohband, S., Dupont, C., Jendrossek, L. E., Markley, C., Rummel, C., van Niekerk, J., Jensen, E., Alessandrini, P., Bradski, G., Davies, B., Ettinger, S., Kaehler, A., Nefian, A. and Mahoney, P. (2006), 'Stanley: The robot that won the DARPA Grand Challenge', *Journal of Field Robotics*, 23: 9, pp. 661–92, http://robots.stanford.edu/papers/thrun.stanley05.pdf. Accessed 15 September 2015.

Turcotte, J. F. and Ball, M. L. (2013), 'All transportation is local: Mobile–Digital–Networked–Technologies and networked orientations', *Transfers*, 3: 1, pp. 119–39, http://www.ingentaconnect.com/content/berghahn/trans/2013/00000003/00000001/art00009. Accessed 20 September 2015.

United Nations Department of Economic and Social Affairs, Population Division (2014), *World Urbanization Prospects: The 2014 Revision, Highlights (ST/ESA/SER.A/352)*, New York: United Nations.

United Nations Educational, Scientific and Cultural Organization (UNESCO) (2002), *Information and Communication Technology in Education. A Curriculum for Schools and Programme of Teacher Development*, Paris: UNESCO, http://unesdoc.unesco.org/images/0012/001295/129538e.pdf. Accessed 10 September 2015.

Urry, J. (2007), *Mobilities*, Cambridge: Polity Press.

Valtolina, G. (2015). 'Sharing, l'ultima frontiera è l'equomobile', *Corriere della Sera - Milano*, 20 May, http://www.selpress.com/unionecommercio/immagini/200515M/2015052029431.pdf. Accessed 15 September 2015.

Wallas, G. (1926), *The Art of Thought*, New York: Harcourt, Brace and Co.

Waze (2015), 'Live map', https://www.waze.com/it/livemap. Accessed 15 September 2015.

Weiser, M. (1991), 'The computer for the 21st century – Specialized elements of hardware and software connected by wires, radio waves and infrared will be so ubiquitous that no one will notice their presence', *Scientific American*, September, pp. 94–104, http://web.media.mit.edu/~anjchang/ti01/weiser-sciam91-ubicomp.pdf. Accessed 15 September 2015.

Wellman, B. (2002), 'Little boxes, glocalization and networked individualism', in M. Tanabe, P. van den Besselaar and T. Ishida (eds), *Digital Cities II. Computational and Sociological Approaches: Second Kyoto Workshop on Digital Cities*, Berlin: Springer-Verlang Berlin Heidelberg, pp. 10–25.

Zipcar UK (2015), 'Find cars', http://www.zipcar.co.uk/london/find-cars?zipfleet_id=33074050. Accessed 15 September 2015.

Chapter 13

Blurring the physical boundaries of the city: Media architecture and urban informatics for community engagement

Glenda Amayo Caldwell and Mirko Guaralda

Introduction

Architecture focuses on designing built environments in response to society's needs, reflecting culture through materials and forms. The physical boundaries of the city have become blurred through the integration of digital media, connecting the physical environment with the digital. In the recent past, the future was imagined as highly technological: Ridley Scott's *Blade Runner* (1982) is set in 2019, and introduces a world where supersized screens inject advertisements in the cluttered urban space. In 2015, screens are central to everyday life, but in a completely different way in respect to what had been imagined. Through ubiquitous computing and social media, information is abundant. Digital technologies have changed the way people relate to cities' methods of supporting discussion on multiple levels, allowing citizens to be more vocal than ever before.

As highlighted by Jennifer Gray (2014: 1), the nineteenth-century architect Dwight Perkins collaborated with social scientists and activists 'to leverage design as a vehicle for social change'. In 2014, two centuries later, architects continue to grapple with similar social dilemmas of rapid urban growth and social segregation. Similarly to Perkins' vision (Gray 2014), architects and designers of today consider how the use of ubiquitous and pervasive technologies can be used as strategies to identify and map out sociological data, also known as urban informatics. We question how architects can use the affordances of urban informatics to obtain and navigate useful social information to inform design. This chapter investigates different approaches to engage communities in the debate on cities, and specifically aims to capture citizens' opinions on the use and design of public places. Physical and digital discussions have been initiated to capture citizens' opinions on the use and design of public places. In addition to traditional consultation methods, Web 2.0 platforms, urban screens and mobile apps are used in the context of Brisbane, Australia, to explore contemporary strategies of engagement (Gray 2014).

Appropriating technology

Mitchell (1996) foresaw buildings turning into large-scale computer screens, a vision similar to the one depicted in *Blade Runner*. Current media architecture typically focuses on digital façades to display information, which provides little opportunity for integration

Figure 1. Circle on Cavill, Gold Coast, Australia. Photo Credits: Mirko Guaralda

and active engagement. Yonge-Dundas Square in Toronto, Times Square in New York City and Circle on Cavill, Gold Coast, Queensland (Figure 1), are all examples of urban areas where screens dominate the space but are not directly accessible by the public. The use of screens in built environments has the potential to engage with local users, but generally contents are controlled from the top down.

Figure 2. Condolence messages for Jack Layton, Toronto City Hall (2011) (source: Mirko Guaralda).

People are naturally driven to interact with built environments. Site observations conducted in Toronto during the aftermath of Jack Layton's death in 2011 reveals how citizens appropriated the architecture of the town hall. Figure 2 is an image of the messages of condolence and sympathy inscribed with coloured chalk on the walls of the government precinct.

This spontaneous memorial was embraced by the local administration, and allowed the community to identify themselves in a specific location through direct interaction with the space and architecture.

Architects as spatial agents

Schneider and Till (2009) suggest architects are spatial agents. As actors in the production of a building, they have to face their social responsibility, realize the consequences of what they create and its influence on the urban environment. They state that the agent is one who effects change through the empowerment of others: 'Empowerment here stands for allowing others to "take control" over their environment, for something that is participative without being opportunistic, for something that is pro-active instead of re-active' (Schneider & Till 2009: 99). The question is the capacity in which architects act as spatial agents. There is an opportunity for architects to consider the alternative ways that design can express agency for the people who live within our urban environments and not be driven by capitalism (Till 2009: 100). We propose that it is the time for architects to reconsider their future, how they need to appropriate media and technology, and for what purposes.

Architecture and HCI

Martyn Dade-Robertson (2013: 3) defines architectural user interfaces (AUIs) as the notion of the built environment acting 'as a mediator between human beings and computational information'. He draws parallels between the disciplines of human-computer interaction (HCI) and architecture. He states that just as computational technology has an effect on the design process and experiences of spaces and places within architecture, that architecture similarly has an effect on the design and development of computer technologies. Furthermore, trends toward ubiquitous and pervasive computing have shifted the focus from virtual environments back to the value of the physical environment, therefore prompting the need for architectural input in the evolution of HCI (Dade-Robertson 2013).

This view is reinforced by Fischer et al. (2013) who argue that architecture provides a form of spatial understanding that can assist in the development of urban HCI systems. Fischer et al. (2013: 39) claim that 'architectural thinking helps focus on the value that public displays could create for a city beyond information and utility'. This is particularly important considering that public spaces can be activated by ubiquitous technology, allowing city users to interact with media façades such as in the interventions 'Discussions in Space' (Schroeter, Foth & Satchell 2012) and SMSlingshot (Fischer et al. 2013).

Media and urban informatics for community consultation

Urban environments are embedded with complex building, communication, information, transportation and social networks that are communicated into tangible information revealing the digital and physical layers of cities through urban informatics (Foth

2009; Foth, Choi & Satchell 2011). Urban planners and designers rely on community consultation processes to promote equity through the collection of local perspectives informing design, planning and policy (Burgess, Foth & Klaebe 2006; Foth, Agudelo & Palleis 2013; Caldwell, Foth & Guaralda 2013). Current consultation approaches are challenged by the perception that these represent a limited part of local societies (Jenkins 2006). The ubiquitous nature of mobile media, social media and urban informatics provides opportunities for community consultation processes to evolve to include a larger portion of local stakeholders (Fredericks & Foth 2013; Houghton, Miller & Foth 2014; Caldwell et al. 2013).

The combination of unobtrusive research methods (Kellehear 1993) and participatory action research (Kindon, Pain & Kesby 2007; Tacchi, Foth & Hearn 2009; Bilandzic & Venable 2011) is used in guerrilla research tactics (GRT) to enhance social research (Caldwell et al. 2015). GRT employs creative research methods by combining unexpected physical artefacts with digital links to online surveys, polls and social media networks in participatory interventions. In this way, it acquires data typically focusing on critical social and urban issues (Caldwell et al. 2015). This chapter takes participatory interventions one step further: it asks how can architects and designers not only use them as a way to engage with the public, but also how architects listen to what the city says to inform the design and creation of interactive public places.

In collaboration with South Bank Corporation (SBC) in Brisbane, Australia, academics and students from the Queensland University of Technology (QUT) conducted urban interventions as part of a 2012 project funded by a QUT Engagement and Innovation Grant. South Bank is the cultural precinct of the city of Brisbane. It comprises the State Library, the art and science museums, a performing arts centre, a tertiary music school and the convention centre; the area also includes the South Bank parklands, hotels, retail and restaurants. South Bank is accessible by a range of public transportation (trains, buses, river boats) and is within walking distance of the central business district. It is a primary tourist attraction and a critical part of the city of Brisbane for all inhabitants. SBC and their place manager were concerned about how the local users of the area perceive it. Hence they collaborated with QUT to seek alternative methods of community consultation.

This chapter discusses how different tools were used to listen to the South Bank community. The project was undertaken in two phases: the initial phase aimed to develop innovative community engagement approaches using urban informatics and new media tools to inform place-making strategies for SBC; in the second phase, the information that was collected from South Bank users was shared with final-year architecture students at QUT, who in turn designed building proposals in response to what the community expressed for South Bank sites that are under consideration for future development. One of the architectural designs is examined to uncover how such community-generated information can influence the design process and the concept of the final building proposal. The primary goal of the project was to promote a discussion from all stakeholders around urban issues affecting the experience of the local community, and to see how different media can be used to listen and respond to local inhabitants' needs.

Methodology

The study adopted an inductive approach in which data was collected through a range of urban interventions. The interventions aimed to provoke citizens' responses to common issues related to unresolved urban spaces, as well as propositions to either modify the cityscape in substantial ways, introduce new buildings or modify the current urban structure. This investigation is based on Lefebvre's theory of perceived, conceived and lived space (Lefebvre & Nicholson-Smith 1991). In particular, the research uses digital media to capture how citizens perceive South Bank by asking them to share their vision for this suburb. Data was collected through the use of traditional research methods and urban informatics tools. These were subsequently compared to evaluate the ways in which participants are likely to share their ideas about urban environments. The objective of the study is to gain an understanding and awareness of people's desires based on their everyday experience of the built environment, as well as how to translate their desires into an interactive architectural space.

Urban interventions

As part of the QUT Masters of Urban Design course, four teams of students (A–D) conducted a series of urban interventions at South Bank between August and October 2012. This section summarizes the urban interventions and some of the key findings that each group encountered through their research process, which focused on collecting citizens' feedback regarding the improvement, activation and enrichment of South Bank.

The researchers in Team A employed an interactive mural wall as their intervention. They used a poster to depict the site that was under review – the Ernest Street rail underpass – with hand-drawn vignettes showing potential designs for this underutilized area of South Bank. The different tools that were included to support the intervention and the collection of data from the public included the project's Facebook site, a Survey Monkey questionnaire and Web platform. Each method of collecting the data asked the public to indicate which design solution (displayed via the hand-drawn vignette) they would most like to see at that site. The participants indicated they preferred the Ernest Street Garden as a design solution for this underpass. A major finding from this intervention was that 'participants were willing to participate in additional consultation if they could see their opinion was making a difference' (Team A).

The urban intervention conducted by Team B asked whether South Bank users would like to see Grey Street – the central vehicle and pedestrian corridor of the area – turned into a cultural boulevard. The researchers combined social media and YouTube to interact with participants. The urban intervention involved the projection of video, film and music clips onto the exterior of the Queensland Conservatorium building, a tertiary music school, to expose the activity that occurs within the building to the public on the street. The urban intervention assisted in attracting participants to engage with the research questions. Their data collection found that 75 per cent of the participants were in agreement with the proposition to turn Grey Street into a cultural boulevard. Through the use of social media, these researchers found that the public participants would contribute photos and images of aspects of other cities which they would like to see in South Bank.

The research purpose for Team C was to 'determine the public attitude towards physical, social, and technological connectivity of South bank to the wider Brisbane area'. In addition to paper and digital surveys, this team created their own mapping application, which allowed current South Bank visitors to draw their journey through the area. The different journeys were collected to indicate paths, destinations and places of avoidance, all of which highlighted the key areas of physical, social and technological connectivity in South Bank.

Team D focused on a range of mapping exercises to interrogate the paths, nodes, landmarks and edges of South Bank. By employing a mixed approach including paper mapping surveys, a chalk drawing by South Bank participants and a digital mapping exercise, the team were able to explore people's navigation behaviour in the area. Their results indicate three urban design recommendations for consideration by SBC. The recommendations included: redesigning railway underpasses to reinforce connections with neighbouring suburbs; redistributing minor landmarks through the area to improve pedestrian navigation; and redesigning the Grey Street and Melbourne Street node to prioritize pedestrian connection to other landmarks and pathways over vehicle dominance.

The overall findings from these urban interventions would assist SBC to reposition this area as an extension of Brisbane's central business district, located directly across the river and connected via pedestrian and vehicle bridges.

Findings

In order to examine the engagement methods and strategies employed by the teams, the urban interventions have been grouped as the first urban interventions (UI-1) and the second urban interventions (UI-2).

UI-1 adopted traditional methods of data collection from South Bank users, involving observations, interviews and questionnaires (summarized in Table 1). UI-2 combined tangible media, such as posters and a mural wall, with applied urban informatics tools, including a digital screen application, interactive projections, social media and online surveys (see Table 2). QR codes were included on the posters placed on the sites in question and on the interactive mural wall, allowing the digital sites to be accessed through mobile devices.

By comparing the UI-1 and UI-2 data in Tables 1 and 2, it becomes clear that a larger portion of people engaged with digital or Web-based data collecting devices, be that through digitally mediated tools or Web 2.0 platforms. In Table 1, the highest number of participants (337) was found to be in the observations part of the study, which is primarily dependent on the researcher and not the participants giving information. In Table 2, higher numbers of participants were accounted for in the online survey (77 participants) and the website (142 views). The method that had the highest number of participants (166) was the interactive mural wall, which displayed drawings of different design propositions for the context; this allowed participants to vote by physically placing coloured dots on the drawing they liked best. The mural wall also had QR codes linked to the Web platform, containing a survey, information and social media surrounding the project.

UI-1 and UI-2 allowed for the collection of specific data in terms of the stakeholders, in addition to more general information in regards to how people interact with the built space. This information was then elaborated upon and incorporated into the design briefs for architectural building developments on three different sites elected by SBC. The design briefs were interrogated and developed upon by QUT final-year architectural design students in 2013. Out of the 150 design proposals developed, six were selected and used as provocations during the third urban intervention (UI-3). Conducted from August to October 2013, UI-3 employed a blended approach that included traditional research methods and urban informatics tools applied in two iterations (UI-3.1 and UI-3.2). In this instance, participants were asked to evaluate alternative architectural design options

Objective	Method	Target Participants	Number of Participants	Researcher
To understand the social interaction within South bank	Interviews	Stakeholders	2	Nicholas Martoo
	Focus Group	Design Students	12	
	Observations	**City Users**	**337**	
To understand how South bank precinct is perceived and navigated by city users.	Traditional questionnaires (including mind map of the area)	City Users	16	Team D Charbel Naim Dan Tweedale Edward Heron Elly Mcgregor

Table 1. UI-1 (traditional tools).

Objective	Method	Target Participants	Number of Participants	Researcher
To understand participants' needs and desire within South Bank precinct	**Interactive mural wall – linked to online survey and website through a QR code**	**City Users**	**166**	Team A Thomas Rowland Josh Townsend Trang Phan Lichen Pan Xin Li
	Online Survey	City Users	12	
	Website	**City Users**	**142 views**	
	Online Survey and building projection	City Users	41	Team B Helen Reilly Thinlay Jurmin William Story Khamis Alzahrani
	FaceBook Page	City Users	14	
	Photo Sharing (FaceBook)	City Users	4	
	Traditional questionnaires	City Users	91	
To understand how city users relate to South bank built form	Online Survey (promoted through flyers), interactive mapping application	City Users	77	Team C Ke Ke Ned Lukies Michael Mitchell Wang Xu

Table 2. UI-2 (urban informatics tools).

for three specific sites set by SBC. Two sets of posters illustrating different scenarios were placed throughout the South Bank Precinct. Both sets had brief information about the project and links to online platforms, where more details were provided and a survey was proposed to participants (Figure 3). The aim of UI-3 was to gather feedback from local South Bank users regarding the design proposals that were depicted on the posters and through the online platforms.

Table 3 summarizes UI-3, revealing that although participants engaged with the posters and accessed the web page, often they did not take the extra step to fill out the survey. During observations, participants were seen to be discussing the posters, but they did not actively scan the QR code and access the website. Data about online platform access shows that 80 per cent of UI-3.1 participants accessed the website through the QR code, while only 55 per cent of UI-3.2 users accessed the specific web page through this path.

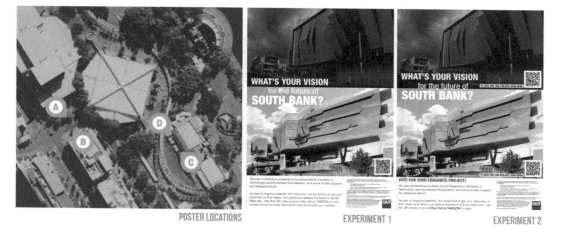

Figure 3. Poster locations and images used in UI-3.1 and UI-3.2 (source: Ruhee Moola).

Objective	Method	Target Participants	Number of Participants	Researcher
UI-3.1 To understand how people engage with stimuli in the public realm	On-site poster with QR code linked to website	City Users	100 (webpage visits during the experiment)	Ruhee Moola
	Online Survey	City Users	0	
	Site observations	City Users	60	
UI-3.2 To understand how people engage with stimuli in the public realm	On-site poster with QR code linked to online survey	City Users	63 (webpage visits during the experiment)	
	Online Survey	City Users	18	
	Site Observations	City Users	45	

Table 3. UI-3 (a blended approach).

UI-3 questioned how static displays such as posters could facilitate public consultation when used alongside online tools. The findings reveal that participants can be directed to online surveys and information platforms through the posters situated in the urban context. However, the engagement of users was dependent upon several factors, including display locations, foot traffic quantity and type, and display design (which indicated colour display preference over grey-scale). Survey responses were more positive about displays situated at particular destinations, rather than in areas of high pedestrian travel. Furthermore, the landing page of the online platform had to present both the information about the research and the actual survey.

Mediated architecture

Final-year architectural design students used the information gathered from the city users in UI-1 and UI-2 to inform the development of building prototypes in which technology could be used in a way to signify users' presence and everyday use of space.

Figure 4. Proposal for an interactive digital façade at South Bank (source: Justin Giovenco).

The students were challenged to consider the use of technology as a driver in the design of the built environment. The design developed by Justin Giovenco (Figure 4) is discussed as an example of how young designers perceive the active use of technology as a way to measure uses and presence in a public environment.

The inclusion of an interactive digital façade in Giovenco's design is suggested as a way to inform citizens, but also to provide an environment that could be easily customized by users. More than a simple screen, an interactive wall is proposed as a way to actively engage citizens; their use of space would inform the images displayed on the façades, acknowledging that a place is mainly made of people and not just of architecture.

Conclusion

The integration of media with architecture is an emergent field that affects the design of physical spaces by incorporating materials with dynamic, reactive and interactive behaviours (Brynskov, Dalsgaard & Fatah 2012). Current examples are largely limited to media façades such as those observed in Toronto and the Gold Coast (Figure 1). In the long-term, these screens seem to become part of the general urban landscape; once the novelty factor has faded, the public accepts them like a common element that clutters our cities. Our research has trialled a way to engage citizens in sharing their perception of an inner city suburb by testing different methods to provoke their interest. These experiences have then been translated in propositions for interactive architecture, wherein engagement and novelty have been supported by the introduction of digital media. The urban interventions run in Brisbane, on the other hand, show how a playful interaction with technology can allow not only data gathering to inform the design process, but also the engagement of citizens in the actual decision process concerning changes in the built form. What was evident from the interventions is that once the novelty factor fades, such interventions are less effective. UI-3 has shown how the number of respondents dropped in the second iteration, and how nearly half of the participants that engaged with the online platform have accessed the system from pathways other than the direct use of QR codes.

The interactive mural wall in UI-2, as well as the informal memorial in Toronto (Figure 2), are examples of direct interaction with a specific architecture. Playfulness and a soft transgression in the use of space have engaged the public as central actors in sharing memories and providing comments. This low-tech approach provides insight about how technology could be applied to gather information and inform the design process; however, relying on users' technology (e.g. mobile phones or tablets) captures only a portion of possible participants.

UI-3 has shown how participants viewed and discussed the posters, but that few jump directly online. Direct access to digital environments through touchscreens, tangible user interfaces and interactive interventions appear to be a more suitable solution to enhance public engagement and community consultation. The proposal by Justin Giovenco provides a possible interpretation of how this interactive playfulness through technology could be integrated in architectural design. An interactive, ever-changing wall could encapsulate the qualities observed in UI-2 and the memorial in Toronto.

Iveson (201) states that there are different experiments being conducted globally which explore the opportunity for mobile media technologies to inform urban governance:

> Many of these experiments involve establishing new channels of information from urban authorities to urban inhabitants, in the hope that city life can be made better by providing people with useful information where and when they need it [...] experiments are also underway which seek to enhance the flow of information in the other direction, from urban inhabitants to urban authorities.
>
> (Iveson 2010: 115)

The opportunity for media architecture to affect not only how information is provided to the public, but how media architecture can reinforce the communication from the public to the designers and decision-makers, is also worth considering and testing further.

References

Bilandzic, M. and Venable, J. (2011), 'Towards participatory action design research: Adapting action research and design science research methods for urban informatics', *Journal of Community Informatics*, 7: 3.

Brynskov, M., Dalsgaard, P. and Fatah, A. (2012), *Proceedings of the 4th Media Architecture Biennale Conference*, Aarhus, Denmark, 15–17 November, New York: Association for Computing Machinery.

Burgess, J. E., Foth, M. and Klaebe, H. G. (2006), 'Everyday creativity as civic engagement: A cultural citizenship view of new media' http://eprints.qut.edu.au/5056/01/5056_1. pdf. Accessed 14 September 2015.

Caldwell, G. A., Foth, M. and Guaralda, M. (2013), 'An urban informatics approach to smart city learning in architecture and urban design education', *IxD&A (Interaction Design and Architecture(s))*, 17: Summer, pp. 7–28.

Caldwell, G. A., Osborne, L., Mewburn, I. and Crowther, P. (2015), 'Guerrillas in the [urban] midst: Developing and using creative research methods-guerrilla research tactics', *Journal of Urban Technology*, 22: 3, pp. 21–36.

Dade-Robertson, M. (2013), 'Architectural user interfaces: Themes, trends and directions in the evolution of architectural design and human computer interaction', *International Journal of Architectural Computing*, 11: 1, pp. 1–20.

Fischer, P. T., Zollner, C., Hoffmann, T., Piatza, S. and Hornecker, E. (2013), 'Beyond information and utility: Transforming public spaces with media facades', *Computer Graphics and Applications*, 33: 2, pp. 38–46.

Foth, M. (2009), *Handbook of Research on Urban Informatics: The Practice and Promise of the Real-time City*, Hershey, PA and London: IGI Global.

Foth, M., Agudelo, L. P. and Palleis, R. (2013), 'Digital soapboxes: Towards an interaction design agenda for situated civic innovation', in *Proceedings of the 2013 ACM Conference on Pervasive and Ubiquitous Computing Adjunct Publication*, Zurich, Switzerland, 8–12 September, New York: AMC, pp. 725–28.

Foth, M., Choi, J. H. and Satchell, C. (2011), 'Urban informatics', in *Proceedings of the ACM 2011 Conference on Computer Supported Cooperative Work*, Hangzhou, China, 19–23 March, New York: ACM, pp. 1–8.

Fredericks, J. and Foth, M. (2013), 'Augmenting public participation: Enhancing planning outcomes through the use of social media and web 2.0', *Australian Planner*, 50: 3, pp. 244–56.

Gray, J. (2014), 'Social practice and the laissez-faire metropolis: Dwight Perkins in Chicago, 1895-1915', *Architecture_MPS*, 5: 1, p. 1.

Houghton, K., Miller, E. and Foth, M. (2014), "Integrating ICT into the planning process: Impacts, opportunities and challenges', *Australian Planner*, 51: 1, pp. 24–33.

Iveson, K. (2010), 'The wars on graffiti and the new military urbanism', *City*, 14: 1–2, pp. 115–34.

Jenkins, H. (2006), *Convergence Culture: Where Old and New Media Collide*, New York: New York University Press.

Kellehear, A. (1993), *The Unobtrusive Researcher: A Guide to Methods*, St Leonards: Allen & Unwin.

Kindon, S., Pain, R. and Kesby, M. (eds) (2007), *Participatory Action Research Approaches and Methods: Connecting People, Participation and Place*, Oxon and New York: Routledge.

Lefebvre, H. and Nicholson-Smith, D. (1991), *The Production of Space*, Oxford: Blackwell.

Mitchell, W. J. (1996), *City of Bits: Space, Place, and the Infobahn*, Cambridge, MA: MIT Press.

Schneider, T. and Till, J. (2009), 'Beyond discourse: Notes on spatial agency', *Footprint*, 4, pp. 97–111.

Schroeter, R., Foth, M. and Satchell, C. (2012), 'People, content, location: Sweet spotting urban screens for situated engagement', in *Proceedings of the Designing Interactive Systems Conference*, Newcastle Upon Tyne, UK, 11–15 June, New York: ACM, pp. 146–55.

Tacchi, J., Foth, M. and Hearn, G. (2009), 'Action research practices and media for development', *International Journal of Education and Development using ICT*, 5: 2.

Epilogue

Edward M. Clift

igital technologies have transformed the modern world. We live in the midst of a great rewiring from analogue to digital that seems to know no bounds. This volume has sought to critically examine the current state of this transformation in order to speculate on its continued unfolding in a future time horizon. Whether the subject is big data, gamification or the sharing economy, digitization is all around us. DNA itself – the building block of life – is becoming translatable into digital forms that can then be recoded using future technology.

The authors whose work has been collected here share a profusion of insight into the contemporary cultural movements that are associated with this global shift in imaging technology. Using the city as the locus for their investigation, they succeed in uncovering a number of revealing instances where a new urbanity appears to be taking shape. Some, for example, have pointed out the many ways that location-based apps change our navigation through and conceptualization of the cities in which we live. Others make an even larger claim: namely that the sum total of all these technological elements is creating a new form of digital or hybrid city that increasingly blends experiential qualities drawn from both physical and virtual realms into the everyday life of its inhabitants.

Any discussion of the city in a philosophical sense hearkens back to St. Augustine's *The City of God Against the Pagans*, written shortly after the fall of Rome in 410 AD. In this treatise, he equates the ideal city with civilization itself, as inspired by religious order. The authors featured in this book – many of them participants in the conference sessions in London and Los Angeles of the AMPS's Mediated City Research Programme – were drawn together by a similar recognition of the city's pre-eminent role as a collective symbol of shared meanings and patterns of life. Modern cities are increasingly becoming a set of hybrid forms that merge city life with digital data, augmented reality, and other technology-enabled features.

The implications of this great rewiring have already been felt in everything from local traffic patterns to international politics. Taxi services (to name just one example) have been completely disrupted by new approaches and solutions to the organization of temporary personal transportation needs. The end result is that cities have lost their mythical monumental form in our imagination, morphing into large-scale malleable objects subject to the electronic flickers of a digital universe. The logic of representation has been turned on its head since the images of the virtual world now precede – or occur simultaneously with – the reality they describe. Communication is more salient than ever in the new social operating system, especially as it spreads internationally through the same digital channels.

Hybrid digital cities are using digital technology to quite literally reinvent the city along the lines of a user interface. Social media has renewed the value of relationships and recreated the affinity networks that had been largely abandoned within cities. At times, it even seems that communication tools have evolved to the point where the anomie of the traditional city has been largely circumscribed. This relational focus is also affecting the kinds of decisions that are made in the deliberative worlds of politics and government. Residents now want to interact with their governmental representatives as easily as they do with each other over social media. Political structures at all levels are having to reinvent themselves along the lines of Gov 2.0 in order to adjust to these changed communication expectations. It can be argued – indeed it *is* argued in this volume – that the desire for interactivity by residents should be elevated to a novel social force, one that accomplishes the task of urban design by crowd-sourcing knowledge from residents or 'end users'.

Cities have always been places where strangers meet and crowds form, but those features are now exploited for the city's own autonomous self-management process. Public health and security are key concerns for cities, and often the first to adopt large-scale technology solutions. This book contains work that expertly outlines this type of interaction through the example of New York City's implementation of a series of apps following 9/11. Apart from efficiently organizing health-related information, these apps served the useful purpose of reassuring the population that the city government both cared about their health and well-being, and was working actively to safeguard them.

It is refreshing to read this book, as its chapters take a close critical look at the many social transformations set in motion by the digital communication revolution. Without losing sight of the many tangible benefits afforded by these technologies, the contributors have together outlined a perspective that is only cautiously optimistic. The digital future they collectively describe is one that can be either filled with the promise of increased efficiency and hybrid connectivity, or plagued by increased surveillance and vastly reduced levels of privacy. Although we can easily imagine a variety of digital futures, it is useful to remember that they can still only be lived in the day-to-day present of our lived experience. We enter new digital territory every day by making a series of small choices that only cumulatively and over time become large ones.

Given demographic shifts and the economic value of new technologies, the rise of the digital city is likely here to stay. Bandwidth capability alone is already recognized as a significant factor in the economic success of entire communities. The number of people living in cities is growing every day, to the point where they now accommodate well over half of the world's population. Since cities compete for human talent (as well as many other resources), it is reasonable to expect their digital footprint to become ever larger. In the process, they become a medium themselves, facilitating with various degrees of intentionality the interaction of the human being with the expanding digital world of data.

Notes on Contributors

Series editor information

Graham Cairns has taught at universities in Spain, the United Kingdom, Mexico, South Africa and Gambia. He has worked in architectural studios in London and Hong Kong, and ran a performing arts company, Hybrid Artworks, with a specialism in video installation and performance art. The author and editor of five books, he has presented papers at international conferences, and published on architecture, film, interior design and advertising. He is director of the research organisation that initiated this Intellect book series, AMPS (Architecture, Media, Politics, Society) and is Executive Editor of its scholarly journal *Architecture_ MPS*. He is also a Senior Honorary Research Associate at the Bartlett School of Architecture, University College London.

Editor information

Carl H. Smith is a senior lecturer in Creative Coding, Learning Technologies and Research, and director of the Learning Technology Research Institute (LTRI), Ravensbourne. He is also a senior research fellow at London Metropolitan University. Previously, he has also been a research fellow at the Humanities Research Institute (HRI), University of Sheffield; developer/research fellow at The Cistercians in Yorkshire Project and HRI; and developer/researcher at The Humanities Advanced Technology and Information Institute (HATII), University of Glasgow. His current research projects include: 'CRe-AM FP7: Creativity research adaptive roadmap', which aims to bridge communities of creators with communities of technology providers and innovators in a collective, strategic intelligence/road mapping effort; 'MATURE FP7: Continuous social learning in knowledge networks', which is part of the Digital Libraries and Technology-Enhanced Learning call to investigate continuous social learning in knowledge networks; and 'Centre for Excellence in Teaching and Learning (CETL) Reusable Learning Objects Project', funded by the Higher Education Funding Coucil for England (HEFCE).

Edward Clift is President of Brooks Institute, a private and independent visual arts college located in Ventura, California. Prior to joining Brooks, Clift was a communication professor and founding dean of the School of Media, Culture & Design at Woodbury University. He is a graduate of the master's degree programme at the Annenberg School of Communication (University of Pennsylvania) and holds a PhD in communication from the University of Utah. In addition, he holds an MFA degree in photography from the Savannah College of Art and Design, and a BFA from the Tisch School of the Arts in New York City. He has published articles on the rhetoric of economics and edited a book on the same subject entitled *How Language is Used to Do Business* (Mellen, 2008). In addition to his work as an educational entrepreneur, he has served as chair of the Burbank Cultural Arts Commission and as education director for the Burbank International Film Festival. Clift is a graduate of California Connections, a professional development programme sponsored by the Southern California Leadership Network.

Glenda Amayo Caldwell is a researcher in the Urban Informatics Research Lab and a lecturer in architecture at the School of Design, Queensland University of Technology. As an early career academic (ECARD), she joined QUT, from the USA in 2009. She has a Bachelor of Science (Architecture) from the University of Michigan, Ann Arbor USA. She commenced a Masters in Architecture at SCI-Arc in Los Angeles and completed the degree in Miami at the Florida International University. She conducted her PhD *Media Architecture: Facilitating the Co-Creation of Place* at QUT. Through her research and teaching she questions the effect of media and technology on the design of architecture and urban environments. Her investigations explore the connection between the digital layers and the physical layers of the city and how tangible expressions of the interrelationships between them create and define new experiences of place, creating hybrid place.

Her research has been published in edited books, international journals and peer reviewed conferences.

Contibutor information

Cristina Miranda de Almeida is an artist, architect and urban planner affiliated to the Department of Art and Technology, The University of the Basque Country (UPV/EHU), and has been a visiting scholar in the research line 'Digital Culture' (IN3/UOC, Barcelona) since 2009. She holds a European PhD in arts (UPV-EHU, 2005), a postdoctorate degree as advanced research associate (Planetary Collegium, University of Plymouth, 2006), an MA in industrial design (DZ-BAI), and specializations in territorial planning (Fundicot, UV) and town planning (IBAM, Rio de Janeiro). She is currently working on the 'Material-ICT' project, as well as collaborating on the book *The Point of Being* (editor with Derrick de Kerckhove), white papers for the SEAD Network, and articles for the *International Journal* *of McLuhan Studies* and *Noema Journal*. Her artwork has been exhibited internationally, including in Taiwan, Rio de Janeiro, Pforzheim, Sint-Truiden, Madrid, Barcelona, Bilbao, Mons and Palermo. Her main research interests are linked to the Internet of Things, and new sensibilities and materialities, specifically when viewed from a transdisciplinary perspective that merges art, architecture, science and consciousness studies.

Georgios Artopoulos holds an MPhil in architecture and the moving image from the University of Cambridge (2004). He conducted his PhD at the Department of Architecture, University of Cambridge (2005-10) – where he also assisted as tutor and research assistant – for which he received a doctoral award from the Arts and Humanities Research Council. Artopolous has contributed to twelve European research programmes and received the Best International Short Film award at the 'Mestre Film Festival', Venice. He has had his work presented at the 'International Biennale of Contemporary Art' held at the Czech National Gallery, Prague; the international exhibition 'Computational Turn in Architecture' at MAV, Marseille; the 'Hong Kong and Shenzhen Bi-City Biennale of Architecture and Urbanism'; the 11th and 12th 'Biennale of Young Creators of Europe'; the '63rd Venice Film Festival'; the Royal Institute of British Architects, London; the BALTIC Centre for Contemporary Art, Newcastle; the London Design Festival; the Ukrainian Institute of Modern Art, Chicago; the ISEA in 2006 and 2008; the British Council, Brussels; the Byzantine Museum and Benakis Museum, Athens; and at many other international film festivals and art exhibitions. His work has been published in more than 23 peer-reviewed journals and architecture books – including *Digital Creativity*, *Architecture_MPS*, the *International Journal Of Visual Design*, *Metalocus*, *Interfaces*, the *Scroope Cambridge Journal of Architecture* and *Architectural Issues* – and in 35 international conference proceedings and exhibition catalogues (including GSM II, eCAADe, ACADIA, ASCAAD, Hellenic Semiotics, Generative Art and others). He has also presented at more than 29 international conferences and exhibitions, including Art Expo, Art Tech Media, ARCO, GIROS, Image: Beyond Media, and others.

Alessandro Aurigi is a professor of urban design and head of the School of Architecture, Design and Environment at Plymouth University. Aurigi was previously head of architecture at Newcastle University, a lecturer at the Bartlett School of Planning and research fellow in the Centre for Advanced Spatial Analysis at University College London. His research focuses on the relationships between our increasingly digital society and the ways we conceive, design and manage urban space to support and enhance place quality. Aurigi has published the multidisciplinary book *Augmented Urban Spaces* (Ashgate, 2008, edited with Fiorella de Cindio) and *Making the Digital City* (Ashgate, 2005). He has also written in international journals, including the *Journal of Urban Technology*, the *Journal of Architectural and Planning Research* and *Urban Design International*, amongst others. He has given speeches in Brazil, Japan, South Korea, The Netherlands, Belgium, Finland, Portugal, Spain, as well as the United Kingdom and Italy.

Nikolas Bakirtzis studied archaeology and social anthropology the Aristotle University of Thessaloniki, Greece, and received his PhD in art and architectural history from Princeton University. His research and publications concentrate on the material culture, historic landscapes and architectural heritage of the early Christian, medieval and early modern Mediterranean. He was awarded a Dumbarton Oaks Junior Fellowship, an Honorary Whiting Fellowship in the Humanities and has been a senior fellow at the Research Center for Anatolian Civilizations of Koç University in Istanbul, as well as a Mellon postdoctoral fellow and lecturer at Columbia University's Department of Art History and Archaeology. During the 2008-09 academic year, he was Cass Gilbert Visiting Assistant Professor in the School of Architecture and a research associate at the Center for World Heritage Sites of the University of Minnesota.

Bakirtzis was awarded a Marie Curie International Reintegration Grant by the European Commission, and joined STARC in June 2009 to direct the research project 'TIEM – Tracing Identity in the Eastern Mediterranean: A digital survey of Late Medieval monuments in the Eastern Mediterranean islands'. In 2012, Bakirtzis was awarded a Princeton University Seeger Center for Hellenic Studies Visiting Research Fellowship.

Fausto Brevi is an associate professor in the School of Design at Politecnico di Milano. He holds a degree cum laude in architecture, and is a specialist in 3D digital modelling and visualization for automotive design. He spent several years training the designers of some of Italy's most important industrial design departments, mainly in the car design industry, including at Alfa Romeo, Fiat, Lancia, Italdesign, Pininfarina, Bertone, Ghia and I.DE.A. Institute.

Fausto has attended several training courses on the techniques of modelling, animation and digital visual simulation, with internships in Toronto (1988 and 2000), Ghent (1991), Santa Barbara (1992) and Paris (1996). He has translated the reference text *Principles of Computer Graphics* (McGraw-Hill Italy, 1987), and is the author of several papers on traditional and digital representation in different fields of application. Focusing on virtual prototyping as applied to industrial design, he was the scientific supervisor of the Virtual Prototyping Lab of Politecnico di Milano's Design Department from 2003 to 2011, and is a member of its D.Rep (Design Representation) and ADD (Advance Design) research groups. He has also been a member of the academic board for its PhD courses 'Virtual Prototypes and Real Products' and 'Industrial Design and Multimedia Communication'.

Fausto has been the director of the postgraduate master's course in transportation and automobile design at Politecnico di Milano since 2009. He is currently managing a five-year research project in collaboration with Volkswagen Group Design entitled 'Moving Milano 2010–2015: Urban mobility culture associated to EXPO 2015', focused on developing electric concept cars for urban mobility. He has been visiting professor at Stanford University and at Università di Bologna since 2014.

Glenda Amayo Caldwell is a researcher in the Urban Informatics Research Lab and a lecturer in Architecture at the Queensland University of Technology, Brisbane, Australia. Her research focuses on the effect technology has on the experience of the city where architectural design methods and theories are combined with interactive media and urban informatics for community engagement. She explores how use of technology weaves the different disciplines of architecture, urban design, media design, interaction design and urban informatics together to create opportunities for social interaction to occur within the digital and physical layers of the urban environment. Of particular interest are Media Architecture, participatory design, community engagement, guerrilla research tactics, and place-making to promote sensitive architecture that responds to the needs of the community.

Melanie Chan is a lecturer in media and communication at York St. John University. Her research interests include contemporary film and literature, cultural geography (space, place and embodiment) and screen theory. She has published articles in journals such as *Cognitive Technology*, the *Journal of Baudrillard Studies* and *Film and Film Studies*, and written a book chapter for the edited collection, *21st Century Gothic* (Cambridge 2009). Chan has also acted as a reviewer for several journals, including *Alphaville* and *Networking Knowledge*, the journal of the Media, Communications and Cultural Studies Association (MeCCSA).

A specialist in transportation design practice and the field of low carbon vehicles (LCVs), **Matteo Conti** works as a senior tutor on the vehicle design master's course at the Royal College of Art. Conti, who joined from Northumbria University's School of Design, acts as a programme manager and is responsible for curriculum development whilst coordinating external projects. His ambition is to successfully combine in-depth research and design practice with applied teaching, in order to provide the best possible learning experience for students and to deliver valuable creative design output to industry.

Conti has been a senior lecturer in transportation and industrial design for the past 15 years, as well as acting as a programme leader and an industrial placement tutor. He has also created various industrial partnerships over the years with prestigious design houses, such as Pininfarina, Bertone and the I.DE.A Institute, to carry out collaborative projects and arrange industrial placements.

Conti's work includes the publication of several academic papers in the field of LCVs, as well as live-industrial collaboration projects, one of which culminated in the exterior redesign of the Avid CU-EV (in limited production) and another for the design of a new electric scooter for Elecscoot (for large volume production). He previously honed his design skills in the marine industry by establishing and managing Stile Mare Ltd, where he worked as a design consultant. Currently, he is working as a freelance designer on the upgrade and launch of an exclusive EV sports car for the UK market.

Lilia Gomez Flores is IMPRINTS' research assistant, and has finished a PhD studying the visual image and interaction of avatars in virtual communities on the Internet. Her research interests include virtual ethnography, cross-cultural studies and marketing in cyberworlds. She has a BA in graphic design and an MPhil in 2D/3D motion graphics, and has presented the outcomes of her research at several national and international conferences.

Aroussiak Gabrielian is an architectural and landscape architectural designer with a background in visual arts and critical theory. Most fundamentally, her research focuses on the relationship between visual culture and attitudes toward, and treatment of, the constructed environment; or how representations of the built environment impact the way in which we see and understand it, and thus shape it moving forward. She is currently a member of the Faculty of Landscape Architecture at the University of Southern California, and co-founder and director of foreground design agency, a transdisciplinary practice operating between the fields of architecture, landscape architecture, urbanism and the visual arts. As an activist practice, foreground acts as a platform to investigate the dynamics of social rituals and ecological processes, with the aim of generating design interventions that promote a healthy public realm and offer enhanced opportunities for enriched participation in the environment. Aroussiak explores the role of representation as an active agent in the design process, and develops new ways of reading and visualizing the spatial, temporal and tactile phenomena of landscape to interpret and structure site. foreground is the recipient of numerous recognitions, including a winning entry in the 2012 Pruitt Igoe Now competition. With her partner at foreground, Aroussiak has authored forthcoming essays about the firm's design research in *Wildproject: A Journal of Environmental Studies* (December 2013) and the *International Journal of Interior Architecture and Spatial Design* (2013).

Mirko Guaralda is a lecturer in architecture at the Queensland University of Technology (QUT). His background includes experience in architectural design, landscape architecture and urban design. Before joining academia full-time, Guaralda worked in industry and local government. He has been involved in a wide range of projects at different scales: from small dwellings and gardens, to new estates and urban strategic planning. He is currently research associate with the Centre for Subtropical Design, the Urban Informatics Research Lab and the Children and Youth Research Centre at QUT. Guaralda's research investigates people-place interaction, with a focus on unstructured activities that support the development of resilient and strong communities. The use of social media is evaluated as an increasingly relevant strategy to structure not only interpersonal relationships, but also the way people relate to the built environment. Gueralda's work studies how communities can customize and appropriate the urban landscape through unplanned uses, guerrilla techniques and bottom-up approaches. In this approach to our cities, media often provide platform to share ideas, connect and organize intervention. Smart technologies also support the navigation of the urban landscape, superimposing new meanings to consolidated environments.

M. Hank Haeusler Dipl.-Ing. (Fh), PhD (SIAL/RMIT) is Discipline Director of Computational Design (CoDe) at the Australian School of Architecture + Design, University of New South Wales, Sydney. He is also a board member of the Media Architecture Institute, a non-profit organization designed to complement the work of established universities and research institutions; and Lead CI of Encircle, an ARC Linkage Grant funded research group investigating responsive transport environments. Haeusler is known as a researcher, educator, entrepreneur and designer in media architecture, digital technology, interaction design and ubiquitous computing. He is the author of seven books, including *Media Facades – History, Technology, Content* (avedition, 2009), *Infostructures* (Freerange, 2010), *New Media Facades – A Global Survey* (avedition, 2012) and *INTERChanging* (Spurbuch, 2014), in addition to over 30 book chapters and conference papers. He has lectured widely in Europe, Asia, North America and Australia, and was appointed visiting professor at the Central Academy of Fine Arts, Beijing, in 2013.

Richard Laing holds qualifications in quantity surveying and humanities, and completed a PhD in value assessment of the built heritage. Since 1999, he has led numerous research commissions, including 'Streetscapes' (Scottish Enterprise), 'Greenspace' (ECFP5, Scottish lead) and 'Urban Connections' (Aberdeen City Growth), and was the RGU lead on CARE North (ERDF Interreg). These projects provided techniques for assessing human responses to virtual built environments. Professor Laing has represented the Royal Institute of Chartered Surveyors on the European Construction Technology Platform, with a particular emphasis on energy efficiency in buildings, and is a member of the EU Smart Cities Stakeholder Platform. His research concerning design evaluation has made a significant and innovative use of virtual models and scenarios to present various designs and environmental interventions.

Claudia Lima is a professor at the University Lusíada Norte in Porto, Portugal, and researcher at the Centre for Research in Territory, Architecture and Design (CITAD). She currently teaches Project III (Architectural Design Studio) at the postgraduate and dissertation level, as well as architectural research methods and thesis design. She received an MA in civic design (2006) from the University of Liverpool, and later a PhD in architecture (2011) from the same university. Her research interests and expertise relate to representations and perceptions of space, inspiring a concern with the urban and architectural narratives that develop in response to technological innovation and transient demands.

Linda Matthews is currently undertaking a PhD at the University of Technology, Sydney (UTS), concerned with the development of architectural and urban design methodologies that utilize the optical logics of digital surveillance systems. The aim of the research is to understand how these systems frame and re-present the city, and to use these virtual urban spaces as a source of qualitative and quantitative information sets that can be digitally reconfigured to generate architectural form. She completed her Bachelor of Architecture degree at UTS, where she was awarded the University Medal, and also holds a Master of Architecture degree (History and Theory) from the University of New South Wales (UNSW) in Australia. She has won a number of significant academic awards, including the prestigious Design Medal from the UNSW chapter of the Royal Australian Institute of Architects. Matthews has recently collaborated with architectural practices to develop a site-specific technique for generating building façades based upon the transformative potential of the digital image. Matthews was awarded a Byera Hadley Travelling Scholarship to the Venice Architecture Biennale, where she undertook research exploring the possibilities of this new technique.

Marta Miguel holds qualifications in architecture and urban design. Her final project was recognized with merit and published by the L'Ecole Nationale Supérieure d'Architecture de Montpellier.

Since 1999, she has worked in Scotland, Portugal, Italy, Holland and Angola. This international experience has given her the opportunity to engage with different cultural approaches towards design and urban planning: in Holland, she designed highly defined *Vinex* urban areas; in Scotland, she developed strategies to deal with the phenomena of shrinking cities; and in Luanda, she designed systems of bottom-up interventions to address sanitary issues related to the fast growth of suburban areas in developing countries.

She has worked as lecturer at the TUdelft in Holland and at The Robert Gordon University in Aberdeen. Her research explores planning challenges, and new ways to manage urban and social development in increasingly complex and dynamic postmodern cities. Her research interests relate to urban evolution and urban dynamics; the formation process and character of both emergent and planned cities; the role of architecture in the human and urban evolutionary process; and alternative pedagogic approaches towards the teaching of architecture and urban studies.

Gavin Perin is a lecturer in the School of Architecture at the University of Technology, Sydney (UTS). He completed his Bachelor of Architecture degree at the University of Canberra, and a design-based research Masters of Architecture degree at Royal Melbourne Institute of Technology. He is currently undertaking a PhD at the University of Technology, Sydney. His main area of academic interest is the role of representation in architecture, and the generative and instrumental effect of the forms of representation on design practice and its artefacts. This work, which is being developed both theoretically and through practice-based research, explores the evolving frontiers of digital design, with the aim of developing new and innovative ways digital media can be used to design built artefacts that function in physical and virtual environments. He is also co-director and founding member of the Locative Media Lab (LML) at UTS, which is engaged in theoretical and practice-based research that explores the evolving frontiers of digital design. The LML offers a unique opportunity for researchers and industry partners to engage with a multidisciplinary team of national and international designers, architects, creative practitioners, theorists and technology experts to address a spectrum of research and design issues.

Kristin Scott holds a PhD from George Mason University; an AM in interdisciplinary studies from the University of Chicago; an MFA in creative writing from Columbia College, Chicago; and a BA in English literature from Smith College. Her fields of research include visual media and digital cultures; urban culture, mobilities and spatial practices; digital urban sustainability; urban securitization and the militarization of urban spaces; the urban public sphere; postmodern bodies and biotechnologies; and science and technology studies. Scott is also a visual artist, and works in photography, drawing, painting and mixed media. Her most recent research focuses on the recent digital technological initiatives of Seattle, New York City and San Antonio. She is examining and considering the discursive practices of each as self-proclaimed 'smart', 'digital' and 'cyber' cities. She considers what economic, political and social factors and goals motivate urban digitality in each city; how each city complicates or problematizes current debates about digital public spheres and open and participatory democracy; the role of digital technologies in the functioning of each city's civil society; and the manner in which abstract, ideological concepts of the 'digital city' articulate with each city's actual digital technological claims and programmes.

Sandra Wilson is a contemporary jewellery designer/maker, researcher and educator. She is co-investigator on a major EPSRC-funded research project called 'IMPRINTS: Public responses to future identity management practices & technologies', from which her chapter draws. Her work is inspired by living systems, and has won awards from the Scottish Arts Council, the Audi Foundation for Innovation and the British European Designers Group. Her work is also in the collection of HRH Princess Anne. Previous research projects have included 'Pulse: The stuff of life' (Scottish Arts Council), 'Evoke: The meaning of jewellery in the digital age' (AHRC) and 'Tempting fate: Jewellery & superstition' (Carnegie Trust).

Quazi Mahtab Zaman is an architect, urban designer and lecturer in urban design at the Scott Sutherland School of Robert Gordon University, and has actively contributed to academic teaching and research since 1992. He was a researcher and postdoctoral fellow at Hong Kong University, and visiting postdoctoral fellow at Oxford Brookes University between 1998 and 2002. In 1996, he was a research assistant for OMA Asia (Hong Kong) and GSD Harvard University, USA (for Rem Koolhaas Masters Studio for the Pearl River Delta China Project); and was associate professor at BRAC University (Bangladesh) during 2002–07. Dr. Zaman was a US Fulbright Senior Teaching and Research Fellow at the College of Art, Architecture and Planning at Cornell University, New York from 2007 to 2008. His research interests include urban design and architectural manifestation in the urban context; New Urbanism; regionalism and regeneration; healthy cities by urban design; vertical urbanism; emerging new versus traditional urbanism in Asia; mega cities (specifically new modes of production of space and theorizing urban congestions project); children-centred urbanism; and public realm interfaces study. He is author of over 50 journal articles, chapters and books, and acts as editorial board member for many journals. He has extensive architectural and urban design consultancy experience.

Marco Zilvetti is a PhD student at the School of Design at Politecnico di Milano, where he gained his master's degree cum laude in product design in 2010. Since then he has been collaborating with major international companies including The North Face, CBRE and Frette, working on several projects in the field of product, interior and graphic design. Following his passion for car design and digital technologies, Zilvetti started his PhD research in 2012 to enhance his knowledge about urban mobility, focusing on driverless cars and future mobility.

A speaker at various conferences, Zilvetti's work includes the publication of academic papers in the field of smart cities, future urban transport and car design, where he can present his transdisciplinary experience. At the same time, he has collaborated with the postgraduate master's course in transportation and automobile design at Politecnico di Milano, providing didactic support about meta-design and scenario building.

As an enthusiast about digital technologies applied to design, Zilvetti has been actively involved in academic activities since 2007, when he started supporting the MB Digital Modelling courses at Politecnico di Milano, first as a MA student, and later acting as an assistant lecturer (2013–14). Since November 2014 he has been a visiting PhD student at the Royal College of Art in order to acquire deeper insights about British society, as well as to complete his research activities on future urban mobility and driverless technologies.

Index